Border

LINES

Caroline
KRAUS

Broadway Books
NEW YORK

Border LINES

a memoir

Names and identifying characteristics of individuals in this book have been changed to protect their identities. The book makes occasional use of composite characters as well.

PRINTED IN THE UNITED STATES OF AMERICA

BROADWAY BOOKS and its logo, a letter B bisected on the diagonal, are trademarks of Random House, Inc.

Visit our website at www.broadwaybooks.com

First edition published 2004.

Book design by Caroline Cunningham

The Cataloging-in-Publication Data is on file with the Library of Congress.

ISBN 0-7679-1403-1

10 9 8 7 6 5 4 3 2 1

For my mother,

Madeleine Martha Caroline Véron Kraus

O the mind, mind has mountains; cliff of fall
Frightful, sheer, no-man-fathomed.

—Gerard Manley Hopkins

The dream took place at my high school track, a quarter-mile oval shimmering in the heat. Its rough rubber boiled beneath me as I slipped on a pair of spikes and scanned the bleachers. An unusually large crowd filled the stands, and I didn't find it remarkable that they were all mothers, rows and rows of mothers, as if our entire town had been emptied of its maternal core, which was now gathered at my high school and awaiting this, the greatest race of my life. They waved and shook hands with one another, flashed nervous smiles, then moved into position to watch us run.

Jeanette Riley was putting her spikes on beside me. In real life, Jeanette had been my most dreaded rival, and I had never beaten her. In my dream, she sent me an amused, sympathetic wink, as if to applaud me just for trying. Four hundred yards of hurdles stretched before us, and the winner would have a ticket to the state meet in Jefferson City. In real life, Jeanette had been there three times. I had only imagined.

I stood behind my blocks, stretching my legs and flopping my arms around like Jeanette did. Her mother hovered as close as the officials allowed, in line with Jeanette behind the low spectator fence. She held her stopwatch and yelled, "Come on, Jeanette, *concentrate*. Don't drink that water—put down the water." Jeanette put her cup of water down. "Wristwatch! Wristwatch!" her mother yelled. Jeanette trotted over and let her mother remove the watch. Mrs. Riley rubbed her daughter's arms and whispered something that cast a shadow over Jeanette's pretty face. They stared at me with a united, steely expression.

My mother entered stage right, behind Jeanette's mom. Her purse was slung over her arm, her big Jackie-O sunglasses were perched on top of her head. She greeted a succession of other mothers and gave a special wave to my best friend's mom. Then she made her way trackside and scanned the crowd of coaches and athletes milling about. When she located me at the starting line, her face relaxed into a smile. Mrs. Riley came then, as she always did, and planted herself beside my mother, who lowered her sunglasses and offered a terse hello.

A serious-looking man with a starter's gun approached, and he gave us the usual prerace instructions. Six other girls were there, but in my dream they were faceless. Only Jeanette mattered.

I crouched down in the blocks and felt my heart drop. We waited, gun raised, poised on our fingertips, eyes fixed down the lanes. Mom gripped the fence as the gun went off, and I hurled myself forward.

Jeanette and I were airborne together over the first hurdle, left leg straight, right curled flat behind us. Just as in real life, she pulled ahead. Jeanette's mother screamed and shrieked and hollered.

Side by side, my mother and Mrs. Riley watched. In the stands, all the other mothers leaned and stretched as we took the hurdles; they strained and shouted, willing us forward.

Jeanette's mother's screams would not stop. They rocketed through the air like a fire alarm. I sped up between the fourth and fifth hurdles and miraculously took the sixth in step with Jeanette. Her shocked expression gave me hope. I sped up a little more.

"Jea-nette! *Move* it!" Mrs. Riley shrieked. "Faster, Jeanette! Faster!"

Jeanette's long legs pumped harder until she came even with me for the next hurdle. Her elbow swung left, striking my ribs as we landed. I stumbled, and, as happens only in dreams, a collective gasp escaped from the crowd. My mother lifted her sunglasses and gave Mrs. Riley a cold stare.

I stayed on my feet, now two strides behind the pack of faceless girls and yards behind Jeanette. As we approached the last curve with only a hundred yards left before us, my mother's alto suddenly came booming across the field, stunning Mrs. Riley into silence.

"Run, Caroline!" she shouted. *"Run."* My legs responded with a magical burst of speed, hurling me past the pack, hot on Jeanette's heels. When we passed in front of the spectators, I was matching her stride for stride.

"Goddamn it!" yelled Mrs. Riley.

"Run!" yelled my mother.

The other mothers raised their voices, too, in a united, desperate chorus, cheering in symbiotic accord with their fleet of daughters, flying madly down the lanes. We were living marionettes, tied by blood to our counterparts bordering the track. We were their younger legs; we ached beneath them like grieved phantom limbs. Our finish line was their victory.

I was a step ahead of Jeanette and then two. My mother knew it before I did, and her jaw dropped in proud amazement. Jeanette shrieked once, and then I clipped the tape, arms raised.

I was doubled over and panting when Mom came to me, hopping effortlessly over the fence. The other mothers came pouring onto the track, too, finding their own daughters, who had appeared from nowhere, springing from thin air like ghosts, all of us gasping for air.

In my dream, my mother hugged me tight. Her eyes were wide and intense. Alive.

I came in from the wilderness, a creature void of form.
"Come in," she said, "I'll give you shelter from the storm."

—Bob Dylan

Chapter ONE

Morning light edged over the horizon as I awoke to the sound of low, urgent moans coming from Jane's room. San Francisco emerged from the night, glistening before me in shades of white, and Jane's howls of pleasure rose with the sun. Below my window, furtive whistles called across Dolores Park, hawking drugs, while Jane's muted laughter filtered through the wall that divided our rooms. I fixed my eyes on the distant Bay Bridge and imagined driving across it for good, soaring east as far as the Atlantic. I imagined a new life in a quiet, charming town she could not find, where I would become stable minded and marry a tall, sensitive man. We would have children and dogs. And money—we would never worry about money. I touched a purple gash above my eye, still raw and wet, and as if to comfort me, Jane knocked three times on the wall. I pulled a pillow over my head, pressed my knees to my chin, and willed the world away.

A few hours later, Jane stood naked in my doorway with a sly smile spreading across her face. I blinked at her perfect silhouette from the cave I'd built with my pillows and waved a small hello. She absently slipped her thumb into her mouth and blinked back at me with warm, curious eyes. Climbing into my bed, she drew my arms around her, squirming like a puppy for the perfect spot. With shallow breaths she sucked her thumb and waited for me to ask about her night.

I said nothing. We lay there in silence, cautious, in the aftermath of battle. I knew Jane was already returning to the fantasy of our strange, platonic marriage, and I was once again exhausted and anxious, awaiting the next disaster.

"Did someone say pancakes?" she asked in a small voice.

I held my breath. She waited.

"Or . . . was it waffles?" she whispered hopefully.

I swallowed hard.

"Honey?" Jane's thumb paused between her lips. She tilted her head to look at me. I met her blue eyes as they narrowed and searched me for clues. Soon she would read my silence, and her sweetness would turn to rage. But I could not speak. November was freezing the air outside, stasis before the spring. And I was dormant, too, stilled by Jane and her stare, frozen by my own inertia; paralyzed by the impossibility of escape.

It was close to Christmas then, which meant that soon my family would be gathering in St. Louis. My father and sister would be dressing the house with greens, a tree, and our beloved Santa, who swings in a hot-air balloon and sings "Fly Me to the Moon." They would recline by the fire, talking medicine, or putter in the kitchen with opera filling the house. My brother would fly in from Washington, D.C., loaded with presents and stories from Capitol Hill, and he'd head straight to the market to buy bagels, yogurt, and five cartons of eggnog, all of which my father would discover sometime in February. My parents' friends would stop by with food and gifts and report on their children, who, I felt sure, were either getting married, having children, or working their way up ladders of success.

And then there was the Void. The Void would envelop this routine, would dull all of the holiday smells and sounds. It would be what was left of our mother, who had died two years before. It would sit across from my father at the dinner table, stroll our gardens, and sleep fitfully on the sofa. I knew this presence well; it was as strong, devastating, and vivid as was my mother's living self.

When I left Jane that morning, I was late to meet a psychiatrist—a woman Jane had found—and I was circling her house when it dawned on me that the wet sensation creeping down my neck might be blood. I touched the spot, and my fingers came back red and sticky. I lifted my jaw to the rearview mirror and turned my head, keeping one eye on the narrow road. Old, economical cars lined the quiet, residential street. This was Berkeley, 1992. In those days, riding in a big Republican car was asking for trouble.

It was a cold, washed-out November, and I was sick. I had gotten used to it, to feeling like I had the flu all the time, but I wasn't used to the cold. The chill followed me everywhere. It hung near me at work, trailed me home, and crawled under my bed covers at night. It didn't seem to bother other people, but I was shivering in my car that morning, even with the heat roaring full blast.

I felt the back of my head again and found the soft welt just above the base of my neck, seeping red on blond. I must have awakened it with my hairbrush, trying to look presentable. I turned the mirror away and cursed. So much for first impressions.

I kept circling the psychiatrist's house; there was nowhere to park. In all of Berkeley there was never anywhere to park, but this once I was happy to delay my arrival. Along with the blood, which had just found my shirt collar, the welt above my left eye was ripe with fall colors. I was on my third cigarette in as many minutes, and

I had nothing but my hand to stop the bleeding. I figured I wouldn't have to say a word when I met Francine; she'd probably take one look at me and pull out her prescription pad.

I paused in front of her house, and then, as if witnessing one of those comets that appears only once in a lifetime, I watched a car pull out of a spot and drive away. I was known to risk lives to claim such a spot. Like a heat-seeking missile, I would accelerate across three lanes of traffic—pedestrians be damned—then slip my Celica neatly between bumpers with a finger's width to spare. This skill had developed over time, after night upon endless night of closing up the bookstore where Jane and I worked, turning away the midnight shoppers, and driving home across the Bay Bridge together, only to search San Francisco's deserted, car-lined streets in vain, with the moon smiling upon our rootless hunt. Eventually I started pulling my car up on the grassy median right in front of our building, leaving it for the parking police to laugh at in the morning. Jane left them notes of explanation, written carefully, eloquently, during the drive home. I stored them in my top desk drawer, next to the piles of tickets I could not pay.

I stared at the open spot, put on my blinker, and smoked. I could either take the bridge back to San Francisco and clean myself up, or park. The first scenario had a lot going for it, except that Jane might be home, and returning bloody, even from an old wound, would just get her going. Then again, part of me suspected that she was somewhere close, hiding in the bushes maybe, watching to make sure I went in.

I took the spot. I waited there and studied Francine's house—a small brown shingled cottage with lights glowing yellow in the foggy air—and wondered who awaited me. I didn't know much about her, just that she had written a book on Eastern philosophy that Jane liked, and on the book flap Jane saw she was a therapist living in Berkeley. The next thing I knew, I was scheduled for an appointment.

I threw mints in my mouth and rubbed lotion on my hands to hide the cigarette smell. The front door of the house opened, and I slid down in my seat. A woman picked up a newspaper from her porch and waved it in my direction. She was tiny, no taller than a child, with long white hair tucked behind her ears. Even from my distance I could see deep crevices carved into her narrow face. She looked to be a hundred years old.

"Coming in?" she yelled.

I sank farther into my seat and pulled sunglasses down from the top of my head. Francine stood on her porch and opened the paper, peering at me over the headlines.

Damn. I wanted another cigarette.

I tried to smile as I hid my stained hand and crossed the street to meet her.

"Caroline," she said. "Hello." Her lips drew back into a lopsided smile, showing long, crooked teeth. Everything about her was crooked—her nose, her chin, her fingers—even her glance.

I extended a clean left hand to her right and felt like a giant as she switched hands, reached up, and gave me a firm shake.

"May I use your bathroom?" I asked.

"Okay," she said, drawing out the word. She peered behind my back.

Inside it was warm, and a fire was making loud cracking sounds in a small living room off the front hall. I thought right away of a hobbit's house, with its small, dimly lit rooms, knitted afghans draped over chairs and sofas, and ancient, wooden furniture cluttered about. For that matter, Francine looked like a wise old hobbit herself, with that long white hair, creased face, and shuffling gait. I had to laugh. Leave it to Jane to find me a hobbit shrink.

I made quick use of her bathroom, which also seemed strangely miniaturized. After rubbing tiny shell-shaped soaps against the back of my head and rinsing away the blood, I lowered my sunglasses. I emerged from the bathroom and felt my way through the shadowy kitchen and study, arriving in the living room, where Francine sat by the fire, reading the newspaper. She pointed to a small brown sofa across from her. The room smelled of burning oak, and I removed my coat cautiously, welcoming the heat.

"I'll let it go this time," she said, dropping the paper as I took my seat. "You are supposed to be here at ten."

My watch read almost eleven. I stood to go.

"I said I'll let it go," Francine repeated. She pushed rimless bifocals up on her forehead like a pair of headlights. There was not a clock to be seen in the room or even a watch on Francine's wrist. Maybe she told time by the sun.

I sat down and found my ballpoint pen with the top that clicks. I had developed a habit of clicking that pen whenever I felt nervous. I never left home without it.

"So," Francine began.

"So," I repeated.

She watched me for a minute, then said, "Why don't you start."

"That's okay," I said. "You start."

A smile rose and fell like a sigh across her face. "Well, you have the advantage over me," she said. "Only you know why you are here."

"I'm here because Jane called you," I said. "It's her idea. Didn't she tell you something?"

"She said you've been . . . *not yourself* lately. I think that's how she put it."

"Not myself," I repeated.

There was a big canvas pillow by the fire and a half-chewed bone on top of it. By the size of the bone, I figured the dog must be big, and I wondered how a big dog would fit into such a tiny house.

Lately. That part made me chuckle.

Francine followed my eyes to the dog bed.

Whatever. Jane would have probably said I was cracking up, and that cracking up, along with a few other things, ran in my family, so Francine should be on the lookout. Jane had read a lot about ailments, and she had diagnosed me with one thing or another just about every month. Earlier in the year she had thought I had digestive problems, and before that I was anemic. I withstood acupuncture, boiled herbs, and weeks of chard, kale, liver, and collard greens before Jane resorted to a shrink.

"What's with the pen?" Francine asked. I had been clicking, and stopped.

"It's comforting," I said, surprised by my own honesty.

Francine paused. "Well then, click away," she said. Her right hand was shaking, and she anchored it in her lap. "So. Jane also said that your mother died."

I clicked faster and looked right at Francine. "Yep."

"When?"

I turned my eyes to the ceiling and stalled. The further away I got from the day, the more I hated that question.

It's not that I couldn't have answered. I could have recited the day, hour, and minute that my mother died. I could have described the eerie order of my parents' bedroom, Dad leaving for his morning run, and the sheer cotton nightgown Mom wore, damp with sweat. Had Francine wanted me to gauge the angle of Mom's head, I could have told it. Or the quality of light? Pale dawn. The world had been silent around us that morning, until my mother began to fight for air and I started to scream.

"Where is your dog?" I asked.

"She's out back."

"What kind?"

"Springer spaniel mixed with something. Her name is Sherry." Francine stifled a yawn, and for a second I thought she might return to her newspaper. "What's with the sunglasses?" she asked.

I should have known that sunglasses always give you away, especially when there is no sun. I removed them.

"Oh," Francine said.

I felt my whole body tighten and seal like Fort Knox.

Jane and I had been passing each other in the hall of our apartment after it happened. She saw the cut and bruise above my eye and stopped, pressing me against the wall to look closer. Her expression had been polite incomprehension at first, followed by fear.

"What the fuck is that?" she'd demanded.

I turned away, even though I had wanted her to see it, to *see* it, finally, in Technicolor. I had hoped my face would speak for itself, but in that moment, as if dropped without a parachute into reality, I realized I'd crossed a bad line. I had entered Jane territory.

She gave me a cutting, dismissive laugh and then went to run a bath.

I followed her.

"I'm not feeling right," I admitted.

The bathroom door closed in my face.

"It won't happen again—"

Jane opened the door. Steam flooded behind her.

"Do you really think I believe that?" she asked. "Do you think I'm blind? Stupid? Look at who you're talking to." She shut the door, then opened it to finish a thought. "You are way out of your league," she added. "Only a novice would do it so it shows." Then she closed the door again.

I waited with my ear to the door.

"I've been thinking . . . maybe I should go, Jane," I said. "I'm not—"

I heard the water shut off.

"Jane?"

I waited.

The door flew open, smashed into my face, and knocked me down. Jane came out swinging. She was on top of me before I could speak, hands around my neck and knees on my chest. Her expression was frozen in terror, eyes wide, teeth bared. The back of my head hit the floor, and the skin split just enough to make me yelp.

I froze beneath her, completely still. She released her grip and stood, disgusted.

"Snap out of it!" she yelled. Her whole body was shaking. *"You are supposed to be the stable one. Lucy and Ethel—remember?"*

I inched away, adrenaline racing.

"It's ridiculous," Jane muttered. She flapped her arms. "No one is leaving. No one is leaving."

She went into the bathroom, and I heard her climb into the tub. I grabbed my purse and stumbled out the door, eventually arriving at Moby's bookstore, where we worked. I hid behind a wall of returns in the back room and spent the night under a desk in the bookstore, drifting between sleep and wakeful anxiety. The next day I returned to our apartment and found Jane naked, curled in a ball on my bed, watching Oprah. She had wetted her own bed in the night, and her arms and legs were lined with thin red razor cuts. I located the pack of razor blades and threw them out. Then I changed Jane's bedding and treated her cuts. Her eyes were wet and glazed, fixed on the television. Her thumb never left her mouth, and she didn't speak until I sat next to her on the bed and said, "I'll stay."

"Good," she said softly.

Then, falling asleep, she added, *"Ethel."*

Ten minutes went by, or maybe it was an hour. Francine was making comments, I saw her lips moving, but I couldn't speak.

"And I've lost my glasses," she said.

"They're on your head." I pointed.

"Aha!" She looked at me, pulled them down, then disappeared.

I heard a door open and then nails tapping on the hardwood floor. A minute later Sherry came trotting in with a tennis ball. She dropped it at my feet and crouched with anticipation. I tossed it back. She leapt, caught the ball, then watched me like a lifeguard. After a few minutes Francine returned with mugs of tea.

"First visits can be awkward," she said to Sherry. She placed the tea in front of me and stirred hers, blowing on the top to cool it. From outside we would have looked like two old friends visiting on a winter's morning.

"Humiliating," I corrected. "Paying someone to listen to me is humiliating." I sipped the tea and shuddered as heat spread through my chest.

Francine sighed. "Exactly. You get humiliated, and I get rich. Very awkward."

I put my palms around the cup, studying Francine. She was either very clever or a crackpot.

She looked at Sherry and said, "Well, okay, not rich."

"Are you a psychiatrist?" I blurted. I suddenly thought it was very possible that Jane had told me I was going to a psychiatrist when really she'd set me up with some lonely grandmother she'd met in a supermarket.

Francine said she was a psychotherapist, which meant she was trained to lead people through therapy but not prescribe medication.

"Do you think I need medication?" I asked.

"I haven't a clue," she said. "Well, actually, I doubt it."

I checked my watch.

"Do you have somewhere you have to be?" she asked.

"Not really. Our shift starts at two. We work at Moby's books."

"Our? We?"

"Jane. Me."

"Oh." Francine nodded. "I love Moby's. Impossible parking, though."

Two points for Francine.

I spooned some honey into my tea, and the sweet, comforting scent reminded me of home and holidays. I wished I could stay overnight. I wished I could stay forever.

"So," Francine said. "Is that blood?" She pointed to my shirt collar.

I was quiet again.

After a while she broke the silence. "I should mention a couple of ground rules. The first is easy, arrive on time. The second is, try to answer my questions, and answer them truthfully, or else we won't get very far."

I nodded, suddenly afraid of not being allowed back.

"Good," Francine said. "Great." She waited. I clicked my pen.

"What was the question?" I asked. But Francine didn't smile.

I chewed a nail. She didn't budge.

Finally I said, "We're not well."

Francine pushed her glasses up on her nose. "Jane and I," I added.

"How do you mean?" she asked.

"I mean she cuts herself, on purpose, with razors. And she gets in trouble with everybody. And I haven't got any money left because she keeps needing more. And I think she'll be fired soon. And I just want her to be okay, you know? I want to prove everybody wrong and make her happy."

I waited for the heavens to open and strike me dead.

"Oh," Francine said.

I kept going. "Her mother is coming, and I don't think we'll survive it. And I can't make rent next month, no way can I make it. And it's so cold. Isn't it cold? Everywhere."

Maybe it was the fire that did it to me, or Sherry snoring at my feet, but I couldn't get the words out fast enough.

Francine took some time to think about this.

"What about you?" she asked.

"Me? But I just *told* you." Maybe she wasn't listening. Jane was carrying a butcher's knife around the house. She was writing poetry that made Sylvia Plath sound cheery. I was too scared to sleep.

Suddenly I started to giggle. It was happening more and more; I would laugh at all the wrong times. It was embarrassing.

Francine blinked at me. I was possessed by a canyon-size grin.

"I know what you're thinking," I said.

"Really?" She leaned forward, intrigued.

"I don't know why I do this," I admitted, covering my mouth.

"Maybe something is funny?" she suggested.

"No. Nothing is funny," I assured her.

I was clicking my pen faster and faster, and for some reason I felt like throwing it right between Francine's sympathetic eyes. I wanted to scream at the top of my lungs. I wanted to smash everything in sight. I wanted to cry. Francine must have seen something in my expression because she raised her hands in surrender and said, "Whoa.

"I'll tell you what I'm thinking," she offered. "I'm thinking that, based on what you've told me so far, there's a missing piece here."

I stayed quiet.

"Are you and Jane a couple?" she asked.

"Well . . . not in the way that you mean," I said.

"In another way?"

"We're . . . *close*," I said cautiously.

"And you're not related. . . ."

"Oh, no."

I waited for more, but Francine was quiet.

I said, "So why don't I just leave, right?"

"Do you think you should leave?"

"Well, I can't leave, that's the point."

"You can if you want to."

"Really, I can't. No, we are not a couple, and no, she's not family, but for some reason we are stuck with each other. It would be easier if there was a category for us, believe me."

"Maybe that's it," Francine mused. "Maybe that's the missing piece. The 'for some reason.' "

I looked at her doubtfully.

"Shall we look for it?" she asked.

"Look for *what?*"

"Well, if we knew, it wouldn't be missing," she noted.

Right.

When I stood at Francine's door to leave, she asked me to bring props next time if I wanted, photographs or artifacts that were significant to me. She said I was on her calendar for the next Wednesday morning, and the next one after that, and the next one after that. I said that was fine with me.

When we stepped onto the porch, I saw Jane's sky blue Volkswagen double-parked beside my silver Celica. Her eyes were closed, her head tipped against the window, facing us. Even from that distant angle I thought she looked rare—not just beautiful, though her intense, poised features were that—but heightened and raw, as if she embodied emotion itself, in all its extremes.

"That's Jane," I said to Francine.

She lowered her bifocals to look, then gave me a supportive smile. I trotted down the stairs with a wave. Francine's figure stayed reflected in Jane's window as I tapped on it. Jane cracked an eye, rolled down the window, then turned my wrist and checked the time.

"Cripes, that was long," she yawned.

"What are you doing here?" I asked.

"I want a full report. Let's get some eggs at La Note." She glanced at Francine and whispered through her teeth. "Why is she still standing there?"

"Because we're fascinating," I said.

Jane nodded. "True."

"And La Note is expensive," I added.

Jane pulled a handful of twenties from her coat pocket and handed half to me. I shoved it quickly in my pocket. I wasn't sure where it came from, but money was money. Money was good. I took this mantra with me to the passenger side and met Francine's eyes one last time before climbing in.

At the café, I did my best to spin a good yarn about my morning appointment, adding the kinds of details Jane loved, like the tiny furniture, my clicking pen, Sherry, and Francine's hobbit face. But the whole time I couldn't shake the feeling that I had done something wrong in there, something traitorous and irreversible.

That night, buried under my giant comforter and piles of blankets, I fell asleep thinking of Francine's crooked mouth saying, "There's a missing piece," over and over again. But my last waking image was of my mother, always my mother, a little more faded every time.

How did I get here?

The city lights dimmed with her face.

And of course, she didn't answer.

TWO

Right away I started pawing through old boxes, looking for suitable artifacts for Francine. I had one of Jane's poems and two pictures of her to bring. In one photo she was sweet and preppy, in the other she looked ready to pull out a gun.

I circled my old trunk, packed with Mom's papers and belongings, and then cracked it open. I'd quietly collected as much as I could after she died, when no one was looking, snapping up combs and lipstick, handkerchiefs, opera glasses, the remains of her Chanel No. 5, pocketing anything monogrammed, secreting her gardening shirts, appropriating her trademark penny loafers. I was the self-appointed keeper of my mother's archival flame, and no one seemed to mind or notice.

I also had reels of 16 mm film, found by Dad in the recesses of a closet he'd never had cause to open before Mom died. As far as he knew, they were the only record of Mom in motion. In the same closet he'd found boxes of letters and assorted Mom memorabilia, and he turned that over, too. I took it hungrily, hoarded it all, stacked it high in my room, and sorted through my loot, cataloging school records, calendars, letters, photographs, souvenirs, news clippings, and private journals. In these remains, I had hoped, lay my blueprints. Scattered clues to guide me on my own.

I took out the film strips and held them to the light. The reels began in Switzerland, 1904, when Mom's father got his first camera. His wedding to my grandmother was there, with plumed horses and decorated carriages. I scrolled past their immigration to St. Louis and, frame by frame, the birth of an American family. Mom turned up as a toddler, serious faced and teetering on unpracticed legs. The films ended with her at seventeen, in long dark braids, rocking in a porch chair, nervously taking her first public sip of liquor.

I put the film aside and moved on, flipping through Mom's school records, calendars, letters, souvenirs, and the curled yellow pages she'd written thoughts on.

I got caught up in the calendars—a lifetime of calendars that she'd kept. There were Smith College datebooks from the fifties, scattered hardbound calendars from the sixties, and, for most of my lifetime, the plain white spiral-bound variety, which had lived on her kitchen desk. Inside these volumes lay the fragments of my mother's life, penciled before me like echoes in her familiar hand. There were early dates with my father, periodic piano lessons, trips abroad, and, eventually, three children born. Her married years were littered with volunteer activities, school events, and countless trips with children to the doctor. There were graduations, birthdays, vacations, and lists and lists of daily errands.

I opened 1983 and was struck by its emptiness. The blank weeks were a record of Mom's emotional paralysis—her hideous trip into depression—and blank months followed when she had been locked behind hospital doors. Periodically Dad's inscrutable handwriting appeared, showing his efforts to fill in as carpool driver, errand runner, cook, doctor's appointment keeper, and social organizer. Mom's first, temporary returns from the hospital were recorded in my teenage scrawl, with big balloons and exclamation points. I saw that Dad had taken over for her final return, writing simply, *Mom home today.* By then, if I had written it, there would have been question marks at the end and not balloons.

Of all Mom's lists and notes, the most consistent entries appeared while I was in high school and college, prefaced by the restaurant name *Bernards,* where her Tuesday ladies group met once a month. I liked to call them her posse. They were a rowdy group of women, several of whom had grown up with my mother in St. Louis, and a few who joined later as fellow new wives and mothers back in the early sixties. Without fail, these ladies gathered for their monthly *Bernards* therapy, and in the summers they also met on Tuesday mornings for doubles tennis. They volunteered together, went to the same parties, and shared family trips. They were an inseparable collection of well-bred suburban housewives, Ivy League educated and independent minded, and as fixed an image in my childhood as winters by the fire, charged dinner table debates, or playing in the woods.

I checked my watch to make sure Jane would be away for a good while longer and then continued revisiting the calendars. I opened 1990 and looked for The Day, in early March. It was just before my birthday—*"Dr. Owen, 3:00."*

I had been with my mother for that spring visit when, at her request, Dr. Owen had put specifics behind what I'd already been told—that the old cancer had come back and now had found Mom's spine. This was not news by March. We had all been home for her Christmas Eve relapse, when Mom's back was seized by such pain in the middle of the night that Dad took her right to the hospital. Since then she had found pills to manage the pain and taken rounds of chemotherapy, but the chemo, Dr. Owen said, was to no avail.

Mom held my hand as I protested with the obvious—that she had done her part. She had lived past the two-year benchmark, which promised that recurrence was less likely than a fatal car wreck. And we had already celebrated. She had sent out letters telling her friends and family, and, I told Dr. Owen, she'd won her second chance fair and square.

Mom's oncologist spoke bluntly, as he knew my mother insisted, when he explained that in spite of this interim victory, the present ache in her back would continue to grow and spread. He said it would kill her, most likely within a year.

Mom was mute beside me after he said this, which was never her style. The only indication she gave of being present was her tightening grip on my hand and then a slight nod when Dr. Owen asked if she was all right.

Mom and I were quiet for most of the ride home. As we drove through our town, glass walls seemed to lower all around us, separating the life of the world from our suspended cocoon of silence. We drove past our grocery store, where Annie waved her broom at us and pointed to her new spread of peaches. We passed a row of firemen sitting in T-shirts and suspenders outside the firehouse, past the high school tennis courts where my mother had won so many victories, then down our lane, vibrant with spring life. The rising hum of cicadas signaled the evening's approach, and as our house came into view—white clapboard with black shutters, lined by my mother's gardens—a long, low wail rose within her. It was deafening. It didn't seem human. I remembered feeling her anguish ripple through me like thunder.

Like all memories, that car ride and my mother dissolved too soon, and I found myself with a tight jaw and moist palms, back in San Francisco, surrounded by a pool of calendars. I realized I had been sitting in the dark, probably for some time, and I closed the calendars and slid them into the box. The afternoon had dropped quickly into dusk, which was a dreaded, lonely moment for me. It told me I should be surrounded by family, setting five places for dinner, and competing with my brother and sister for parental attention. It left me vaguely unsettled and slightly worried.

As I reached for a light, the phone suddenly rang. I jumped and lifted the receiver, expecting to hear Jane's voice. Instead, a maternal hello carried across the line. It was Helen Burns, charter member of the Tuesday Group, checking in.

"Is this a good time?" she asked.

Still half inside the car with my mother, I gripped the phone and offered a pathetic squeak.

"Oh *dear*," Helen said. "That doesn't sound good."

Helen was at our house often, but especially in that spring of 1990—the first spring after I'd graduated from college and the last season that my mother would see. We lived in a state of surreal suspension then; everything had an air of The End. We held our collective breath, and had it not been for Helen and the Tuesday Group, I believe we would have all expired from the tension alone. That spring I had a hard time leaving my mother's side. When she napped, I lay in my father's spot beside her and waited for her to wake up. And when she did, I was grateful. I pretended not to notice when she cracked an eye open and watched me for a while. Her hand would eventually drift over to my head and stroke my hair. We had lots of conversations that way, unspoken games that grew into a sort of telepathy.

Because of my mother's health, various substitute fourths rotated into the Tuesday morning tennis games. One day my mother put me on the phone with Helen, who'd invited me to be their fourth the next morning. And since my mother's expression looked final, I said yes.

Mom loaned me her tennis dress and racket, and as we cooked dinner that night she described what I was in for. Helen would be the first on the scene, she said. She'd have a thermos of water, and she always remembered to bring the balls. And I should watch out for Frances Lipp; she was the lefty ringer of the group. I shouldn't be lulled by her gentle smile, which would disarm me right before a backhand whizzed past my ear and down the line. Joan Kelly, she added, had more energy than the group combined but a little less accuracy with her strokes.

"Joan's gift is in retrieving," Mom said. "No matter where the ball goes, her little legs will get her there, and the ball always comes back. So don't underestimate Joan," she warned, throwing carrots into a pot, "she'll drop it an inch over the net."

The group assembled early the next morning, and since my mother was still asleep when I left, I couldn't confirm that the dress she gave me was *supposed* to reveal my underwear. I marched bravely up the hill to the court, feeling the chill of late March air, tugging at the dress, and wishing the whole thing were over. The ladies were warming up when I arrived, embroiled in debate.

"You want to buy a *what?*" Helen was saying as she fired a volley at Joan's feet.

"You think it's a bad idea," Joan said, tapping the ball miraculously back over the net.

"Well, I think you might examine what the horse *represents*," Helen said, ducking a zinger from Frances Lipp. "I mean, a *horse*, Joan? Really."

"I don't understand," Joan said, breathing hard.

"Well, it's obviously a replacement for something," Helen said.

"Oh, Helen," Frances groaned.

"Tell the truth, Joan," Helen said, "are you and John . . ."

Joan made a *ppfft* sound and waved to me. I waved back, pretended I hadn't heard a thing, and trotted onto the court, feeling younger by the second.

"Praise the Lord, she's here," Joan said. "I'm all warmed out."

"Caroline's on my team," Helen announced. "Young legs," she added, patting me on the back.

I eyed Frances at the net and felt a surge of competitive adrenaline.

"Shouldn't Caroline get a chance to warm up?" Frances asked, smiling at me. Mom was right, she had a sensational smile.

"Nope," said Joan, "too late." And with that she served one hard to my right.

The ladies talked about their children and summer plans, tuitions, politics, and hot flashes as I hurled myself around the court in a desperate attempt to keep up. They never seemed to move, just a poke here and a swat there and I was on the ground, panting. After one particularly daring dive, I remember Helen looking down at me and shaking her head.

"It's not that serious, sweetie," she said, plucking the ball from my hand. "Did you take lessons from your mother?"

I smiled. That was a compliment.

"When you get older, you learn to econ-o-mize," Helen continued. "You realize you'll get there whether it's at top speed or a turtle's crawl, and the result is exactly the same."

"Helen," Joan called, "if you had twenty-two-year-old legs, we'd be looking at a puff of smoke right now."

"Whatever," Helen said, marching back to the baseline.

I brushed myself off.

"Just for the record," Joan said to me, "your mother defeated Helen on this very court—*with one lung.*"

Helen chuckled, then seemed to lose her concentration. She bounced the ball to serve, and after a while she said, "What is it, five to three?"

Frances and Joan didn't answer. I fixed my eyes on the ground.

"It's four all, you cheat," Joan finally said. And before I could blink, a ball whizzed past my ear.

. . .

"Water break!" Frances announced after the first set was over. "Let's change sides."

"I don't know what you think you'll gain by changing sides," Helen teased, opening her thermos and taking a long drink. "We've already beaten you on every side."

Frances shrugged, eyeing the water with anticipation.

"How are Madeleine and Grant doing?" Frances asked. She tossed her racket in the air and missed catching it. Helen snickered as it clunked to the ground.

"Fine," I said.

My brother and sister were fine as far as I knew, which wasn't very far at all. Madeleine was swallowed by the demands of medical school and living in another part of St. Louis. Grant was a busy lawyer in Washington, D.C. I didn't hear from them much.

"How's your dad?" Joan asked, twirling her racket. She caught it fine and grinned at Frances.

"He's all right," I said cautiously.

"He has a lot on his shoulders," Joan observed.

She was right. My father spent his days spotting cancers under his microscope and his nights caring for one of its victims. He was, by then, world famous in pathology. A side effect of his trade was that he usually got the task of telling family and friends exactly what disease they had and most likely how it would claim them. For years he had dutifully counseled people he loved—his mother and father, his in-laws, his closest friends. Then one day he slipped a slide under his microscope and saw his wife's disease, its familiar, awful cells marshaling their forces against her.

"Speak of the angel," said Frances, waving toward the road. My father drove past us, on his way to work. He waved back.

"Is your mom alone now?" Helen asked.

"Oh no, there's a nurse," I said. "Dolores."

"Dolores," they repeated in unison.

Frances dropped her racket and took a seat on the court. "Hand me that damn water, Helen, or I swear I will expire," she said, then added a smile.

"Does your mother like her?" Joan asked.

"God help Dolores if she doesn't," Helen remarked, passing the thermos to Frances with a matching smile.

"Oh, they have their battles," I said. "Dolores watches TV."

"Is that bad?" Joan asked.

I nodded. "Soap operas. All day long."

"Good God in heaven," said Frances, finishing off the water.

"Poor Dolores," Joan sighed. She took a seat beside Frances and started to stretch.

I nodded again. Behind my mother's back, Dolores was also fierce. One day when I'd skipped coming home from my first bookstore job for lunch, Dolores took me aside, bony finger raised to my nose. "Your mother got dressed for you," she hissed. "She waited."

I didn't tell Dolores that it was hard to get home and back in the hour I was allowed or that I'd been getting flak for coming back to work late. You don't look in the eyes of someone like Dolores and speak at all. You just make sure it doesn't happen again.

Helen pulled a pack of cookies from her gym bag. "Energy," she said, passing them to me.

I took a seat, wondering what had happened to the tennis game.

"I wish someone hadn't killed the water," Joan said loudly, taking a bite of cookie.

A figure emerged from the house overlooking the court and waved. "What are you guys doing?" she called.

Helen waved the cookies in the air and beckoned.

"Bring water!" Joan called.

Mrs. Reese, the owner of the tennis court, disappeared into her house and returned with lemonade.

"So who's winning?" she asked, winking at me. "They pooped out, didn't they."

Helen withdrew her cookies, indignant, and said, "Did not."

"Well, fine," said Mrs. Reese, taking a seat on the court. "So what are we talking about?"

We never did play a second set that day, and if my mother's friends had anywhere to go, they didn't show it. They reclined at my feet and talked, and, slowly, they pulled me from the shadows. I remember realizing that these women had known my mother long before I came into the world, and some even before she met my father. They had circled their wagons when Mom's depression struck and pulled them tighter, years later, when the cancer came. They had chased down doctors, healers, and alternative bookstores, looking for cures. For a while my mother ate pounds of carrots, put crystals in her pockets, and listened to visualization tapes at their insistence. Throughout my father held his tongue, knowing that the reality of the disease, and the improbability of miracles, made no difference to these women.

I thought of Mom propped up in bed at home—just a hundred yards away—probably cursing Dolores.

"Let's go see Monny," Helen said.

"Righto, exactly what I was thinking," said Joan, creaking to her feet. After a stop inside Mrs. Reese's kitchen to collect bags of food, I followed the Tuesday Group down the hill to our house and hoped with some anxiety that my mother would be in the mood for company.

"Monny!" four voices called as we entered.

Dolores froze at the sight of us and disappeared.

"Well, that was easy," said Joan, striding into the kitchen.

With military precision, the women unloaded milk, bread, fruit, Tupperware, and packages of cooked food. Helen pulled a bouquet of cut flowers from her bag. "They'll perk up," she said, pulling a vase from Mom's cupboard and filling it with water.

The ladies formed a single line and headed past Dolores into my mother's bedroom. I was about to enter, ready to help if she didn't want company, when I heard a hearty, unmistakable laugh that rarely sounded in our house anymore. When I peeked around the corner—nose to nose with Dolores—I saw my mother surrounded on her bed by three sweaty women. They were wearing handmade crowns with the title TUESDAY GIRLS printed across them.

"So did Caroline put up a fight out there?" I heard my mother ask.

"She threw herself all over the place, if that's what you mean," Helen replied.

"That's what I mean," Mom said proudly.

There was a long silence.

"So then . . . what's the news?" Mom finally asked. She spotted me then, in the doorway, and held me in her eyes. When I felt myself suddenly wanting to cry, I turned away with Dolores and followed her to see what the kitchen fairies had brought.

Mom died a few months later, on a Tuesday morning. I was supposed to be a fourth that day, and when I didn't show the ladies might have sensed it. They would have been warming up on Mrs. Reese's court when the ambulance came down our lane, followed by Dr. Owen's car, then my aunt's, my sister's, Reverend Michael's sedan, and the hearse. They must have gathered then, eyes fixed on the road to our house. I imagine they stood there for some time.

I know that when I finally emerged—after the minister had said his words, after I had seen my mother's body for the last time, and after our family had finished colliding in grief—three ladies stood in our driveway, waiting. They were shouldering tennis bags full of soups and flowers, and they were holding on to each other for dear life.

Two years later, when Helen reached me that evening in San Francisco, she must have heard the weight of the world in my voice.

"What's wrong?" she asked. "Are you in trouble?"

I took a deep breath.

"I . . . No. I'm okay."

"Not convincing," Helen said.

Just then I heard a car horn outside and saw Jane parking. I drifted in thought, until Helen called me back. "I don't mean to be rough, Caroline," she said, "but no one hears from you. You're like a ghost out there."

I leaned my forehead against the window and watched Jane sing along with her radio. *Here she comes*, I thought. *My best friend, and my worst enemy.* She lifted something from the backseat, and my heart sank. *And she's bringing pizza and a video.*

Helen's voice returned. She seemed worlds away.

"Hey? Are you there?" she asked. "See, it's happening now—"

If one can experience a feeling of combined terror and love, I felt it then, hearing Jane's keys find our door and then her searching voice calling me as she entered.

I pushed the box of calendars into my closet as her feet came padding down the hall.

"I know, Helen," I said.

Jane poked her head in and winked at me, pulling the pizza and a movie from behind her back.

I heard silence on the other end, not a good sign from Helen. "I've got to go," I said quickly. And without hearing her good-bye, I hung up.

Chapter THREE

Jane and I once figured out that we had moved to San Francisco simultaneously, in the spring of 1991. She had taken the northern route from Massachusetts through Wyoming and Montana, and I followed southern roads from St. Louis through Oklahoma, past the Grand Canyon, and on into the Mojave Desert.

After Mom died, I had started imagining that she watched me from high places, like city roofs or the tops of trees. I imagined she was urging me to leave home, even though saying good-bye to my father felt dangerous, and the image of his tall, silent figure waving in my rearview mirror would haunt me all the way to California.

Governed by Dad's good sense, I'd flown out to San Francisco in advance and made a surgical strike, renting the first place I found, a one-room studio in the Haight-Ashbury district. I landed a job at Sorrell's bookstore, fifty miles south of the city, near Stanford University, and to Dad's amazement I was back in a flash and quickly packing.

To most of my family, my decision seemed sudden. For me, it

was overdue. After Mom's funeral in June, my brother flew back to his life in Washington, D.C., and my sister turned back to the distractions of medical school. Dad got back to work as quickly as possible and was gone from the house early every day. Meanwhile, I spent the summer days lying on the roof in my bikini and long nights watching television. When the weather turned cold, I wandered our house and prowled my mother's belongings.

I was twenty-three, and the life that stretched before me had no shape or substance in my mind. The plans I'd had all my life faded to nothing as I baked in the sun, replaying old scenes with Mom, letting them roll behind my sunglasses like home movies. I watched us on the patio in spring, when I was still young enough to think our two acres and family encompassed the world. Mom had pulled weeds from between bricks while I plugged a fountainhead with my finger, releasing the water and then plugging it again. She had paused as I, drunk with some strange happiness, announced that I would live in St. Louis forever. When I was married, I told her, I would have a house next door. I would see her every day.

"I'd love that," Mom admitted. "But there are a lot of exciting places in the world outside of St. Louis." She waved her hand, as if to suggest the range of possibilities.

"I don't want to see them," I'd replied.

Mom said, "After I went to college, I almost moved to California."

I unplugged the fountain and crossed my arms. "Really? Why?"

"Well, there was a young man . . . ," she ventured. Then she paused, unsure of how to develop that story for my ears.

"Dad?" I asked.

When Mom shook her head, my smile faded.

"Your father wasn't happy about my going," she whispered playfully. "But I'd only ever lived in St. Louis. And there was the young man . . ."

"So what happened?" I demanded.

"Oh. My car broke down in Kansas City. And by then I was pretty anxious about leaving my mother, your aunt Estie, and my brothers. And your father, too. I think I was a little scared. . . ."

"And you changed your mind," I said approvingly.

"I did." Mom smiled.

"And see, aren't you glad?"

"Well. I'm awfully glad I married your father," she said. "And I'm glad *you're* here," she added, winking. "But sometimes I still think about California. Sometimes I wonder who I might have been if I had gone."

Under the summer sun, I replayed that story. I replayed it until it grew into a mission, and then it became a plan. If my brother had his law career, and my sister her medicine, if my father had his work, if all of my friends were bouncing around the world and finding love, then the least I could do was aim past Kansas City and find this place called California.

I had high hopes for San Francisco. I'd read that Joan Baez lived near Sorrell's and often visited the store, and I figured if she liked it, I would, too. I also fancied myself an up-and-coming hippie—I had a guitar, and I was gloomy—which fit in perfectly with my image of the city. Best of all, only a few people there knew me, so I'd have plenty of room to change everything about myself.

Looking back, I see San Francisco as a curious siren. Almost everyone I was about to meet had migrated west for their own vague reasons, following some strange instinct that promised hope. It was a place that seemed ripe with possibility; I was already envisioning my new life as a writer, filmmaker, and all-around free spirit. And Jane was pointed west then too, already transforming her problems and past into fiction.

My drive began well enough. I was fueled by the prospect of adventure and the anticipation of a new and better me who would surely materialize as I crossed each border. Maybe I'd learn to *play* the guitar that was crammed into my backseat or become a genius filmmaker with the Super 8 resting on my dashboard. I wondered if I might fall in love with a young poet or have an affair with a Berkeley English professor.

The fantasy began to fade in Oklahoma. Solitary hours wore on me, and I fell back into old habits of talking to myself, of pretending I was a stand-up comedian, or Blanche DuBois, or Bruce Springsteen. I found new meaning in the song "Born to Run," which I belted out my window and into the open sky, rewinding and singing it again until my voice was raw. Later, and suddenly, I was struck by tears—heavy, hiccupy tears that wouldn't subside even when exhaustion set in. I wondered if this was what Mom had felt in Kansas City—the transiting sense of being caught between what you've left and lost, and the unknown ahead. As I drove, nothing I filled my mind with, from counting seconds between the power lines, to singing with the radio, distracted the growing uneasiness inside me.

I paused long enough to point my Super 8 at the Grand Canyon, then made my way through the rest of Arizona and into the vast, vacant Mojave. I didn't see a soul for hours, and with the desert sprawled before me, I became desperate for a sign of life. I was squinting hopefully at a glassy image materializing in the distance when my car hood suddenly made a popping sound and a river of oil oozed up my windshield. A loud cracking noise was followed by a brief shudder, then my little Celica limped to the side of the road in a cloud of steam and quit.

While I sat in the noon heat, pondering my next move, Jane was speeding up north. She had hitched a ride with a friend, and I can picture her reclined in the passenger seat, bare feet stuck out the window the way she liked to do. Depending on her mood, she might have been working the radio and singing along or braiding her hair and reading Anne Sexton or Hemingway.

When it came to authors or artists, Jane was drawn to people who had either gone crazy or killed themselves. Doing both was ideal. She had spent some time herself in a place she called the "loony bin," and I later wondered if her habit of drawing razors across her arms and legs might have started around then. I was never present to see, but Jane said she held her breath when she cut herself, piercing her skin just enough to hurt but not so much as to leave visible scars. The minute she exhaled, she said, everything felt better.

"Imagine sinking into a hot bath on a cold night," she would later tell me. "Over and over again."

Jane didn't talk much about the times she was sent away, and since she talked freely about everything else, I imagined it was pretty bad. Stripped of her razors, and confined with people at all extremes of mental distress, she said she took residence by a corner window lined with wire and sat there all day, thinking of what, I never learned. But later—on the occasions when Jane felt thwarted, threatened, or betrayed—I'd see her take root by our apartment window in the same way and detach with such frightening completeness that I wondered if part of her wasn't still latched to that loony bin, frozen in time.

But as she rode west with her friend, I know Jane was thinking things were about to get better. I'm sure we both did, as we crossed the country that April.

My car breaking down did dent my optimism, though. It was a perfect, if obvious, metaphor. I had apparently "blown my head gasket," which is the predictable result when flying through a scorching desert at one hundred miles per hour with the windows down and air-conditioning on full. Like my poor gasket, emptied of its oil and cracked in two, I sat broken in my shack of a motel room, in the middle of nowhere. And I was exhausted. I had walked a mile to an emergency phone, called for help, and trudged one mile back to my car. An hour later, a man in a lumbering pickup arrived and said he'd "hitch me right up," which I hoped would mean "go back and get a nice clean AAA tow truck" but really meant "put a chain on my car and drag it to a motel/auto shop fifty miles outside of nowhere." His name was Elmer, and he was completely bald on the top of his head, with a fringe of thin blond hair dripping down to his shoulders. His face was ageless and tan and lined by the sun.

"We got no television or phones," Elmer warned as we pulled into his small encampment. A tin sign hung over what looked like a barn, and it read ELMER'S AUTO BODY/OVERNIGHT. Next to the barn there were six little green cottages made of thin wood.

"You can have number five," he said.

I must have started crying then, because I remember Elmer calling his "boys" out to "look at this." Four men of varying ages emerged blinking from the barn, and they lit up cigarettes while I sat on a tire and wept.

"Head gasket," Elmer said to the boys. They nodded and started opening beers.

"Got to go way on to Appleton for that," one man said. "Radiator?"

Elmer patted my car hood. "Probably shot to hell." He asked one of the boys to show me to number five.

A wind started kicking up as I stepped inside the room. It blew right through the walls and tossed my hair. The fellow who led me in said he was Louis, and he watched me from the doorway as I sat on the bed with my purse on my knees and tried to look composed.

"Are there other people here?" I asked.

Louis looked puzzled.

"Are there other guests?"

He chuckled. "Naw. Not many folks come out this way. At least not on purpose. We go home on the weekends ourselves."

I used every ounce of strength not to entertain Louis with more tears. He seemed to be waiting for them to come.

"Got a quarter?" he asked brightly. He pointed to a coin slot beside my bed. "Pop one in there and it shakes." Then he winked and shut the door behind him.

After a while I wondered about food. I had been watching Elmer and his boys through my window, waiting to see if they ate. Finally I stepped outside and approached the barn. They were sitting on crates, eating sandwiches and drinking more beer. Elmer said hello. I asked about the food and he said they cooked in their rooms, but that I could order pizza because a number was scratched on the glass in the phone booth outside. I backed out of the barn and went to find the phone booth, fighting harder winds. I spotted it way out in the desert, leaning a little, a good quarter mile away. When I arrived at the booth, anxious and out of breath, I found messages carved into the glass like the last words of some lost civilization. I half expected to see a pile of skeletons at my feet.

I located the Domino's number, ordered a large pizza with three Cokes, and then returned to my cottage window to wait. Sometime later a dot appeared on the darkening horizon, growing into the shape of a white Honda civic. I rushed out to greet my hero, who looked to be barely sixteen, with a sloping smile and bad skin.

"One large and three Cokes," he said, touching his cap. I downed an entire slice as I paid him.

"Goddamn," he said, impressed.

"I'm stranded," I said. "Please don't go."

The boy laughed. "Elmer's okay," he said, climbing into his car. "Just watch out for the other guys. I hear they get kind of restless." And with that, my link to civilization peeled off into the distance.

After finishing half the pizza and two Cokes in my room, I went back to the phone booth. By now the wind was furious, and my long hair went horizontal as I stepped in slow motion across the sand. I had a radio in my room, and a newscaster had said that a record-breaking windstorm was in progress, reaching speeds of up to seventy miles per hour. He said the space shuttle *Atlantis*, which was due to land that very afternoon, had to keep orbiting because of the wind. When I finally made it inside the phone booth and finished spitting out mouthfuls of sand, I dialed my father collect. The minute I heard his voice I started to cry again, loud and hard, until he finally had to shout over the phone.

"Are you hurt?" he yelled. "Where are you?" That released a whole new level of sobbing, matched only by the howling wind.

"I am going to wait until you stop," Dad yelled.

I imagined him on our blacktop with a megaphone, calling across the miles between us. After a while I slumped against the phone booth and quieted.

Dad's voice was calm. "Where are you, Caroline?" he asked.

"I don't know," I said.

"You don't know?"

"Correct."

"Do you know what *state* you are in?"

I looked around.

"Well, it's pretty windy."

Dad cleared his throat. "Well, that's not a lot to go on."

Having not yet ascertained if I was bleeding, drugged, or kidnapped, my father was probably losing his patience.

"Elmer's Auto Body/Overnight," I said, squinting at the sign. It was shaking in the wind. "I'm in the desert, that's for sure. Probably California. They said my car blew the something gasket."

Dad sighed. "Is there someone there I can talk to?"

"Why?"

"Because California is a large state, and I'd like to know exactly where you are."

Bless him, I wanted to know that, too.

"I think everybody's sleeping off their beers," I said. "I'm staying in a one-room cottage next to a barn where five men seem to fix cars. Last I saw, they were pretty drunk."

"Oh, God," Dad said. "Don't wake them."

"No, I won't."

"Is there a number where I can call you?" he asked.

"Well, it's a phone booth," I said, "and the number is gone."

I began scratching my name into the glass with a key. I put it under an inscription that read "Welcome to Nowhere." Dad and I were quiet on the phone.

"So is Gayle there?" I asked. She was Dad's first attempt at dating, and last I'd checked they were making progress.

"No," he said.

"Oh. Did you eat dinner yet?"

"Yes."

I was quiet again.

"Pasta," Dad added.

I finished my name and started on Mom's.

"Are you missing Mom tonight?" I asked. It was a stupid question, but I wanted to hear him say it.

"Every night," he said.

The names Caroline and Monny—short for Madeleine—were now permanently recorded on the glass. I started on Dad's name, Frederick. I already felt sorry for the next person who found himself standing in this phone booth, reading the names of other lost travelers as they dialed for pizza.

"Anyway, check the news tonight," I said, changing my tone.

"Why?"

"I'm in the middle of the world's biggest windstorm, and the space shuttle can't land. If they show a map, you'll know where I am."

On that note I signed off and hurled myself through the wind back into the cottage. On my way, I saw one of Elmer's boys taking a cardboard box out of the trunk of my car. He set it on the ground and opened it.

"Hey!" I yelled, but my voice came back at me in the wind. I saw him pull out several books and my wooden box of letters, which were too precious to send with movers. I ran toward my car, this time pushed by the wind, and skidded to a stop inches from the man. His shirt said CLEM. "What are you doing?" I asked. "That's mine." I had to shout over the wind.

Clem nudged the box with his foot. "Just curious," he said. My Swiss Army knife was sticking out of Clem's pocket. I reached for it and he batted my hand. I stepped back. Clem folded his arms, amused.

Feeling suddenly, completely alone, I bent down and cautiously picked up my box. Clem sat on a crate with beer and pretzels and watched me while I shuttled the contents of my car into my room.

During the night I hung on to my mattress and waited for the roof to fly off. The wind rushed against my face and howled through the slats in the walls. I was tempted to relocate to my car but thought I might encounter one of Elmer's boys or get swept into the heavens on the way. Later in the night I thought I saw shadows passing my window. Then I was sure I heard voices. After one said my name, I leapt up, pushed my bed in front of the door, and sat on it until morning.

By the time light appeared, the wind had stopped. I stepped outside and saw bottles and cans all around my door and faint shoe prints embedded in the sand. I set my jaw and went directly to the barn to ask Elmer when my car would be ready. He thought for a moment, then estimated that I had at least two more days before I was going anywhere, probably three. The boys stood behind Elmer and unanimously agreed.

My mouth was open in horror when, of all things, a police car rounded the corner and pulled right up beside us. A uniformed fellow stepped lightly out of his cruiser and walked over. He was on the older side and rugged, way over six feet, with a big round gut. His badge said "Officer Hunt."

"Are you Caroline Kraus?" he asked me.

I said I was.

"Well, your daddy called us last night over in Appleton, and he asked us to check on you."

Elmer pushed his cap back on his head and looked at the policeman.

"She's fine," he said. The boys were hiding behind an old junk car, not too eager to be seen by the law.

"I see she is," the policeman said. He walked toward the junk car and sent the boys flying in all directions. Then he looked at Elmer and said, "Where do they think they're going? Clear across the desert?"

Elmer stood, scratched his chin, and said something about my car maybe getting fixed sooner. Maybe under an hour.

"That's good news!" The policeman looked at me. "Isn't that good news?"

I watched the boys skirt around the cottages, grabbing duffel bags and shouting at each other, and thought that it surely was good news.

I waited in the police car while Elmer tinkered with mine. After talking to Elmer privately, Officer Hunt joined me. From time to time, the police radio squawked about this or that problem at a faraway residence or traffic light, and Officer Hunt's eyes narrowed as he listened, and then he relaxed. After a bit he turned to me.

"Good parents," he said.

"What?"

"Looking after you all the way out here."

"Yeah," I said, "but my mother is dead." I looked away, confused by my confession.

"Oh," Officer Hunt said. He cleared his throat and squinted at the sun. I felt like holding his hand, he looked so hurt.

When Elmer finished, he asked for $800, all the money I had in traveler's checks. He said he didn't believe in "plastic money," so I signed my checks over as fast as I could, shook hands with Officer Hunt, and tore away.

Elmer's shop was still visible in my rearview mirror when three squad cars appeared, then flew past me, lights ablaze. My heart pounded. I wondered how close I'd come to any number of horrors. I wished I could throw my arms around my father, who must have stayed up all night looking for a police station somewhere in the California desert, near a place where a space shuttle apparently couldn't land. I said a prayer for the Officer Hunts of the world, who troubled themselves with girls like me, and accelerated west. I didn't realize it then, but I was leaving the last zone of my father's protective reach. And it must have been terrifying for him, to know his youngest was moving away so fast, crossing borders he could not see or hope to understand.

I fueled up and drove all day, arriving in San Francisco late at night. My little studio was dark—the basement floor of a three-story Victorian at the steep top of Masonic Street. It had one big window with a partial view of passing feet. Which was a strange perspective—over time I would come to see my neighborhood as an energetic population of shoes.

I unloaded my car into the tiny room, collapsing in a pile of clothes and boxes and falling sound asleep until morning.

Over on Castro Street, Jane was in her temporary lodging, an apartment belonging to her friend. She was probably curled in a ball, secretly sucking her thumb. When the sun rose we would both wake to our new surroundings.

We had both arrived. Both driven as far as we could.

FOUR

Growing up, I learned pretty quickly that I had two strengths to speak of. They were unremarkable in a global sense, but solid. Enough to get me by.

It turned out I was coordinated. On playgrounds I outran most anybody—boys included. And if I wanted to put a ball in a goal, net, or basket, I could dribble around ten people and do it. I took my awards and trophies and clung to my place at the top, mainly because in classrooms I was more acquainted with the other end. Numbers baffled me. Facts slipped from my distractible mind, and laws of science swirled like hieroglyphics on the page. Only one area really clicked, and that was books—books with stories, not numbers. Turned out I had a knack. I saw meaning in, around, and beneath the words. I disappeared into them and emerged drunk with inspiration. It made sense, too—stories were a portal into dreams, and dreaming was my preferred state of mind.

Along with reading, I added writing to my short list of activities. Making up my own stories provided satisfying alternative worlds, tailored to my adolescent moods. I mined the fertile fields of schoolyard politics, raw childhood emotion, and the peculiar, frightening, and generous teachers I encountered. I watched it all from a safe distance, recorded it, received some notice and applause.

It shouldn't have been funny, but we had all laughed when a classmate's father was arrested. The story was he'd been caught in a state of "indecent exposure," which put him in jail for three days. Our third-grade teacher had to call a class discussion to stop our loud speculations as to what indecent exposure meant, which had driven our classmate to tears.

In the fifth grade we heard about a girl at another school whose older sister was killed in a car crash. That same year, a sixth-grader lost both his parents, one three months after the other. In my detached eyes, this was all grist for the mill. As far as I was concerned, any real calamities might as well have happened on TV. I never once imagined that the horrors I heard about could seep into my reality. If anything, I took pleasure in seeing the bullets repeatedly miss our home. It reinforced my feeling that the Kraus family was invincible.

I was too young to understand that no one is spared forever, or even for long. Had I looked more closely at the people around me, or with wiser eyes, I might have seen that little cracks were everywhere—in my friends' families, in families that were just like mine. I might have discovered that divorces were troubling kids I played with, that secrets loomed in the most fashionable households, and that accidents, embarrassments, and losses were talked about all the time, but in hushed adult voices, kept low to protect younger ears. When my luck changed, I was unprepared. I never had the chance to look over my shoulder and say good-bye.

My turn came in tenth grade, when Maggie Johnson died. Maggie was a sophomore like me, went to a Catholic school two towns over, and we were serious rivals on the playing fields. Whenever I saw the number eight—in math class, on billboards, on license plates or signs—I always thought of Maggie's green-and-white jersey, whizzing past me with a hockey ball tight on her stick. She was considered the greatest athlete ever to grace St. Agnes Academy, and to my growing envy, the *St. Louis Post-Dispatch* took constant notice of her.

Maggie and I began as enemies, two opposing forwards equally driven to score. We swore to our respective friends that we didn't like each other and exchanged the requisite dirty looks when we passed on the field. But really I enjoyed our competition. I was awed by Maggie's talent. I snuck to her games against other teams and hid myself behind the bleachers, cheering her on.

Maggie wore a long brown ponytail, and her thick, sturdy frame made some girls mistake her for slow. When she blew past them like a comet, they realized too late they were wrong. Where I was reckless and overreaching, Maggie was clever, quick, and cool. And when we were combined on a special all-star team that tenth-grade year, we became a formidable pair on the forward line.

At first we were cautious, unsure how to act after battling each other for so long. My muscles resisted passing the ball to her open stick, and if I did, she scrambled with surprise. Neither of us was content to assist at the goal, as we were both groomed to be the one who scored, and it was only when our coach forced us to practice alone that we developed our rhythm, and then caution turned into friendship.

By the time our all-star team traveled to California for the Thanksgiving tournament, Maggie and I were inseparable, giggling allies. We sat together on the airplane and listened to Elton John, sharing headphones. Elton's song "Funeral for a Friend" became our anthem that November—we had decided that opposing teams would be the unfortunate "friend" when we got done with them.

Maggie scored herself a hat trick there, while college scouts took notes, and I scored a pair of goals, too. We were on top of the world on the plane back to St. Louis, and when we hugged good-bye at the airport, we swore to stay in touch.

The next time I saw Maggie was a few weeks later, at one of her basketball games in early December. I waved when she came jogging onto the court, but she didn't see me. I stayed long enough to see her score sixteen points and then took off for home. Two days later I got a phone call from Katie, a classmate of Maggie's and the goalie on our all-star team. I was reading in my bedroom when I picked up the phone.

"Maggie's dead," Katie sputtered.

"Huh?" I said. "Katie?"

A strange whimper followed.

"Hello?"

"Did you hear me?" she wailed.

"What did you say?"

"Maggie is dead."

A pause.

"Ha ha," I said.

A nervous giggle from Katie.

"You're sick," I said. "Is she there?"

"Caroline. She was killed last night. On Highway forty."

"Oh, shut up," I said, closing my book. I waited with the phone to my ear. "Katie. Come on. You'd better stop it right now."

"I'm not joking."

"No, I just saw her. I saw her play against Villa."

"I know, I saw you," she said. "I'm on the team."

I said, "Damn it, this isn't funny," and waited for Maggie's voice to come on the line.

Katie whimpered again.

"Oh, God," I whispered.

"You're the first person I called," she said. "I'm sorry. I'm not good at this."

I kicked my bookshelf, sending a mountain of paperbacks onto the floor. Then I dropped the phone. When I screamed, my sister, who was home for Christmas, came running. She saw me hit the wall before I pulled my bookshelf down and then stepped aside as I raged past her.

Mom was in the basement. When she saw me trip down the wooden stairs, she dropped an armful of laundry. "What's *wrong?*" she gasped, catching me. "What's happened?"

When I told her, her body froze around me like a shell.

Maggie was in the *Post-Dispatch* the next morning, in a big obituary. A full page remembered her as a popular, gifted young girl and one of the best athletes to play upon our midwestern fields. I stared at her sly, grinning picture, stared at it as though she might come back. I read the obituary twice and then read it again. I hadn't known she was a scholar or that she had two older brothers and a little sister. I hadn't known that the college scouts from California were already calling. Or that, as her mother was quoted, she had plans to be a psychologist. That was news to me.

The article said Maggie had died late at night on a snowy highway, not driving but running across four lanes after her car had broken down. Three friends were with her but too scared to make the dash. They had seen Maggie slip, and then headlights coming fast through the night, and then she was knocked high in the air. She landed under a second car and was run over by a third.

I remember thinking that was all wrong. She had been so fast, so brilliant on her feet. I had never once seen her slip.

On the day of her funeral, just before Christmas, a letter arrived for me with Maggie's name on the return address. My mother pulled it from her apron pocket and choked when she handed it to me. Inside I found a note and pictures I'd sent Maggie of the two of us in California. She'd put devil's horns on my head. The note read, "Hey—thanks for coming to my basketball game. I came to see you after, but you were gone (?) And thanks for the pictures . . . they ruin our image, though (heh heh). You keep it in the archives, okay? Maggie."

I touched the thick paper and smelled it, hoping to catch some living remnant. I saved the envelope and put the note beside it in a special album, with Maggie smiling on the cover. Pictures of her went up around my room, along with every article about her death. It was my first shrine. The beginning of everything and the terrible end. A dead friend's letter, addressed to me.

That year, like all teenagers, I changed incrementally, into someone new. For a while, my writing turned dark and mean, with characters suffering graphic, bloody deaths. The high school journal editor wouldn't print them, saying the newspaper preferred the funny stories I'd submitted before, the ones with happy endings. He said to let him know when I started writing those again.

At first I stopped showing my writing to others, and then I stopped writing altogether. I had lost my powers of concentration, so that words in any form became a challenge not worth the effort. So instead I watched movies. I snuck late night TV at home, and went to the theater every weekend, or as often as my parents would allow. In movies I disappeared the way I had in books, only the images came to me ready-made, preserving my energy. And when I realized I could count on sound and picture to relieve me from my thoughts, like a helpless addict, I fell in love with film.

In such a volatile time as adolescence, when the course of a developing mind is still so mutable, Maggie's death must have set my rudder askew. For months I was beset by a new, existential confusion, long before I had any idea what "existential" meant. I drifted. And carrying an almost physical sense of loss, I found myself far from solid ground when the next bullet came, and made a direct hit.

It was one year later, on Thanksgiving night, and a jury of

family members was at our house to witness it. Uncles, aunts, my grandmother, and cousins were all present, so there was no denying it had happened.

Uncle Dee had mimicked Grandmother Moser's Swiss accent, and Mom twirled with a plate of cheese and crackers in her hand, eyes on fire. "Stop it!" she shouted at her brother. "Stop it stop it stop it!" She threw down the tray. "That's our *mother*, Dee."

The room went silent, save for a small giggle that escaped from my sixteen-year-old cousin, Heidi. Mom whirled around and faced the giggler. "You think it's *funny?*" she shouted. Heidi cringed and shook her head, but another giggle escaped.

"Monny . . . ," Grandmother said.

Mom pointed at Heidi and said, "You don't have any right."

Heidi edged away and then ran down our hall. To everyone's astonishment, Mom chased her, shouting and waving her fist. Then Dad chased Mom. Then my grandmother hauled herself up and trailed Dad, and I sprinted after them. I found everyone crowded in my brother's bathroom, with Heidi cornered on the toilet, weeping. Dad held Mom back and said, "Stop it, Monny," into her ear.

"Vat is vrong?" my grandmother wheezed. She was out of breath, gripping the shower curtain.

Mom seethed and shook, her eyes fixed on Heidi. Then she burst into tears, turned, and fled for the rest of the night.

The rest of us went on with the turkey-and-pie routine. Everyone was on edge, looking over their shoulders for my possessed mother. Grandmother made an awkward but well-meaning toast, in which she reminded us to be grateful for all we had. She was our last living grandparent and as such held high office in our hearts. We went back to our sweet potatoes, cranberries, and stuffing, determined to be thankful.

By December, Mom had stopped leaving the house. Dad said she woke herself up crying at night, and when that woke him they talked about anything Dad could think of that was good, trying to chase away her depression. She told my father that a sadness was gripping her, a paralyzing ache in her chest. She confessed to thoughts of suicide and asked him not to leave her sight. If he stepped outside to empty the trash or get the paper, she watched him from a window until he returned. Meanwhile, Mom's doctor delivered medications to help her sleep, to block her thoughts before they warped into something lethal.

I kept going to school. But as I walked across the street each morning, the better part of me stayed behind, where my mother disintegrated with alarming speed.

She had stopped coming to my hockey games, though I still maintained the improbable hope that she'd appear in the stands, healed by some divine intervention. Each time, her absence threw me. She had played a mean center forward herself at my age, and I had come to rely on her thundering voice running with me as I chased the ball, willing me toward the goal. Sometimes she had been alone on the sidelines, bundled against the weather on wooden bleachers. Other times Dad was there, too, along with cheering crowds, and still her voice had found me.

It was a bad sign when she stopped coming, and as her emotional systems shut down, her moods took on a contagious sense of gloom. On the morning of my last hockey game for the season, Mom was crying at breakfast. When I walked out the door with my book bag, she was still in tears.

I was distracted when I suited up for the game, and preoccupied when the starting whistle blew. When I raced toward the ball I landed on it, cracking my ankle and turning my knee. In my young life I had never felt such pain. It shot up my leg, through my gut, and into my brain like burning metal.

I fell. And in that suspended moment—when spectators gasped and jaws dropped, when all eyes were on me, blinking and widening, adjusting to the scene—I saw a figure in the distance, gripping her purse like a football, running full-tilt toward the field.

Seconds later Mom was crouched at my side. She assessed my swelling leg and ankle and determined correctly that I could not walk. She held my hand and singled out two senior boys to carry me to our car. She kept her head down as other mothers called after her, and she took a deep breath before putting our car in gear.

We headed straight to the emergency room—Mom pale and shaky in the driver's seat, and me moaning in the back. Then I started laughing. I laughed so hard that she almost blew a red light. She hit the brakes and turned around, looking at me.

"You *came*," I said, gripping my knee. "You're better."

Mom's expression was vacant, sick. My smile faded.

"Aren't you better?"

We stared at each other. Her jaw quivered.

"But you came," I said.

She looked as mystified as I felt.

The light turned green, and Mom hit the gas. We drove in silence, then I saw tears on her cheek. I heard her mutter, "Come on Monny, come on. Come *on* Monny. Come on . . ."

Looking back, I remember that day with wonderment. I carry it with me, dusting it off whenever I need to remember that once I had someone who could track me down when I was in trouble and bring me to safety, even as she crashed.

Chapter
FIVE

A thick fog greeted me when I cracked an eye to my first morning in San Francisco. It was eerie how it seeped and hung, turning the Victorian houses across the street into vague, muted impressions. I camped out at my window for a long time, watching feet pass on missions I guessed based on their shoes. Black laced oxfords were headed to the financial district, orange pumps for shopping, flip-flops taking a day at the beach. High-tops on skateboards rushed past, and combat boots walked in pairs. Penny loafers had not shown up until late in the afternoon, when I finally ventured out.

I opened my door and shrieked. A man stood on the other side. He screamed and clutched his chest. A tiny hairless dog hopped in the air beside him.

"Honey," he gasped.

"Jesus," I said.

"I'm Gary," he explained. "From upstairs." He took a breath and said, "You scared the life out of Jackson," which I understood to mean his dog.

"Jesus," I said again.

Gary peeked behind me into my studio, and I closed the door quickly, stepping onto the walk outside.

"Headed somewhere?" he asked.

I looked around. The fog had lifted. People walked with purpose, and I envied them their destinations. "I thought I'd find a grocery store," I said.

"The closest market is right up there," he said, pointing. "But it's expensive. The Safeway is better. It's down the hill past Haight, two blocks."

"Oh."

"So you're new to the city?" he asked. His navel was visible below a cropped purple shirt. A little jewel was pierced inside. I nodded at the jewel.

"Is there a good bookstore nearby?" I asked. "Or a café?"

"Ah," he said with recognition. "Do you have a map?"

I did, and I showed him. "It's a long walk," he admitted, "but City Lights is here on Columbus in North Beach. Vesuvio's Café is next door." I brightened, having read about those exact places. He studied me and added, "You'll probably be wanting to stand at the corner of Haight and Ashbury, right?"

His tone had turned accusing, so I shrugged, although that had been on my itinerary.

He sighed and tapped the map showing the intersection, right around the corner. "I warn you, though," Gary said, "there's a Gap on the corner now, and a Starbucks. Alice doesn't live here anymore, if you get what I mean."

I could tell Gary was already disappointed in me. I must have seemed like a cliché, just another misguided arrival playing hip until reality set in and the appeal of pretend poverty wore off. Later he said he saw it all the time, kids like me who moved to the Haight district expecting to see Janis Joplin stepping out of her pink Victorian and into a psychedelic Porsche on her way to Jimi Hendrix's house.

Before sending me off, Gary pointed to a few areas I should avoid. "Everything else is paradise," he said. "You can't go wrong."

I looked up and down the street again. Consulted the map. Gary followed my eyes north, south, east, and west. "Go that way," he suggested. He nudged me and pointed down the hill. "Play nice, and be home before dark."

I folded my map and got moving.

It was exciting, the liberation I felt, and sad. I was free to go anywhere, do anything, be anybody. I had no attachment to restrain me, no expectations to reward. Everything was there, and everything was new. The remains of my family were far away, each on their own separate course. Nobody was watching. Like a boat slipping unnoticed from its dock, I set off down the street, unmoored.

You know you're not right when everything you've dreamed of is before you, and it all seems dull. I looked in the window at City Lights bookstore, where authors I admired had become legends, and forced myself to go inside. I sighed at the shelves of books around me, where I had imagined myself standing just as I was, blossoming by osmosis into a new Great Voice. Now the shelves of genuine great voices cowed me. I smiled at the clerk, pretended I was late for something important, and left.

Next door, Vesuvio Café was also known for harboring writers. I went inside and moved past smoky tables and colorful walls to a small round table. Maybe Ginsberg had sat there, or Kerouac, or Neal Cassady. I bought coffee and opened my notebook. *You're here*, I told myself, *do something.* But when my thoughts stalled somewhere between "do" and "something," I left again, this time for home.

I finished unpacking, soothed by the mindless purpose of small tasks. I played records, made tea, and organized my books by genre, author, and size. Photographs went up in a flurry of hammer and nails, and as darkness fell, I tugged at my lamp chains one by one, until the room swam with cozy yellow light, like a submarine. Outside, I thought, the blinking houses and streetlights could have been passing ships.

The next morning, as I dressed for my first day of work, I reviewed the pictures on my walls. I had hung them so unevenly that it actually looked intentional. On one wall I greeted my brother, sister, Mom, and Dad, with their familiar expressions forever suspended in photographic time, as ethereal and distant as childhood.

In each photograph I lingered on my mother. My infant arms circled her neck in black and white as I peeked over her shoulder. In color, my father kissed her on their anniversary. My sister stood beside Mom in Paris and whispered in her ear. My brother hugged her from behind with a red apple in his teeth.

On another wall, pictures of my friends suggested privileged, happy lives—attractive kids with infectious smiles, contraband beers at parties, locked arms at football games; all with bright futures, all grinning with the lightness of possibility.

I left them, paused in front of my mirror, and gave myself a parting look.

Wear lipstick, Mom would have advised.

I found some and colored my lips.

And remember who you are.

That had been her favorite. Like on *Hill Street Blues*, when the captain said to his men, "Let's be careful out there," Mom sent me out with, "Remember who you are." I had heard it first when I was nine, before Little League soccer tryouts. As the only girl showing up—in the whole history of that particular league—I had needed some prodding.

"You belong out there as much as any boy," Mom had said.

And as she adjusted my old girls team uniform, I remember

thinking, These are her rules, not theirs. Earlier, when she had cornered the Little League chairman during his son's baseball game to get me the tryout, Mr. Hanson had made the fatal mistake of replying, "But Mrs. Kraus, girls have their *special* place—"

If he'd only known that this placating attempt would double her determination.

"They don't want me," I'd complained as Mom marched me to our car. "They won't pass to me."

She threw us in reverse and muttered, "They will. They will when they see you play."

Just before my turn came to dribble down the field and shoot on goal, Mom jogged to where I waited in line. So that the boys would plainly hear, she said—and with great seriousness, as if I were about to deliver a nationally televised speech:

"You can do it, honey. *Remember who you are.*"

I was half out my door when the phone rang. Grateful for the delay, I ran back to get it.

"You made it!" Aunt Estie cried. "I heard about your desert adventure."

Aunt Estie was Mom's younger and only sister. She was up on a third wall, in a photo from the late fifties. In it she was young and tan, grinning under wavy blond bangs and stunning in her bathing suit at the beach. My mother was next to her with a matching pageboy haircut: handsome, but not quite as gorgeous. Tolerant, but not grinning.

Like me, Aunt Estie was the youngest in her family and the only other relation I could trace with blond hair. Whenever Madeleine and Grant claimed I was adopted, I pointed to Aunt Estie as evidence of my belonging.

As different as I was from my studious, practical sister, Aunt Estie was different from my mom. She seemed perpetually content, even tempered, and optimistic. Like me, she had grown up behind a serious sister, whose moods shifted suddenly, without warning. Still, they ended up best friends, with houses on the same street and children rising through the same schools together. Growing up, I took it for granted that Aunt Estie was a natural, if more forgiving, extension of Mom. When she told me to sit up straight, wait before crossing the street, finish my peas, or stop biting my nails, I didn't distinguish roles.

Until Mom got sick. Then my allegiance broke, and I hated the sight of her. Aunt Estie was wise to this, but in spite of my attempts to discourage her, she had arrived every day at lunchtime with the same determined smiles and a little chicken salad or special dessert. She gave me a friendly nod as she passed, but her legs did not pause before she reached her sister.

Now that Mom was gone, my aunt found herself in the impossible position of worrying after me like a mother, without direct authority to intervene. In response I was generally detached and clearly ungrateful. As we spoke on the phone, I could hear her trying hard to tread the line.

"Have you unpacked?" she asked.

"Pretty much."

"Found a grocery store?"

"Uh-huh. But I'm starting work today—I'm late, actually."

"Met any neighbors?"

"Oh. Yeah. Upstairs."

There was a brief silence while she fished for more questions.

"Caroline, it's so brave what you're doing, going so far away."

Aunt Estie had seen me hysterical with fear when it came to leaving home for camp and college, so her words were sincere. But truthfully, it wasn't brave. Giving my aunt an inch would have taken more fortitude. But she was too close to mother territory, which set me on edge.

"What are you going to do today?" she asked. "Oh—you're having your first day at your new job! Are you excited?"

"More late than excited. . . ."

Another silence.

"Say, are you going to try that film course?" she asked.

"What film course?"

"Your dad said you want to take a course—movie writing? Was that it?"

"I might go over to Stanford and pick up an application. Anyway . . ."

"You need to go," Aunt Estie finished. "I know."

It took me forty-five minutes to commute to Sorrell's bookstore. I shed clothes as I drove south to Palo Alto, where the cool city fog was replaced by suburban heat.

In its heyday, Sorrell's had been home to Neil Young, Ken Kesey, and the Grateful Dead. John Steinbeck had visited from Salinas, and in the 1960s Fred Sorrell had housed secret protest meetings and draft card burnings in his back room. Now their celebrated faces lined the store walls in black and white, their crimes and rebellions transformed by time to myth.

I stared up at the photographs as I entered the store and bumped squarely into Faye, one of the old-timers who had known Fred Sorrell before he died. She was large and loud, with dark, wiry whiskers on her chin and fourteen years of bookselling and hard drinking behind her. Her last name was Einhardt, which was an old money name in the East. Everyone at the store speculated about why she chose to live in a seedy one-room apartment in East Palo Alto, where gunfire was a ho-hum event. For some reason she took pride in her elected poverty. She made an art out of scraping by.

"Oh, hi," I said, surprised. "Sorry, I'm starting here today . . . Caroline. Caroline Kraus?"

I had worn a dress for my first day, and by Faye's expression I could see it was a mistake. "Going to a ball?" she asked.

She had on a black T-shirt and dirty black jeans. I looked down at my dress and cursed.

"Back there," Faye said, jerking her thumb toward a door. "Eyes forward."

The back room was hectic. Boxes were stacked to the roof, with more coming in, and teams of young bodies cut them open and put the books inside on carts. Led Zeppelin played through a radio that hung on a coat hanger from the ceiling, and people rushed around me, laughing, complaining, yawning, and talking. I caught the eye of Tom, the man I'd interviewed with, and he waved me inside his office.

Tom's laid-back style put me at ease right away. He had long black hair pulled into a ponytail and a thick goatee. He sat on the edge of his desk and chewed on a bagel with a bemused, almost medicated, expression of calm.

"How was your trip?" he asked. "No car trouble, I hope."

"Oh, I had a little car trouble," I said.

Tom yawned, his eyes rolling back in his head, then he came back to earth with a thump. "Well, you're here."

I nodded.

"I'm going to put you out on the floor later," he said. "Today you can label. We're way the fuck behind on labels."

"That's fine," I said.

"You don't have to dress up, you know," he added. "This isn't Bank of America."

I nodded again.

Tom finished the last of his bagel and sat down. "This is a special place," he said, pointing a finger at me. "We're still fighting here . . . know what I mean?"

I had no idea what he meant.

Tom sighed.

"Right," I said.

"I was a CO," he explained.

"Is that right?" My expression told him I was still lost.

"Vietnam? I was a CO."

"Oh. A commanding officer?"

Tom stiffened. *"Conscientious objector."*

"Ah. Not the same," I said.

Tom was disappointed in me already.

"Fred Sorrell took me in back then," he said. "And I've been here ever since. Now his son runs the place. You'll meet Martin later."

I was wondering how I could retract my commanding officer comment.

"So what's your position?" Tom asked.

"On . . . Vietnam?"

He nodded.

"I—it was a bad war," I said.

Tom whispered, "And I have news for you—it's far from over."

I started in the back room, sticking scanning labels on books for inventory. Around me people were packing and unpacking, and Jerry Garcia sang about riding his train high on cocaine. I matched labels with books under the supervision of River. She seemed to think the task was challenging.

"I always forget to check the title," she told me, "and then all hell breaks loose at the registers." She sighed. "Consequently, the register people hate me."

"I'm sure that's not true," I said.

"I just can't see the point of wasting so much paper," she moaned, scowling at a sticker. "People just peel them right back off and throw them out when they get home. And then there goes a forest. No more oxygen. Poof."

I kept my head down, matching stickers to books.

"I suppose I resent the labels," River mused. "Maybe, subconsciously, that makes me put them on the wrong books."

A commotion at the door caused me to disengage from River's epiphany. An elderly man had entered and was swarmed by affectionate hellos. He was stooped and bald, with round wire-rimmed glasses, a long hooked nose, and a permanent look of mischief in his eyes. He wore a tattered sports coat and khakis, and wrinkled paperbacks poked from his pockets. He spotted me right away.

"Who is this?" he asked River.

"Isaac, meet Caroline," River said. She put her hand on my shoulder. "First day."

Before I could speak, Isaac hugged me. "Welcome to the last of the great independent bookstores," he said.

"Isaac is our celebrity," River said.

"No, no," he said, stepping back.

"A bona fide celebrity," River went on. "Ask him about Martin Luther King."

"Or Jerry Garcia," a voice called from across the room.

"Or Joan Baez," said Tom, smiling behind me.

Isaac beamed.

River was putting labels onto my stack of books in what seemed like a random fashion, which made me nervous. "People actually come to the store just to glimpse this man," she said. "They lie in wait for him."

I moved my stack of books away from River. "Do you know Joan Baez?" I asked Isaac.

"Sure, I know Joanie," he said. He breathed hard, and the corners of his mouth pulled into a grimace. "You'll meet her. She comes by." He took my hand and patted it. "But that's boooring," he crooned, "tell me about *you*." He moistened his lips and gasped for air.

Before I could launch into my short biography, we were out the door and settled in an adjoining café. Isaac talked about late night meetings with Dr. King, hearing Joan Baez sing for the first time, when she was still in high school, and the good and bad changes he saw in American culture since the sixties. He said he could tell I was from the Midwest, because I looked "undiscovered." He said he could help discover me, if I was open to it.

Of all the people who worked at Sorrell's, my favorites were Nick, Angela, Julian, and River. They were always in good moods, and each had entertaining peculiarities. Nick was a tall surfer whose single flaw seemed to be vision that required Coke-bottle glasses, even when riding the waves. He regularly pocketed his specs, because of vanity, I supposed, and then wore a perpetual squint, walking with his arms slightly raised to deflect any surprise objects. Angela was into holistic everything and astrology, and she smelled like incense. Julian was a gifted guitarist, with a keen interest in drugs, especially the sort that would turn the world into his own personal cartoon. The only time he wasn't on a synthetic trip, according to Angela, was when he played guitar.

River was big on cycling. Under her faded cotton dresses she wore racing shorts with a thick, padded rear, and she was armed with a formidable pair of legs. You wouldn't have guessed it, though; from time to time she and Julian found ways to get high during work and then seemed transported from our workaday world. Somehow, Julian managed to pack and return books to the right publisher. And somehow River avoided pedaling into signposts on her way home. Angela said it was because they were Libras—their analytical sides balanced everything out.

In contrast, I was deemed "too quiet" and "broody," as Nick liked to say. Angela thought she knew the solution. "Caroline needs to get high," she announced. "Yesterday."

I had never been high, and they believed this was a tragedy in the making. Given the right combination of chemicals, they promised, I'd be transformed. And the idea was appealing. Transformed could only be an improvement. Transformed was good.

The site of my transformation was an outdoor concert in Golden Gate Park. The field was jammed with people, and along with Faye—who had caught wind of our expedition and tagged along— we made a human chain, following Julian through the crowd. He stopped to buy the goods from a man holding a candy tray, then we continued forward, weaving our way toward the stage. We carved out a blanket-size spot and squeezed onto it. Faye lit a cigarette and started talking up a guy who eventually passed her the joint she'd been eyeing. But I was not to smoke the joint. My friends had something else in mind.

As I lifted my camera and focused it on the stage, Julian opened a thermos and dropped some tablets into it. Ever the gentleman, he passed it to me first.

I sniffed the contents.

"Kool-Aid," he said.

"With what?" I whispered.

"Ecstasy," he whispered back.

I peered inside the thermos.

"You drink it," River said.

"What will it do?"

Angela said, "What do you think? It's called *ecstasy.*"

That did sound promising. I said a prayer and took a swig. Then the thermos made its rounds, and I watched everybody closely to see what happened.

An hour passed, and nothing. Then tendrils of heat snaked up my arms, and my heart seemed to expand in my chest. A band had been playing music I didn't like, and suddenly I loved the music so much that I started swaying and smiling. I looked at Julian and realized I loved him, too. And I loved Nick, and Angela, and even Faye. I put my arm around River.

"Lookie here," River laughed.

"I don't feel a damn thing," Julian said glumly.

"Me either," said Nick.

Faye was stoned on pot and couldn't have cared less.

"This sucks," said Angela.

I swooned with joy. The crowd, which had been making me nervous in its closeness, was full of wonderful souls. The shirtless fat man blocking my view was stunning in his beauty. Faye took a drag on her stinky cigarette and breathed perfume.

"She's fucked up," Nick said, looking at me.

I looked at Julian. A small fear was growing.

"Well, Caroline," Julian said. "Enjoy."

His words were like an instant jinx. As suddenly as the pleasure had begun, I went numb, and the earlier sensation gave way to anxiety. I tried to look cool as my jaw started clenching and unclenching without my permission. Then I imagined little ants running up my spine and out my ears, which wasn't pleasant at all.

"I feel funny," I murmured.

"I'll say." Angela sighed.

"No, really." I was starting to sweat.

"How much did you put in, Julian?" River asked.

Julian's subsequent look of concern made the ants pick up speed.

"Oh." I clutched at my feet. "Oh no."

River tried not to laugh. She said, "Caroline. Honey. Take it easy."

I shook my head. The music faded into a tinny echo.

"Perfect," Julian groaned.

I looked at River and said, "Make it stop."

"Make it stop?" Julian shrieked. "That's good shit."

"Calm down, Julian," Faye said.

"Just don't worry," Angela advised. "If you worry, it gets bad."

I put my head in my hands. Now I was worried about worrying.

"Shit," Nick said. "She's going down."

I locked my head between my knees, afraid to move.

The next thing I knew, I was being half carried through the crowd with Nick and Julian on either side.

"Stop moaning," Julian whispered in my ear.

I saw a few policemen standing at the edge of the field and started to wave my arms at them, but Julian caught my wrists. "Do you want us to get arrested?" he hissed.

As we stumbled on, my mind split into three places. One was the fuzzy, happy place I'd felt at the beginning, the other was horrifying and dark, and the third was me, watching it all happen. The last one broke free and took off running.

I ran all the way home and flung myself on my bed, landing like a corpse, arms spread. Nerves jumped in my head like little spark plugs. I couldn't say for sure that I'd been transformed, but the experience definitely had my attention. My brain seemed capable of such extremes, excursions I'd never wanted before or imagined. From horrible, irrational visions to ecstatic, boundless joy, I'd had no idea such potentials resided in me. I was still breathing hard when I realized that the walls were moving in—on conveyor belts, I thought—to squish me. That sent me out the door and onto the street, running again.

Gary was walking up the hill with groceries, and he called hello as I sprinted down an alley. I ran for an eternity, expecting to arrive at the end of the earth, or at least the ocean. By dusk, the throbbing in my chest faded, my mouth went dry, and I felt myself coming back. I held on to a mailbox and looked around.

"Hey!" I yelled to a passing cab.

The cab eased up next to me, and I climbed in. "608 Masonic Street," I panted.

"608 Masonic Street," he repeated.

"Is it far?" I asked. I pulled bills from my pocket. "I have this."

"Let me guess, a yellow Victorian, with roses in the front," he said.

I gave him a suspicious nod.

"Uh-huh. You sure you want a ride?" he asked, pointing down the street to my apartment. I followed his hand and frowned. All that time I had been running in circles and didn't even know it.

As I stepped gingerly from the cab and aimed myself down the hill toward home, I made a mental note. No more drugs. I needed *something*, but I had seen enough of my mind from the inside. My gray matter had revealed itself as fundamentally fragile and too easily changeable, which was as frightening as it was oddly hopeful. Hopeful, because I did still want change—something equally rich and vivid to fill the vacancy where my mother had lodged. The trick would be to find different means. Perhaps an external diversion; a more tangible guest.

At work, Julian and the gang thought my meltdown was hilarious. They watched me slink into the store the next morning, with my aching jaw and hollow eyes, and applauded.

"You're a veteran now," Nick beamed.

"Super," I said.

"Julian clawed his leg once," Angela boasted.

Julian raised his shorts and showed off tiny scars lining his thigh. "I thought there were spiders," he explained.

I raised my shirt and said, "Ants."

More applause.

Later, I was chewing on a blueberry scone when Joan Baez wandered up and asked me where the philosophy section had been moved. My eyes widened in awe, and I chewed and chewed, raising a finger while I swallowed. She had a wide, embracing smile, tall white teeth, and warm laugh lines. She looked brilliant in her brown vest and jeans, as if she'd stepped right off an album cover, with the same dark hair but shorter, with real, living, radiant eyes. Joan's image had hung on my wall since I was a teenager, standing next to Bob Dylan, holding a big flower beside a poster for peace. As I chewed, the living version waited.

But as soon as I swallowed I felt a surge of inexplicable sadness, and for all the world I couldn't speak.

Joan glanced at Carla, the bookseller standing beside me, and Carla stepped in, leading Ms. Baez away. I crouched behind the register, mortified.

"Hey," Tom whispered above me. "What happened? What did she say?"

I wiped sudden tears on my sleeve and said, "Philosophy."

Tom crouched beside me and said, "Okay, I don't get it."

A ring of heads appeared. Everyone waited. Isaac frowned at my blown encounter and loudly asked why I was on my knees. I had no reasonable explanation. Not for my posture or for the sudden attack of gloom that had gripped me upon seeing Joan Baez. It was as if any jolt to my emotional system—happy or sad—collapsed everything. As I searched for a brilliant bit of dialogue to assure everybody I was fine, I reeled in my own confusion. Had I the power of cinema, I would have dropped through the floorboards that minute or evaporated on the spot. Better yet, I would have rewound my life to age fourteen and started the picture over.

After her Thanksgiving performance, and my rescue on the hockey field, Mom's moods spiraled further from her control, into even more irrational extremes. She transformed meals into an emotional obstacle course. She would, for instance, ask my father to please stop scraping his plate before she screamed. She'd add that plate scraping made her sick. As did the smell of the rotten food before us and my habit of tilting back in my chair. The room was too cold or too warm. Dad's attempt at conversation irritated her, and his silence drove her mad.

Periodically, Mom set out to repair the damage. She'd be extra funny, or extra thoughtful, which kept us alert. "I cleaned your cleats," she'd tell me. "I put flowers in your room." If I didn't react with genuine glee, the flowers were thrown into the trash, along with the shoes.

For Dad, Mom would sometimes dress up on a lark and hide in the kitchen closet when his car pulled in at the end of the day. As he walked in with his briefcase, with me directed to smile and look calm, she would jump out behind him like a jack-in-the-box and hug him around the waist.

Through it all, and to my amazement, Mom resisted smoking. She had quit a thirty-year habit the spring before her breakdown, and soon after, the first signs of her depression appeared. It had been a miracle when she quit smoking. And a nightmare. After she quit, she turned into a gum-chewing monster. Her brain had required cigarettes to function, and once the poison was withheld, her moods went haywire. Lots of people can quit and keep their sanity, but with Mom it seemed more complicated. Maybe smoking had kept her most troubled feelings at bay all those years, because when she stopped, up they came like a geyser.

On my sixteenth birthday, for instance—just after I'd blown out my candles and my fork was poised over cake—Mom remarked that I was getting fat. "And you shouldn't wear tank tops with those arms," she had added.

Had I been the star in my own movie, I would have thrown the cake at her and shouted something brilliant. Instead I just stared.

"Eat your cake," Mom barked. She pushed a piece at me. "Eat your cake eat your cake eat your cake."

I took a bite.

She pushed wrapped boxes at me and said, "Open your presents." I dropped my fork to open one.

Dad was in Colorado at a pathology meeting, and my siblings were at college. I eyed my mother with caution.

"Thank you," I said, unfurling a long afghan. Mom had knitted it herself, in shades of yellow. My sister had a green one, Grant's was brown, and the one in my parents' bedroom was ocean blue. I had finally earned my own.

"I meant to have it for you last year," Mom said.

"I love it," I said, holding it up.

"Next present," she commanded.

And so it went.

Like a long-distance swimmer resisting air, she plowed through the short-term misery of life without nicotine and kept her mind set on the larger victory of physical health. And after all my years of throwing away her cigarettes, while loudly declaring that her smoking was killing me, I told myself that the least I could do was be supportive. So I made sure Mom was stocked with her chewing gum, and I hung on with Dad through her rages. But when the finish line came, when the worst of her cravings had finally passed and she no longer thought about smoking, she still looked defeated, as if the toxins that had left her body had taken with them her last line of emotional defense. She cracked at Thanksgiving, then briefly rallied, and by December she finally broke. And as her bright mind finally dimmed, my own mind, as if attached by some fetal cord, also withdrew.

It was early morning, just before Christmas, when my father helped Mom shuffle down the hall, whispering to her as she cried. I watched from the top of the stairs near my bedroom as Dad talked softly to her and buttoned her coat for the ride to the hospital. She seemed emptied of everything—of blood, bones, organs, and thought. I whispered down the stairs, "Hey, Mom."

Dad's face appeared.

"Hi, Caroline," he said.

I waved.

"We're going to the hospital," he explained.

"Is she staying?" I asked. It was strange, talking about Mom as if she weren't right there.

"I think so," he replied. "I'll call home and let you know."

"Should I come?"

Mom's eyes turned upward to Dad.

"Maybe not," he said.

. . .

I followed my parents to the garage and waved them off in my pajamas. Our neighbor was shoveling his walk next door, and when their taillights were gone, I saw him lean on his shovel, peeking at our little drama. My black Labrador, Sam, sat down beside me, ready for a run.

Later, as Sam and I headed for the woods, with me on my bike and his legs barely touching the ground, I told myself it wasn't such a surprise. Ever since her appearance at my hockey game, I had returned from school to find my mother dissolving, slumped at her desk or in dark rooms, weeping for no reason she could explain. With that much water and emotion flowing out of her, something had to break.

I visited her on Saturdays, usually alone. My brother and sister were away at college, so they had to worry from a distance, and my father was with Mom most every day, so Saturdays he took a break. I remember feeling a strange thrill before I went in, when I was searched by hospital security. They checked my bags and pockets and inspected everything I brought. I liked to fantasize that I was part of a clever scheme to break Mom out, with a nail file, maybe, or a cake knife hidden in my jeans, just like in the movies.

Two layers of locked doors hissed and sealed behind me before I spotted Mom, waiting like a hopeful child behind a long glass window lined with wire. She was usually in her robe and pajamas, but sometimes, on good days, she wore her old Smith College sweatshirt.

We didn't talk much during our visits; her thoughts were slowed by medication, and her speech was thick. But once she took me on a tour of the ward. I met people with anorexia, schizophrenia, and manic depression, and I witnessed paranoia, obsession, and frantic neuroses in full, frightening bloom. I played Ping-Pong with a man named Henry who claimed he was God, and when he finally drifted away, muttering, Mom poked me and said, "Now you can say you beat God at Ping-Pong."

I joined Mom's crafts class and played group dominoes. She waved her arms around in an exercise class and played volleyball, and sometimes I would watch her—the woman who had so carefully guided my life—vacantly serve to people so zonked on lithium that the balls bounced right off their heads.

I brought her magazines like *People* or *Life*, anything that had pictures and was easy to read. I also made tapes of music, which she insisted on calling records, and once she made my eyes pop by asking if I might be more "current"—to maybe include the Go-Gos or David Bowie next time. I found out later that she'd been sharing tapes with a girl named Ellie who starved herself because of an eating disorder, and who'd introduced my mother to worlds beyond Peter, Paul & Mary, Simon & Garfunkel, or Mahler and Bach. I was a little jealous of that suffering girl, who seemed to know certain pieces of my mother better than I did and whom Mom looked after in ways I longed to be looked after again.

One Saturday, when I was sitting alone in the TV lounge, Ellie came to the doorway and lit a cigarette. She opened her eyes wide and peered at me through a nicotine cloud. Then, as if on the brink of a major discovery, she parted the smoke with her hands.

"Well," she said, "you are *definitely* Madeleine's." She nodded her head until I nodded, too, and then she snapped her fingers. Her voice was soft and southern.

"Caroline?" she guessed, continuing forward.

"Yep," I said.

"The athlete?"

"Right."

"The dreamer . . ."

"Um, okay."

"And the movie expert."

"Well, I suppose."

"You're the baby." Ellie pointed her cigarette at me.

"Not so much anymore."

She took another drag, held it, then opened her mouth in a big
O, flinging circles of smoke my way. She winked, as if to
acknowledge how nifty the collapsing circles were, then sauntered
over to the couch and sat beside me. I was reminded of when my
mother had smoked, when her sturdy hands had smelled sweet with
tar, and when I always knew that she'd just been close or on the
phone.

I wondered what Mom liked about Ellie. Her eyes looked sleepy
and dull, and she wore strange clothes—a pajama top over tiny
shorts and then high heels. She caught me assessing her and poked
me in the ribs before I could look away.

"Scary place, huh," she said, nodding again. She dropped the
cigarette on the carpeted floor and turned her heel over it. I heard
my mother's voice in the hall, deep and velvety, and Ellie heard
her, too.

"She's getting better," Ellie said. "She washed her hair
yesterday. *Herself.*"

It scared me that that was a victory.

Then, as if passing me a secret code, Ellie whispered the word
"Doppelgänger," and waited for me to react. After a few moments
she said, "She says you are her *doppelgänger.*"

"Oh?"

"I didn't know, either," Ellie admitted. "But leave it to Monny
to have a dictionary right in her room—I mean, who would bring a
dictionary *here?*"

"They'd have to be crazy," I agreed.

Ellie laughed. "Right," she said, "good one."

I was curious about the word.

"It means 'a ghostly counterpart,' " Ellie said. "What do you
think about that?"

I thought that didn't sound so good.

"Keep in mind she's on medication," Ellie added. Then a voice came from the doorway.

"Hey, you two," Mom said. Her hands were on her hips. She was dressed in street clothes—a brown wool skirt, white sweater, and heels—and her thick brown hair was clean and coifed. She wore pearls, which she had to check out of the hospital safe, and pink lipstick. With those hooded blue eyes set against brown, almost black hair, I thought she stood out among the others. Jane once said that Mom had a poignant face, and she was right. Mom's was a face that had to be startled out of sadness, but when she smiled you couldn't help but smile with her.

Ellie waved.

"Have you eaten yet?" Mom asked her.

The corners of Ellie's mouth twitched.

"There's food still out, but they'll take it away." Ellie stood and walked toward the door. "And no more smoking," I heard Mom whisper. Ellie touched Mom's arm, then slid past her and trotted away.

"Hi," I said, bouncing a little in my seat.

Mom leaned against the door frame. "Hi, sweetie."

"You look nice, Mom."

She touched her skirt and smiled. "Want to take me out for a while?"

I leapt to my feet. "Really?"

"Really."

"But is it okay?" I looked up and down the hall, "I mean, is it *allowed?*"

Mom pulled a piece of paper from her purse, upon which I saw the words *Day Pass.*

"Five hours," she said, replacing the paper. "Enough time to go to the pictures and then lunch. If I know you, there must be at least ten new shows out there you want to see."

I loved the way she said "go to the pictures" and "shows." It made them seem so grand. She touched the top of my head and said, "Okay?"

I could have jumped up and down right there or torn through the ward spreading the news. Here was my mother—and she even *looked* like my mother—and I had her for the whole afternoon.

I had not yet conquered the art of driving a stick shift, and as we jerked along the road to the theater she cringed, eyes wide, lips tight. I was too busy talking to notice that she'd been quiet. I caught her up on the new boy I was pining after, relayed that I had finally made a passing grade in chemistry, and vividly described the two hat tricks I'd made during soccer season. She looked worried when I let it slip that I'd also been hit by a baseball right in the head, and after that she couldn't stop twisting her hands. As we drove I didn't give a thought to whether the familiar landmarks we passed were a comfort to her or a terror. All I cared about was the normalcy of it all—my mother in her fine wool skirt, fishing in her purse for ticket money, the two of us leaning over the glass candy counter selecting treats, and then the mad dash to make the previews.

I should have asked why she was so quiet. Instead, I chattered on and threw popcorn in my mouth, as if taking one's mother from a locked ward to the movies happened every day.

As the movie began, I slid down in my seat, grateful, as always, to be transported. Mom disappeared quickly and without a sound. I didn't notice her go at first, and even when I did I told myself she'd just gone to the bathroom. Later, when she didn't return, I tore myself away and walked into the lobby. Empty. I looked in the bathroom. Also empty. I walked outside and looked around. Next to the door I spotted a gray-faced old woman who seemed to be wearing my mother's coat. Coming closer, I saw that she *was* my mother. She was watching the door and waiting, hugging her purse. Her expression was desperate and apologetic. My heart slid to my throat and cracked.

"I'm not ready," she whispered. "I'm definitely not ready."

I felt like throwing my head against the wall.

Even as I found her shaking by the door, I silently cursed the fact that not one normal day was granted me. As I steered us away from the theater and toward our car, I had the nerve to still hope for hamburgers, fries, and a milkshake—three things that would have made my medicated mother vomit. But her eyes told me no, so I sighed and helped her into the car.

We drove back to the ward with the radio on. I found one of Mom's favorite Glenn Miller tunes, and she tapped her finger against the window in time. Her face was turned away from me, her nose almost touching the glass. As we passed other cars, with other mothers and daughters, I wondered if the seams were only splitting in our car. Maybe seams were splitting all over. If anyone had looked our way, they would have simply seen a handsome mother in her late forties tapping absently against a window. They wouldn't have heard the funny humming that joined the tapping, or known that she was tapping faster and faster, and long after the song ended.

Chapter SEVEN

After the Baez incident, I knew that there was a short in my emotional circuits. Too often I was moved by TV commercials. Dusk made me frantic. I stuttered randomly. Not finding a parking spot made me homicidal, and my favorite occupation was sleep. Also, whenever serious or sad subjects came up, I laughed. I laughed and giggled and all but slapped my knee. At the same time, anything legitimately humorous escaped me. When I started feeling physically unwell—felt my chest growing tighter and tighter, until simple breathing required concentration—I considered a phone number I'd been carrying in my wallet.

"Just in case," Dr. Singer had said at my going-away party in St. Louis. He'd held out a paper. "If things get tough in California."

Dr. Singer had been Mom's psychiatrist. I equated him with mental breakdowns, which were not my intended future. "I don't think I'll need that," I'd said.

"It helped your mother," he reminded me, folding the paper into my palm. "It's just in case."

I waited until my shift was over and went into Tom's office to make the call. A woman answered, "Dr. Martin's office, Alice speaking."

"Hi," I said. Then, as happened too often, my mind went blank.

"Hi," she repeated.

"Oh. I'm calling to make an appointment," I remembered.

"Your name?"

"Caroline Kraus," I whispered.

"Have you been here before, Carolyn?"

"Caro*line*. No," I said. "Dr. Martin was recommended. By Dr. Singer. In St. Louis."

"That's fine, Caroline, we'll set up a time. First, though, what would you say is your chief complaint?"

"My chief complaint?"

"Your reason for coming."

"Oh."

"Caroline?"

"Can I wait and tell the doctor?" I asked.

"Okay. That's okay. How about next Monday?"

I looked at Tom's staff schedule taped to the wall and found my name scheduled for the afternoon shift. "I can come in the morning," I said.

"See you Monday morning, then. Nine o'clock?"

I listened to Alice breathe, and nodded.

"Caroline?"

"Nine o'clock," I agreed.

"I'm going to hang up now," she said. "Have a good day, Caroline."

Had I thought to look closer at Tom's schedule, I might have seen a name printed near mine that Monday, with "Interview" printed next to it. It's funny to me now. The day I saw my first psychiatrist was also the day I first spotted Jane.

.   .   .

I was nervous to meet Dr. Martin, and I took hours to get ready, which was unheard of for me. I was more likely to fly out the door with a chocolate stain on my shirt and tags still on my clothes than sit quietly before a mirror. But that morning I studied my reflection, and I carefully inspected my face and teeth. My skin looked good, and my teeth were white and squeaky. Even my hair did not argue with me. When I was very young and too small to object, Mom had pinned me down before school and braided my hair, ignoring my howls of pain as the braids got tighter and tighter, pulling my face into a permanent look of surprise. She had said that my hair could be attractive if I paid attention. It had a mind of its own but was blond and full, which was an asset, she promised, that would someday attract any number of men.

I had kept it short through most of high school in retaliation, but it was past my shoulders by the time I moved to San Francisco. That morning I pulled it back with a barrette and practiced expressions of nonchalance before the mirror. Then I brushed my eyelashes with mascara, lined my lips with a soft red pencil, and colored them in.

I had trouble deciding what to wear. I'd collected my mother's clothes after she died, stuffed them in my closet, and squished my own to the side. I liked having her skirts, slacks, and shirts hanging there, even if they were two sizes too small. They waited as they always had, with quiet elegance, pressed and clean, ready for my mother to finish her tea and dress for the day. I chose one of her blue paisley shirts for my psychiatric debut and a pair of my wrinkled khaki pants, then slipped my feet into her old penny loafers.

I considered my shrinking figure. True, I'd always wanted to be thin. Long ago I'd rejected my athletic build and dreamed of becoming a waif who nevertheless and somehow ate huge, satisfying meals. Now I couldn't eat at all. I cinched my belt and wondered if the psychiatrist would be concerned about my weight. I wouldn't mind if she worried. Surely, I thought, mine was a compelling case—I was twenty-four, my mother had just died, I had trouble eating and sleeping, and I was shadowed by a strange, disembodied feeling. Disembodied might catch her attention. She might even struggle not to cry in the face of such a terrible story. Maybe her notes would describe me as tormented and brilliant; perhaps she would dedicate her professional life to healing me, to understanding what it was that was slipping away in my head. If I was lucky, she might even find out where it went. I wanted it back.

San Francisco was still a new city to me then, and I left my apartment early to allow time for getting lost. I cruised through Haight-Ashbury, past young kids playing homeless on the street, then past the real homeless, who eyed those kids like lunch. I had chosen my neighborhood thinking that the aimless hippie culture was romantic, but I should have known I wouldn't fit in with the strung-out bodies shuffling along Haight Street. Not because I was better off; I just couldn't stand looking at the way I felt all the time.

I drove to the crest of one of San Francisco's famous hills and paused to admire the view. The Golden Gate Bridge was just to my left, the Bay Bridge to my right. St. Louis was 1,863 miles to the east, and the Pacific lay behind me. With all that space, it was hard to believe that there was no direction in which I could point and call home.

I checked my map. Dr. Martin's office was in Pacific Heights, apparently dead ahead. I released the clutch and coasted down the hill, flying in neutral right through two green lights and a yellow, arriving at her door like a kid in a wagon, fifteen minutes early.

The receptionist stood as I entered. She wore a flowered dress, and an inspirational blast of new age music rushed over me.

"Hi!" she chirped. "I'm Alice."

I giggled. I felt positively giddy from running all those lights in neutral, and the surge of synthetic music, combined with her exuberance, went to my head. Alice giggled back and handed me some forms. As I filled them out, I began to feel even better. I was not, to my knowledge, psychotic, suicidal, paranoid, obsessive, in the habit of mutilating myself, or on drugs. This was encouraging.

Alice escorted me into a dark, wood-paneled office and directed me to wait for "Mary-Lou." My optimism waned. "Mary-Lou" did not suggest a thoughtful, shrewd-but-gentle doctor with half-glasses and a wall full of academic degrees. I wondered if I was about to meet a cheerleader.

I browsed her bookshelves. There were books on all the conditions I'd just denied, as well as books on schizophrenia, Alzheimer's disease, personality disorders, anxiety, and depression. The last two caught my attention—I experienced them pretty constantly. But did I really deserve to be on the same shelf as schizophrenics? Where did the spectrum begin and end? My psyche suddenly felt like a mine field. I stepped away and looked at a less threatening shelf dedicated to hypnotism. I reached for a book titled *Secrets of the Buried Mind* and heard a voice behind me. I spun around, inches from Mary-Lou, who had either materialized from thin air or entered through an actual secret door. She shook my hand and replaced the book, noting the title. I imagined a red flag flying into my file—*Has Buried Secrets.*

Mary Lou was petite, with long red fingernails, so long that they curled at the end. She had a short, careful coif of brown hair, wore a leather miniskirt and tights, and walked with purpose atop perilously tall heels. She gestured toward an easy chair facing her desk.

I took my seat and waited. Mary-Lou also waited. We sat in silence. A clock ticked behind me. Mary-Lou smiled. I smiled back. More time went by. I considered whether or not this was some kind of newcomer's test. I fished my trusty pen from my pocket, brought it to my cheek, and started clicking the top. Surely, I thought, the clicking would stimulate conversation.

"Okay," I said finally. "Am I supposed to start talking?"

"*Would* you like to start talking?" Mary-Lou asked.

I resumed clicking. We stared at each other. This was not how therapy sessions were portrayed in any movie I'd seen. Where were the carefully delivered sets of questions and insights that gradually and mysteriously revealed the source of my distress? I looked around. The shades were drawn, which I found irritatingly metaphoric, and I saw nary a framed degree. Instead, lonely ocean scenes dotted the walls.

"So . . . do you hypnotize people?" I asked.

"Good question," Mary-Lou said, raising her pencil. "What interests you about hypnosis?"

Click, click, click.

"Well, does it work?" I tried to smile.

"Hmn," she said, turning her eyes to the ceiling. "Are you concerned about whether or not I will hypnotize *you?*" She prepared to make a note, carefully pinching her pencil so that her nails didn't get in the way.

I suspected that saying yes would label me paranoid, so I said no. Mary-Lou squinted at me. I began to wonder if she was intentionally answering my questions with a question.

"Anyway, I don't think you can do that against my will," I said. "Hypnotize me, I mean." I shifted in my seat. "So no, I'm not paranoid." I bit my lip. Mary-Lou made a note. Her victory.

"So where did you get your M.D.?" I asked. That should result in an answer.

"Are you concerned about my qualifications?" she returned.

I started clicking again and checked my watch. Mary-Lou glanced behind me at the clock.

"Okay," I said, "I would really like you to make a statement now." I started clicking faster. "You are answering my questions with a question."

Her eyes narrowed. "I can see you're agitated," she said. "Why is that? What's on your mind right now?"

Two questions.

"If you would just make a statement," I said, pleading.

"Caroline, I'm here to help you," Mary-Lou said. "Is that statement enough?"

"Ah!" I pointed at her. "Question."

Mary-Lou sighed. "I ask questions," she said, "because, believe it or not, *you* have the answers."

Perhaps she was having a bad day.

"Okay?" she added, preserving her rhetorical record.

The hour ended as badly as it began, with me muttering something about the lunatics running the asylum and Mary-Lou chewing on one of her expensive nails. She didn't even ask if I wanted to schedule another appointment.

"I can see you're unhappy, Caroline," she said, walking me to the door, "but ninety percent of this comes from your cooperation."

I climbed in my car and rested my head on the steering wheel. I wanted to shout—to anyone who would listen—that things were falling out of place in my head, that my confidence was gone, that I went home from work and crawled into bed, that nothing gave me pleasure anymore, not food, movies, books, or friends. That the place where I was standing was vast and hollow, and there wasn't another soul in sight.

Mary-Lou missed her chance, and so did I. I could have lowered my pen for a moment to describe how hopeless I felt or mention that my mother had recently died. I could have explained that she had delivered two good-hearted children into adulthood but had left before the third knew where her own body ended and her mother's began.

Mary-Lou might have told me this was grief. She might have said that millions of souls have stood where I was and that millions more would come after I left. She could have warned me that the human mind was tricky and I oughtn't to follow it to the dark places. But she didn't. And it would be a long time before I had the courage to ask for help again.

I drove to work after that visit, went straight to the biography section, and took a seat on the floor. I was immersed in other lives when I saw a striking woman sit at a corner table. She pulled a book from her bag and started reading. After a while, she was joined by Tom. She seemed to be in her mid-twenties, spoke with articulate confidence, and looked like she'd walked right off the pages of a J. Crew catalog. I peeked at her through the bookshelves and listened to her describe undergraduate years at Harvard, a close family, art awards, and photography exhibits. She pulled it off beautifully and was hired on the spot.

A week later, Jane showed up for her first day at the bookstore. True to form, Isaac pulled her to his chest and said, "Welcome to the last of the great independent bookstores."

I remember that she wore a bright blue silk shirt that day, because it matched her startling eyes. She wore loose, light-colored khakis, and her thick, dark blond hair was pulled into a long ponytail. She had one crooked tooth in an otherwise perfect smile and a smooth, confident voice.

Later, she spotted me lurking in the stacks and walked directly over, throwing out her hand. Her eyes were warm and direct, and she smiled the way old friends do after being too long apart.

"I'm Jane," she said, "and *you* are hiding."

I returned the smile.

"What are you reading?" she asked, tipping the cover of my book.

It was *An Unknown Woman*, about someone who moves to an island for a year and supposedly discovers herself. I was thinking it was an appealing idea.

"I would have been impressed with that story if she hadn't brought the dog," Jane said. "The dog was cheating."

I decided not to tell her that I had just been imagining myself on Nantucket in winter with a Labrador. "Well, the dog is a pretty big part of her resolution," I countered. "In fact, I think the whole point of the story is the dog."

Jane laughed. "Shows what you know," she said.

She lingered for a moment, studying me. "I'll be hiding over in fiction if you want to make a case for the dog," she said, and backed away with a wave.

Chapter EIGHT

While Mom was on the locked ward, I came home from high school not to emptiness, but to my best canine friend, Sam, whose quivering black body stayed perched like a sentry on the roof of his wooden house, scanning the horizon for my slow figure. I'd arrive at Sam's gate, slugging textbooks and all the worries of adolescence, and I'd drop my load and set him free. His energy required one lap around our house at full speed before he came to my side and waited to hear the plan. A bike trip to the creek was usually in order. I'd watch him crash into the water and swim with engineered elegance, his body twitching with joy, and after a while I'd sneak off on my bike just to watch him catch up. We were endlessly entertained by the woods and trails around our house and hard-pressed to make it home before the sound of Dad's tired call reminded us of dinner.

If I'd been a worrier, I'd have worried that Sam's nature was not always sweet. He was a determined dog, strong willed and strong bodied, and he made his own decisions. He came to my call if it suited him, and that usually suited me until he started roaming into neighborhoods I had to find on a map. Sometimes he came home bloody and limping, with a forlorn expression or queasy smell. He'd scratch to be let in, then drain his water bowl before jumping onto his window seat and staring out the window.

Even so, Sam brought me through the worst of high school, and he seemed as relieved as anyone when Mom returned from the hospital, breathing life back into the house. By the time I confronted leaving home for college, I knew he would have a reliable companion in her.

Before I left, Mom and I made a deal—she would look after Sam, and I would make the most of her tuition money. Dad had paid for my siblings' education, but Mom had been emphatic about sponsoring my four years with her first, "postdepression" job. After decades of raising money for Smith College as a loyal volunteer, she had been hired to do the same on a salary by Washington University's Medical School, in St. Louis. She had proudly shown me her first office with a door and demonstrated definite ambition to understand, if not use, her first computer. Armed with a healthy mind, stable job, and renewed hope, my mother turned an eye to me—a precarious student and wary child—as her next frontier to settle. She said she was determined to see me through a successful tour of college. My graduation, I understood, would be our victory.

In the summers when I came home, my parents and I took to gathering at the top of our yard for cocktails in the evenings. We'd frequently sit on the hill overlooking Mom's garden and discuss weighty issues like tennis or snapdragons. I had to be on my toes, though, for a sudden switch to the great battles of World War I or gender politics—no Kraus should be caught uninformed.

On an August evening after my junior year, as we gathered on the hill, tanned and fatigued from long days in the garden, I nursed my Coke while Sam pulled restlessly at a lead strung around a tree. I'd come home to find that his roaming days were over, after a series of "accidents" that included biting our neighbor's hand—a surgeon's hand, no less—and Mom had warned me that he was on thin ice. She said he'd started attacking the little yappy neighborhood dogs that seemed to insult him just by living. In my company he had passed them with a snarl or a bark, but now, she said, he was compelled to draw blood. As a result, Sam became a prisoner—in a run, on a leash, or pacing inside our house—and preventing his escape was a full-time job.

As we sat atop our hill that August evening, the light changed into dusk, and cicadas and crickets held forth with a comforting low hum. My father's finger toyed with my mother's hand, and as they often did, they drifted from me into their own inaudible private code. Mom's depression had been vanquished, and the cigarettes, but in the second week of my freshman year, a new shadow had appeared, a darker, more malignant spot, spreading across her left lung.

At first, Mom had refused to relinquish that lung. Over this we battled long distance, with me hogging the hall phone at my dormitory, pleading.

"It's your only *chance*," I'd said.

"Chance for what?" Mom wanted to know.

"For *life*," I cried. "What *is* this, Mom? You've never backed down before."

She waited to be sure I was done, then said, "It's about the *quality* of my life."

I had listened vaguely, uninterested in anything but the right answer. In another time or setting I might have understood, I might have even agreed. But at twenty-one I was unwilling to endorse my mother's sure and rapid death, even if that was her preference. So I pleaded. My father urged. My brother implored, and my sister coaxed. We came at her from all sides, and still our mother stayed firm.

The window for surgery had almost closed when Reverend

Michaels came to our house. Few people had inspired or awed my mother as much as this man, who had already seen her at her abject worst, in the gallows of depression, stripped of her precious structure and control, locked behind glass and wire. Reverend Michaels came right away when Mom called him, lumbering up our brick walk to the front door, greeting her with his amused, affectionate southern drawl. They spent the afternoon together, privately discussing her choice. Maybe Mom knew he would be honest with her, would not try to persuade her either way. She said he let her talk herself into it, just by listening. By the time Reverend Michaels left her at the front door, moving crablike to his church sedan, she was mentally gearing up for surgery.

At the top of our hill, Mom swilled her Johnnie Walker and leaned into Dad. Now she had one lung. One lung left and a suspicious new ache in her spine. Sam butted the tree behind us, strained at the lead, and growled. She turned from Dad to me, suddenly praising my profile.

"And you have a beautiful mouth," she added.

I squirmed with pleasure. My mouth was about all I had left after the fifteen pounds I'd put on at the cafeteria tasty-freeze.

Sam growled again and then shrieked. He leapt against the lead I'd not secured, and it unraveled like a bad dream. Cocktails hit the ground as Sam hurtled down the hill, teeth bared, aiming for a woman and—*Christ*—another yappy dog. My mother barked at me to run, but I was already on my way. I chased the end of the long lead as it swished against the grass, trailing Sam's demented pursuit. I dived to catch it but missed. He leapt at the dog, now in the woman's arms, and his teeth found skin instead of fur. Mom arrived with all of the steam one lung allowed and shoved Sam hard with her foot, reaching for the catatonic woman. My mother's expression was so angry, so final, that I was compelled to shout, "No!" to whatever she was thinking.

Weeks passed. Mom and I gardened and walked, gardened and walked, and every day she found new words to compel me to have Sam put to sleep. He stayed locked in his pen, maintaining an anxious vigil on the roof of his house, watching us come and go. We were in the garden when I asked Mom how long she would try to persuade me to do the impossible.

"Until it is possible," she replied, throwing a spade into the soil.

"Then I'll take Sam to college," I said.

She nudged her glasses and eyed me.

"Then you'll need an apartment," she returned.

Dirt flew around her spade.

"You'll need a job."

I hadn't thought of that.

"I'll quit school," I threatened. "I'll work at Burger King."

Mom threw a tomato plant at the ground and lowered a stare.

"Then I'll save a lot on tuition."

The days wore on. We explored every option. Farms refused Sam because he had attacked animals, and our neighbors wearied of his threatening presence. One day I found an anonymous note in our mailbox: *Get rid of your dog.* Mom took it from me and marched next door, where she knew the note had been written. I stood in our driveway and watched her posture go rigid as she spoke to Mrs. Stein at the door. I saw Mom's hands curl into fists and Mrs. Stein's smile fade. The next message I found was an apology. And this time it was signed.

Mom's determination to end Sam's life did not waver. Gardening with her became silent torture, and then dinners were quiet, and then the house, wherever I went, was stilled. The more stubborn I got, the more she withheld conversation, unless it included my surrender. Finally one night I knocked on her study door, craving a smile, a word. She lifted her head from letter writing and smelled victory.

Mom knew that decisions like these can't have time to breathe. She asked Dr. Millis, the vet who had once called Sam "supremely intelligent," to come as soon as possible. When he arrived the next morning in his white pickup, Sam and I were at the creek. Sam raced in circles, intoxicated by freedom, then tumbled into the water with glee.

I smiled at his splashing in forgetful reflex, then panicked when he suddenly turned from me and started for home. I grabbed my bicycle and shouted after him, but he loped steadily over his familiar route, aiming for breakfast. I chased him through the wooded path, catching sight of his hind legs as he snaked and sniffed his way, then came roaring out of the woods into our yard. Sam trotted past the vet's pickup and offered a curious sniff before entering his pen for a drink of water. Mom was already there, waiting.

I hit my brakes and dropped the bike. Sam stood panting beside her, and they both looked at me from behind the wire fence.

"He's sick," Mom had tried to explain in the weeks I had lobbied for his life.

When I had produced a barbed choke chain and muzzle as my solution, Mom had backed away, alarmed. "*Never*," she hissed, throwing them in the trash. "That's no life for him. That's misery."

Now she leaned down and whispered in Sam's ear, and he pressed his body into her.

"Time to go," she said, nudging him through the gate.

Sam's coat was wet and warm in my arms. The vet sat on the window seat beside us, and I hugged Sam to my chest, hoping he didn't know what was coming. Mom stood close, with her palm under Sam's chin. I kept thinking I would stop it from happening, would shout, or scream, or run for the hills, but I didn't move, except to hold him tighter. Dr. Millis pulled something small from a leather bag, and Sam and I recoiled. For a moment I held a conscious, living, breathing body; he had rescued me, slept beside me, tested me, and loved me. Then I watched a needle slip into his soft flank, and quick as a thought he was gone.

In the days following Sam's death, I thought of a book I'd read in grade school called *Where the Red Fern Grows*. In it, a legend evolves after a boy and girl die together in a snowstorm. When their bodies are found the following spring, a red fern has sprouted between them. According to the legend, only angels could plant a red fern—it was a sign of exceptional love, it marked hallowed ground, and it never died.

In the book, two dogs—Big Dan and Little Ann—have this kind of rare attachment. When Big Dan is killed, Little Ann dies soon after, of grief. They are buried in the fall, side by side, and by spring a red fern has joined them.

When Sam died, I still believed in signs and messages. I believed in man's power to write his own ending, conquer the finite, and return after death.

And two years later, on the morning that my mother died, I went to the bottom of our hill where Sam was buried and wondered about my sign. I told myself that they were *not* gone. They were *not* dead. I had to believe that my red fern was somewhere underground, waiting to be born. I did not know in what form I would find my sign, but I would look until it came. Maybe I'd see it in another dog or shadowed in the moon. I might find it in a passing stranger. Or maybe even a friend.

At Sorrell's, Jane circled and observed our pack, sometimes with amusement, sometimes with longing. We did the same. Her looks had Nick and Julian excited, but they were too afraid to say much beyond hello. At lunch breaks in the back room we gathered, and before long we were discussing Jane at length.

"I asked her where she was from, and she said, 'The East,'" Angela reported. "'The *East*,' as if she didn't want me to know."

"I bet she's from New York City," Nick said. He pulled his bleached hair into a short ponytail, then let it loose.

"She plays field hockey," River noted, as if this provided an important clue. "I saw field hockey sticks in her car."

"And she's got the body for it, too," Nick continued.

"I play field hockey," I said, perking up.

All eyes turned doubtfully to me.

"In college," I explained. Since no one seemed impressed, I added, "Division *One*."

Nick said, "No offense, Caroline, but you look more like you played chess."

I shrank in my chair, puzzled.

"*Nick,*" Angela moaned.

"No offense," he said again.

I thought maybe it was my glasses. They were recent. Possibly my glasses made me look like a chess player. I doubted that chess players were synonymous with beauty or on Nick's list to date, which even in the midst of hating him was disappointing.

Julian cleared his throat. "Jane is trouble," he announced. A slow smile crossed his face. We waited for more, but that was it.

"Well then," River said. "The Sphinx has spoken."

"I'll sign up for some of that trouble, thank you," Nick remarked. He stood up and pushed a bowl of soup into the microwave.

Jane walked in behind him and reached past me for a paper bag in the refrigerator. When the room went silent, a flicker of anxiety crossed her face.

"Hey, do you play field hockey?" I asked brightly.

Nick coughed.

"Halfback," Jane answered. She looked at Nick and added, "I can also play chess." Then, to Angela, "We do it all in the East." Then she walked out the door.

Angela put her hand across her mouth and whispered, "Shit, she heard us."

River punched Nick. Julian started to giggle.

"I played center forward," I ventured meekly.

That broke them all into giggles. So I left, in search of Jane.

She was sitting with her back against the store on the sidewalk outside, chewing a homemade sandwich. When I approached she straightened, surprised.

"Hi," I said.

She smiled.

"They can be really tiring," I said. "Sorry."

"I could care less what they think," she said.

"*Couldn't* care less," I corrected. "If you *could* care less, that would mean you do care." Sometimes I channeled my father that way. He was a stickler for language. "Unless you *meant* to say you care," I added. "In which case—"

Jane stared at me midswallow. It seemed wrong to either stay or go at that point, so I folded my arms and looked at the sky.

"You've been watching me," she noted.

"What?"

"Every time I turn around."

"I don't think so."

Jane fished a green apple from her paper bag and said, "Uh-huh." She glanced at the vacant spot beside her. I took a seat.

"So . . . how's it going so far?" I asked.

"I don't know," she sighed. "Too soon to tell."

"You have to get in with Faye," I advised. "She runs the show."

"Oh yeah? I was guessing that was Isaac."

She had a point. If Isaac liked you, people showed respect. He liked most women, though, especially the pretty ones.

"Why does the guy—what's his name? With the wild blond hair?"

"Nick."

"Why does he squint half the time? He almost knocked me over."

"He gets tired of his glasses," I explained. "He's a good guy. Normally."

"And River?" Jane crunched her apple and cocked her head.

"A little spacey. Really sensitive. She cries if a line forms at her register."

"And you?"

"Me? I wouldn't know how to begin. . . ."

"Oh. You're *complex*," Jane said.

"Let's say that," I agreed.

She threw her apple core toward a distant trash can. It made a satisfying *clunk*. She said, "Well, let me try.

"You are a born peacemaker," she surmised, "coming out here to see if I was crying over being talked about. You look worried a lot. You'll have lines on your face if you don't buck up. Still, you're pretty funny, too. In an awkward sort of way. I heard you quote Pauline Kael the other day to impress a customer—something about the auteur theory, which cracked me up. I guess you're one of those people who *studies* movies. Which I don't really get, but it shows some . . . intellect."

Jane looked to see if she was close.

I said, "Huh."

She winked.

"Well, fine," I said. "Let me guess. *You* are . . ." But after a pause I shut my mouth. I really had no idea.

"An enigma," Jane said. "Ha."

I felt a tingle in my gut, the kind you get when someone new seems endlessly perfect and clever. She checked her watch and said, "Lyle is making my life hell."

He was training Jane on the registers. Lyle was not perfect, or clever, and he was not forgiving. Each register had to add up exactly, with initials logged in and out. Frequently, Lyle came streaking through the store with his roll of tape flying behind to find the poor souls behind the initials and scare the life out of them. I had been nabbed twice already and was subsequently relegated to shelving.

After lunch I watched Jane and Lyle as I organized the travel section. Jane tried hard to learn that newspapers were entered by a special code, greeting cards by price plus an x, magazines by another code, and books by ISBN, except for special cases, like remainders, which were treated like newspapers, unless they were remaindered games, which had a whole different inventory system. Jane wisely asked if bookmarks were like cards, and Lyle threw up his hands.

"Let's start over," he groaned.

If he had only known that Jane's mind was not suited to mundane procedures, that she couldn't add very well, that in general memory was a problem, he could have saved them both a lot of time.

"There are blanks," Jane eventually admitted. "All over my brain. Basic grammar, geography. Most of school. Whole years.

"That's why I like art," she explained. "Nothing empirical, nothing to remember. Just naked expression, and the moment."

Like me, Jane liked to read on the job.

"No reading," Lyle always barked, passing her bent head.

As a rule, Jane's hearing didn't work when Lyle was around. Consequently, he would stop in front of her after a couple of tries, unwilling to let his authority go unnoticed.

"What if a customer asks me about this book?" Jane would say. She might have been reading *The Tibetan Book of Living and Dying.*

"Not likely," Lyle would reply.

I did my reading unnoticed, in the stacks. I was one of the few employees who had welcomed shelving duty for that very reason.

"I'm going to keep reading," Jane announced at a Friday morning staff meeting, after one too many rounds with Lyle. She stood up and said, "We should all read, so that we can talk intelligently about what we sell."

Lyle looked pissed. Tom squirmed. Isaac was sleeping in the front row.

"Read at home," Tom said sympathetically. "Or read on your lunch break."

"We might as well be a chain store, then," Jane complained. "We might as well be selling bras."

"Here, here," Isaac said, suddenly awake. Then his head drooped, and he was back to sleep.

After the meeting, Jane saw me stacking the chairs and came

over. "You can read while you're shelving," I whispered. "Sit behind a cart."

Jane smiled.

"The how-to section is quiet," I added.

"You know it's not about the reading," Jane said. "It's about being told *what*, *when*, *and where* to read. That's just fascist."

I threw up the last chair and laughed.

Jane looked me up and down. "So," she said. "Do you play field hockey?"

I said I did.

"Are you good?"

"I'll score if it kills me."

"Ah, a forward," Jane said. "Well, I'm a defender. I'll die before I let anyone score."

We made a plan to play on our next day off. I was to come by her place in the morning, and then we would walk to a field on the Stanford campus. When I came to her door an overweight nanny answered, clutching a crying infant, a telephone, and a formula bottle, and she motioned me in. The house was airy and light, a one-story cottage with tan wood floors, a grand piano, classic appointments, and a practical, comfortable mood. After the nanny shouted her name, Jane emerged in pajamas—thin white cotton with tiny red roses. She smiled shyly and waved.

"Am I early?" I asked.

Jane stretched her arms up high and yawned, showing her tight stomach and the wide undercurve of her breasts. Her hair was rumpled, hastily put in a ponytail, feet bare, with pink-painted toes. The nanny passed between us with the howling baby, heading for the kitchen.

"Need any help, Martha?" Jane asked.

Martha grunted and kept walking.

Turning to me, Jane said, "Want some tea? Orange, blackberry, red zinger . . ."

"Orange," I said, leaning my stick in a corner.

Jane pointed me to a long white sofa and left the room. I sat down and scanned the room—modern wall art, family pictures, baby toys, and shelves of books.

Jane came back with two cups of tea and extended herself on the sofa, placing her small feet against my thigh. Toes wiggled as I blew on my tea and tried to look casual.

"Is it a gorgeous day?" she asked, yawning again.

"Pretty flawless," I replied.

Jane said, "Cripes. It's always sunny here. I need a storm. A good, rollicking thunderstorm."

"Winter will be here soon," I pointed out. "Maybe it gets awful then."

"I hope so," Jane sighed. She poked my thigh with her toes.

"This is a nice place," I noted, staring at the ceiling.

"I have that room," she said, motioning behind her head. "The house belongs to a couple—Jason and Katherine. Katherine is fantastic. Jason can be a dick, but he's not around much. They're both doctors. Actually, neither of them is around much."

Jane brought her knees to her chin and looked at me. Her body was all softness and curves, a small, well-proportioned frame shifting fluidly under cotton pajamas, like a cat.

"How did you find this place?" I asked.

"Boring story," Jane said. "Let me get dressed, and we can go."

I hung on to my teacup as she shot up from the couch and disappeared.

At the field, I produced the game ball awarded to me in high school for scoring the most goals. Jane read the inscription, which said just that.

"I guess you *are* pretty good, then," she said with amusement, dropping the ball on the ground. She wiggled her stick around it, then passed it over the grass to me.

I did think I was pretty good. I pulled the ball back with my stick, then dribbled it in the air, tossing it high and catching it on the tip of my stick. To put fear in her heart, I casually flipped it into the top right corner of the goal.

"Did you play in college?" I asked.

Jane squared off in front of me, her stick low, eyes on the ball. "No."

"Did Harvard have a good team?"

"How would I know?" she asked. Her eyes stayed fixed on the ball.

"But didn't you—"

"Come on," she said, tapping the ground with her stick.

I put Harvard on hold and made a sharp run to her left.

Jane plucked the ball from my stick and sent it thirty yards down the field. She shielded her eyes to watch it.

I retrieved the ball and started again, this time keeping the ball tight on my stick. Jane shadowed me as I darted forward and back, left and right.

"Are you going to do something?" she asked.

I made a hard sprint to her right and flicked the ball hip level at the goal.

Jane stopped it dead in midair. Yawning, she passed it back.

I was officially irritated. With a mighty grunt I scooped the ball over Jane's head and sprinted past her as if my life depended on it. With a dramatic lunge, I slammed the ball into the goal and went skidding on my stomach across the ground.

Jane watched me stagger to my feet. "Well," she said, suppressing a laugh. "I didn't expect *that*."

. . .

When we walked off the field, the outcome of our match was obvious. I was sweaty and panting. My shirt and shorts were covered in grass stains, and my knee was bleeding. Jane looked ready to start. She drank a little water and squinted thoughtfully at the bright sky. A thin trail of sweat rolled across her forehead.

We decided to take a walk and took off through the sunny neighborhoods, pausing to admire the big fancy houses and wide lawns. Eventually we stopped at a bench on a shady residential street. Jane tucked her legs beneath her and said, "So what happened yesterday? You came out of the bathroom and your face was a catastrophe."

"Talk about watching people . . . ," I said.

But Jane was already distracted from that train of thought, so I happily let it go. With great interest, she was tracking two middle-aged men in business suits walking on the opposite side of the street. "Graphic designer and linguistics professor," she said, nodding.

"Friends since high school," I agreed. "Grown apart now."

"The one with the briefcase is the professor. He got married last year. His wife bought it for him—"

"After he got his first job out of college."

"I guess they were college sweethearts. Now the professor doesn't play basketball with the graphic designer anymore. They meet for lunch once a month and pretend to still be friends."

"Billiards," I said.

"Huh?"

"They play billiards. Basketball went out with the designer's knee."

Jane giggled.

A young man and woman took seats at the bus stop across from us.

"Ed's just lost his job," Jane said sadly, nodding at the man.

"And Marlene is pregnant." I sighed.

"They live in a trailer, near Half Moon Bay."

"Really?"

"They inherited the trailer from Marlene's dad, who passed away last June with a coronary brought on by a congenital defect. Instead of finishing night school, Marlene married Ed and moved into the trailer."

"Why did she give up night school?" I wondered.

"The oldest reason in the world," Jane replied.

"Ah." I nodded.

"The school got flooded."

We broke up laughing.

"Ed worked at the diner on Stinson Beach," I continued. "Until he had to leave."

"Because the diner got flooded?"

"Don't be silly. It's on stilts."

The couple across from us looked in opposite directions and didn't speak. The woman packed and unpacked her purse, and the man stared down the street. He wore a plain white T-shirt and working pants. The woman's cotton dress looked handmade.

"They're a couple," Jane said.

"You think? They haven't said a word to each other."

"Exactly. They know they'll be sitting there every Saturday for the rest of their lives, so there's no hurry to talk."

"Ed and Marlene," I said.

"Ed and Marlene," Jane agreed.

We occupied the bench for a while longer, watching pedestrians come and go. I felt utterly relaxed, as if Jane and I had already passed a long history together. Any pretense of politeness had already gone, was shed in unison, like an unnecessary skin. No matter what I said or did, I felt intuitively that Jane would accept and understand me. If I jumped up and down like a monkey and sang "The Star-Spangled Banner," she would either join in or applaud.

At work, we were soon addressed as a single unit. We turned into a "they" as in "Where are *they*?" "Have you seen *them*?" "Did *they* shelve fiction yet?"

It was River who noticed that we were also dressing the same, which is to say that I had accepted Jane's tutorial on better fashion. I bought cotton khakis and Birkenstocks, thin-collared cotton T-shirts, and expensive silk blouses. I acquired a closet full of new clothes, to clothe a new me.

"What are you, independently wealthy?" Jane had asked one day as we shopped.

"Sort of," I admitted. There had been a sizable inheritance when Mom died.

Jane became alert then. She *really* looked at me. A slow smile followed, and then a grin.

Chapter TEN

Mom's investment in my college tuition paid off. I graduated without notable honors, but on time, in May of 1989, and she was right there clutching her William and Mary program, cheering with my family. In our photo together we each have tight fingers on my diploma, and Mom is beaming beneath my tasseled cap.

After college, I shipped my life home and joined my parents in the middle stages of worry over the return of cancer. The cells were ominous, but by that summer she had shown no other symptoms and was still fit. Except for the odd moment, we pretended she was fine and kept on going with fingers crossed. But instead of taking off for some adventure, or diving into graduate school, I elected to take my first postcollege job at a small bookstore close to home and settle into my old room. Mom was conflicted about this. On the one hand, she wanted me to move on as my friends were doing, to higher studies, careers, or travels. On the other hand, time was probably short for us, and none of those things held much meaning in comparison.

The first thing I did after dropping my bags was inspect the house. Right away I found a cordless phone, which was new and surprisingly advanced for my parents.

"Your father leaves it all over the place." Mom sighed. "It rings, and I have to start running."

I ran my finger across a new fireplace mantel in our living room.

"Do you like the new color?" Mom asked. "I think it's cheery."

"Very nice," I said.

What I was thinking, however, was that my parents had survived without me. By all accounts they had even enjoyed being alone together, which gave me pause.

I hadn't been home long before Mom caught Dad and me whispering about her approaching birthday, in August.

"I know what you can give me," she said, stepping solidly between us.

"A tennis match," she said to me, pointing up the hill toward the Reeses' court. To Dad she added, "You're on your own."

So on the morning of what would be her last birthday, we walked up to our neighbor's court and waved at Mrs. Reese by her pool before warming up. I was worried about making Mom run with her one lonely lung and careful to aim my shots right at her racket. Her dress hung loose, and she huffed a lot, but soon I was three games down.

When we met at the net for water, she mopped sweat from her face and neck and said, "You out of shape? Tired?"

I felt a competitive twinge and told it to go away. "No, Mom," I said. "I'm trying really hard."

"Even if you did try, I would beat you," she challenged.

That did it. I decided to go ahead and win one game.

Mom's serve was not hard, but she was tricky with spin, and she preyed on my hopeless backhand. I lunged at her first two serves and found only net. Changing tactics, I moved to the middle of the baseline so she'd have to take my forehand. She tossed the ball up and fired it at the far right of the service box. An ace.

At 40–love, I got serious. I blocked the ball just over the net, but Mom came steaming forward, tipping it back, for game.

"Okay," I said, passing her to change sides.

"Okay," she answered.

I served hard, right into Mom's body. She deflected the ball with surprise, and it flew behind her. She grinned and moved over for the next point.

I served and volleyed, ducked and dived. Mom placed her shots carefully, painting the lines and making me run. She lunged and hit overheads, she ran.

"Five to four," she said, preparing to serve for the set. I was drenched and hungry. We had been playing for hours, with two sets split between us. I decided to finish out playing my hardest to see if she really could do it.

Mom stayed on my backhand like a terrier, and she chose what she ran for. When she had me at match point, she paused at the service line, heaving. "Your game has picked up," she called.

"Quit stalling," I called back.

Up by the pool, I noticed Mrs. Reese was shielding her eyes, watching us. Mom trudged back to the baseline and prepared to serve. I watched her toss the ball high in the air, her arm stretched to the sky and her knees bent before springing. I had seen it a thousand times, since I was big enough to hold a racket. I had studied it and practiced against her for years before finally winning a game. She had briefly celebrated that milestone, then declared a rematch.

Mom's legs bent and released. She sent the ball spinning into my body and rushed the net.

Out of self-preservation I pulled my racket in front of my chest, sending the ball high above her. With one great overhead she delivered the ball back to me like a rocket, winning the match. For a moment we were both stunned. Then Mom raised her arms in victory. I came to meet her at the net, and as our sweaty bodies collided, I knew I'd never have a match like that again, not with anybody. Mrs. Reese applauded as we gathered our water and towels, and we curtsied in front of her, the way they do at Wimbledon before the queen. Then we walked down our hill as we had all my life and speculated on what Dad had out for the birthday lunch.

By October the suspicious ache in Mom's spine had been confirmed as cancer, and the following Christmas Eve she awoke in the night with such pain that Dad took her to the hospital before the sun was up.

In late January, Mom resigned from her job at the medical school and stepped down from the various volunteer committees that she chaired. By February she stopped going to church, and the ministers came to her.

Dolores arrived in March. And in these last months before she died, Mom noticed with some anxiety that her days no longer required dressing or the to-do lists she had lived by, except to schedule and record medications. After breakfast, she read the newspapers, cleaned her dishes, and then sheepishly retreated for a nap.

Sometimes I napped next to her or reclined on Dad's side of the bed, reading. Mom had started reading prayers about dying and had almost memorized C. S. Lewis's *Screwtape Letters*, which depicted a conversation in letters about God's battle against evil and the fate of man's soul.

One morning when I joined her, the usual books were in a drawer, and I could tell that she had something else on her mind. She was on her back in bed, eyes partly open, when she said, "So what are your plans, Caroline?"

"Plans?"

"Yes, *plans.*"

It killed me when she did that. She meant after she was dead.

"Still film school," I said glumly, thinking of everything she would miss.

"Well, you've logged enough hours in front of movie screens. . . ."

"See—I told you it wouldn't be wasted."

"Directing?" she asked. "Writing?"

"Writing. Maybe screenplays, or reviews. And I'd like to make documentaries."

Mom was quiet. Her face clenched and then released.

"Mom?" I asked.

"It hurts," she said, exhaling. "Boy."

When her body relaxed, I returned to my book.

"Documentaries," Mom murmured. "Why? What about?"

"Because I can do it mostly myself," I said, dropping my book. "The writing, the filming, the editing. I wouldn't have to deal with actors, or big sets, or all the hype."

Mom turned an amused eye toward me. "Right," she said. "That would be rough."

"I like screenwriting," I said. "But in the end, it's the director's story. I haven't decided on a good subject yet, though."

Mom said, "Maybe your grandmother—she wanted to write a book about her life. I have the notes somewhere . . . about growing up in Switzerland and coming to America." She caught her breath. "Did I ever tell you that my father forbade her to speak to us in anything but English?"

"Yep," I said. She had been retelling lots of family stories lately, tilling old ground.

Mom closed her eyes again and squeezed my hand until the next spasm passed. When she released she said, "You know what I always thought you'd be good at?"

"What?" I asked hopefully.

"A police detective."

She nodded, agreeing with herself.

"A *what?*"

"Because you notice things," she said. "And you're agile. In case you had to run or leap over fences."

"Leap over fences?"

"Detective Kraus," Mom said.

"Are you serious? I could get *killed.*"

"You'd have a gun," she said. "I bet you'd be a good shot."

"A *gun?*"

"Like Columbo. Or no, like Angela Lansbury in *Murder, She Wrote.*"

"She's like eighty years old," I shrieked.

Mom had made me watch that show with her every Sunday night so that I could testify that she'd solved the crime before Angela. It later occurred to me that perhaps *she* wanted to be the police detective.

"Everyone was young once," Mom said.

"I don't want to be a police detective," I said firmly.

"That's okay," she assured me. "It's still good to have those skills."

Chapter ELEVEN

Despite my apparent sleuthing skills, Jane's background remained largely a mystery to me and the rest of the bookstore staff. In my experience, when getting to know people, I'd first learn the basic statistics, such as where they went to school, where they grew up, what movies or books they liked, and so on. But Jane worked the other way. She dug from the bottom, presented her guts, and watched your reaction. Jane's boundaries were strict, but opposite. She withheld the basic facts, common life data. As a result, she seemed simultaneously remote and intimate, blocking superficial queries like hockey balls, then taking us each on our own exclusive journey, into her most intimate thoughts and experiences.

If Jane was like a modern Wizard of Oz, presenting lesser mortals with quick answers to their dreams, then I was a predictable Dorothy, clicking my pen and longing for a home that didn't exist. Jane gave me her constant, maternal attention. She made sure that I ate enough, laughed enough, knew that I made a difference in her world, and was, exclusively, hers.

And Nick made a believable Cowardly Lion, stumbling through the store with his hapless bravado. Jane gave him shoulder massages at the register and told him that his thick blond mane was very sexy. They traded surfing stories, and she promised to teach him how to sail.

And Faye was our Tin Man—a crusty old hippie with a ticking heart buried beneath her tough mouth and defensive candor. Jane confided in Faye. She said she'd escaped a rich East Coast family, too, and had also left millions behind on moral principle.

We were all Scarecrows at various times. If we had brains, we routinely checked them at the door when Jane was present. When you know someone's most private thoughts on God, sex, politics, and death, and when that someone seems to know you better than you know yourself, it's hard to remember that you never caught their last name.

Still, there were some people who didn't fall for Jane at all. Carla, the woman who had rescued me from Joan Baez, stayed as far from her as she could. When there was cause for them to intersect, Carla was careful with her words and deaf to the few advances Jane made to know her. Very quickly, Jane did not like Carla.

Barbara, who was in charge of the returns department and the mother of four teenage boys, was also immune. Jane brought her presents for a while, but Barbara only looked at Jane over her bifocals like a scientist studying a bug and said, "No, thank you, dear.

"Just address the boxes right next time," she'd add. Then Barbara joined Carla, and several others, in Jane's penalty box.

In one of our early conversations, I learned that Jane was a Scorpio. She explained that Scorpios were highly sexual, physically intense, and fundamentally crazy. She said she had been in the "loony bin" periodically during high school, and I gathered that she empathized with anyone who felt similarly robbed by life or had become lost because of tragedy or injustice. She talked about the writers that she loved, and I noticed that the ones she mentioned had all either publicly suffered or killed themselves, like Dylan Thomas, Hemingway, Anne Sexton, Virginia Woolf, and Sylvia Plath.

Otherwise, what I had was sketchy. She was from a town in the East. She had heard of Pauline Kael. Somewhere she learned to play field hockey.

"I have parents," she allowed.

"Really," I said.

"Yes."

"Hobbies?"

"I despise the very idea," she replied.

"Things that you do when not at work?" I rephrased.

"Depends on my mood. I paint. Take pictures. Have sex. I like Oprah."

Then she said she was tired. Questions exhausted her. My turn.

"I'm a Pisces," I said, taking her lead.

She brightened. "Well. That explains it. We're water and water. We merge."

She was partly right. Astrology books actually say that a Pisces will *sub*merge in the presence of a Scorpio. Which is not our strong point. If you take the stars seriously—as most Pisceans, being drawn to any cosmic excuse, will do—Jane was actually an astrological threat. But Pisceans are also nonconfrontational. So I let that go.

"Older brother, older sister," I continued. "Grant's a lawyer in Washington, D.C., Madeleine is a medical resident in Boston."

"Ugh. How boring," Jane said. "Were you adopted?"

"There has been speculation," I admitted.

"What do your parents do?"

"Dad's a pathologist, and Mom is dead."

Jane paused. "Dead?" she asked.

I felt the dawning of an unwanted smile. The corners of my mouth twitched, and I prayed I wouldn't laugh. Jane watched, transfixed by the contortions overtaking my face. Finally I burst out laughing. She looked truly surprised.

"That is a *strange* reaction," she said.

I doubled over.

Jane giggled, too, looking to me for explanation.

When I calmed down, we watched each other cautiously. But Jane couldn't resist. She opened her mouth and said, *"Dead."*

Again I was possessed. Like a wind-up toy, I went into hysterics. I was like the creepy Joker character in *Batman;* after being dumped into a boiling chemical pit, he came out with a permanent grin.

At around eight each morning, I started getting wake-up calls from Jane. Her sleepy voice seeped into my equally sleepy brain, and she'd tell me about the weird dream I'd just starred in or what she planned to wear to work. Sometimes she'd say she'd just successfully pleasured herself, which meant the day was off to a good start.

The morning calls were a welcome change from my previous routine, which had been to watch my clock, then hit the alarm before it rang. I'd usually dressed with the *Today* show, worked on looking presentable, then watched feet pass until it was time to leave.

Jane put an end to all that. After we hung up, I got dressed fast, knowing she was waiting for me. All day long, I felt as though something exciting were happening, something momentous and new. I could feel myself changing, gathering confidence under Jane's wing. Throughout Sorrell's, the phenomenon was amazing. The ripple effect of Jane's affection had people falling over one another to know her better. And as we all fell in various forms of love, Jane made sure everyone knew I was her favorite. I basked in her reflected glare and saw my social stock rise to unearned heights. Suddenly I was attractive, too. I was someone so rare that Jane Lowell had singled me out.

For a while, Jane had Tom believing she'd joined Mensa, and Lyle apologizing for how he'd nagged her. Faye fetched her coffees, and before long she was encouraged to read on the job or take long breaks when she was tired. Everyone wanted her happy, because then she spread her joy. That was Jane's best skill—getting the world to pause, pivot, and reverse itself, without ever knowing.

There was one morning when a fancy-looking woman approached Jane and me at the information desk. Jane had been reading Anna Quindlen's *New York Times* column aloud and sighed loudly at the interruption.

"Do you have books for boys?" the woman asked politely.

"Boys? Do you mean children's books?" I asked.

"Well, he's nineteen."

"Oh. Then no."

Jane rested her chin on her hands and waited.

"Books *about* boys?" I suggested. "Maybe *Catcher in the Rye?*"

"Is that what they read?" the lady asked.

"How about *Playboy?*" Jane suggested.

The lady stepped back. I coughed.

Jane went back to the newspaper.

"Just a book," the lady said. "Any book. That a boy would like."

"How about Faulkner?" I suggested. "Faulkner is right there in fiction, under 'F.' " I pointed. "Maybe *The Sound and the Fury.*"

"Hold on—girls like Faulkner," Jane warned. "I don't, but some do."

The lady looked between us, confused.

Normally, I would have been more helpful to this poor woman, but with Jane as my audience, I took on a new personality. I said, "Now that I think of it, there *are* no books for nineteen-year-old boys. It's a void." I turned to see if Jane was laughing.

Instead she shot me a dark look, then gave the woman a sincere smile. She said, "Don't pay attention to her. Let's look in Travel Essay—has he read Kerouac?"

When they returned, the woman was laughing and touching Jane's arm. She leaned across our desk for almost an hour, talking with Jane about books, her old college days, and the trials of having a nineteen-year-old boy. After she checked her watch and gasped at the time, she asked Jane why someone so gifted was languishing in retail.

"Good question," Jane said, pointing at me for some reason.

"Can I see your photographs sometime?" the woman asked, handing Jane her card.

Jane said, "Sure, Karen," as though they'd known each other for decades.

When the woman left on a carpet of exhilaration, I could see it in her face, in the giddy smile that lingered as she stepped out the door. She'd just been Janed.

One evening I searched the store for Jane after our shift was over and found myself unusually worried about not being able to say good-bye. I worried about where she was and especially whom she was with. Then I worried about why I was even bothered. When I stepped into the parking garage and saw Jane sitting on the trunk of my car, I almost tripped I was so relieved.

"Hello there." She smiled.

"Hi," I said.

Jane hopped off the trunk and said, "Heading home?"

"Yeah."

She tugged at the handle of my passenger door and said, "I'm coming."

"Oh . . . ?" I looked around the garage.

"I walked today," she replied. "Come on, I want to see your place."

I got in, pushed open her door, then had the fleeting worry that it was midnight already and I'd have to drive her home.

"Ignition," she suggested. "Then reverse."

I looked at the stick shift. "It *is* late, though," I said.

She patted the dashboard and said, "Giddy-up."

It occurred to me that I'd been living a pretty boring existence, if having fun after work seemed so foreign. I told myself that this was exactly what people my age were supposed to enjoy, and I was damn lucky to have Jane rescuing me from an early social retirement.

"*Reverse*, honey," she whispered.

I happily obeyed.

Honey, I thought, backing us out. Only one person had called me that before, and she had given birth to me.

"Is that your mother?" Jane asked. She was turning in a circle, staring at my walls of pictures. I nodded and stepped closer, ready to narrate. I liked the way she examined my room, the way she stood for a long time before every picture and stooped to see the treasures I'd laid on my bottom shelves. In my experience, few people cared to look, when all around them were mysteries and clues: a shelf of battered wooden boxes, a field hockey stick, a pair of old canes, cases of books, an antique desk, an old horseshoe wrapped in brown paper, a crude wooden sailboat, old record albums, and, tacked to the door, my child's drawing, found by Mom, whose smooth handwriting underneath reads, *I love you!*

Jane touched the drawing. I hovered.

Mom gazed at us in all her poses, with elegant smiles, schoolgirl braids, melancholy distraction, and always, always, those hooded blue eyes. It registered on Jane's face that every picture contained my mother.

"Wow," she said. "It's a shrine."

I stepped back, embarrassed. I hadn't thought of it as a shrine.

More of a gallery. A record. I retreated to the opposite side of the room until Jane called me back. She pointed to a solemn image of my mother as a child, suffering beneath pink bows and tightly braided hair. It was a picture of a girl who wanted desperately to go climb a tree. "Now that one reminds me of me," she said approvingly. "I would have liked your mother."

"You don't have much poetry," she noted later, running a finger along my books.

"I like fiction," I said. "And screenplays." I pointed to three whole shelves of screenplays, next to a full shelf devoted to Pauline Kael.

"Not *boys'* fiction, I hope," Jane whispered, moving on.

"No, no," I whispered back.

"What was your mother's name?" she asked.

"Madeleine," I said. "But everyone called her Monny. Madeleine Martha Caroline Véron Kraus." I said it proudly and was rewarded by Jane's impressed nod.

She looked at a picture of my mother sitting on a rock and said, "Hello, Monny."

"My mother's mother had *eight* names," I added, then waited to be asked.

"Go ahead." Jane sighed, smiling.

"Maria Magdalena Wilhelmina Waldburga Von Reding Von Biberegg Véron Moser." I folded my arms and grinned.

"I take it she wasn't born in St. Louis," Jane said. "Any relation to the Von Trapps?"

"They were *Austrian,*" I said seriously, as usual, missing the joke.

To complete my show-and-tell, I handed Jane a leather journal from beside my bed. It had a small picture of my family, with Grandmother Moser taped to the first page. I was about five years old, sitting chubby cheeked and proud in my mother's lap. "This is all of us, in Michigan," I said. "That's my grandmother."

"Good Lord," she said. "The Swiss Family Robinson meets Norman Rockwell, USA."

. . .

I had rooms full of furniture, books, and memorabilia, but most of Jane's life fit into two large blue and yellow duffel bags. She had a small collection of expensive clothes, a small collection of music and art, and one box of books.

When I toured her room for the first time, she watched me from the doorway, thumb nearing her mouth, resting on her bottom lip.

"You *are* an artist," I said. I lifted some sculptures from a cardboard box. Clay hands, heads, feet, and faces sat among colorful painted tiles.

"Actually, my friend Nelle made those," Jane said. She pointed. "My stuff is over there."

I crossed the room, passing windowsills lined with rocks, fossils, jars of sand, and blue glass. A makeshift desk was covered with Jane's writing, a few watercolors, and sketches.

"Take anything you want," she said, walking away. "I'm going to make us orange tea."

I glanced at one of Jane's poems, a draft in pencil with crossed-out lines and additions. The poem was about being abandoned and falling in love. There were metaphors of blood and broken limbs, drowning and gasping for air. I looked at another poem, titled "Rage," and then another, happier piece called "California."

I turned my attention to some matted photographs leaning against the wall with the initials *jrl*. "And you're a good photographer," I called, flipping through the pictures. There were children, lots of children. And landscapes. And nudes. The nudes were male and female, full of arched backs, reaching arms, and hidden faces.

"What does the 'r' stand for?" I yelled toward the kitchen.

"Rainier," Jane said, in the doorway again. She put her thumb in her mouth and blinked at me. "No relation to the prince, though." The words were muffled over her thumb.

I stared at her for a moment, then laughed.

"Don't," she said.

I hiccuped, then covered my mouth. It was odd, but Jane actually made having a thumb in her mouth look stylish. Her bottom jaw moved up and down ever so slightly, and her eyes softened. It wouldn't be long before this was as natural and comforting a sight as seeing her smile.

She brought her thumb to her cheek and held it there, gazing at me as if I might disappear. I felt my whole body relax under her stare, and then something loosened in me.

I was suddenly like Alice, slipping down a new, exciting rabbit hole.

Chapter TWELVE

On days when Mom felt better and was itching to get out of the house, she had an oxygen tank that went with us, which I had named Betsy. Betsy was green with white trim, and she rolled inside a steel harness. Before outings, Mom put on lipstick and selected a piece of jewelry, "to give it a walk," she said. Before stepping out the door, she inserted Betsy's plastic tubes into her nose and turned to me for approval.

This was a tricky moment. Mom's hair was permanently flattened in back, and the plastic tubes smeared her lipstick. Her left shoulder dipped, and she was terribly thin.

"Well, say something," she would huff.

"Perfection," I learned to reply. And that got us out the door.

In the car, Mom always put a seat belt around the oxygen tank. She was afraid Betsy might explode, and she hated the idea of exploding on the way to Saks Fifth Avenue.

It was early spring, and Mom was determined to replace all of my "ratty" summer clothes, even though I'd assured her the ratty part was intentional. She sat with Betsy outside dressing rooms as I paraded past in slacks, sundresses, and skirts.

"Why won't you wear any color?" she complained. "Black and beige, black and beige . . . you're not in the army."

"I like earth tones," I said.

"You like black and beige. Two tones."

Mom advised me to hold in my stomach and pick up my feet when I walked. She asked me when I would stop biting my nails.

"It's a self-manicure," I explained. "I'm experienced."

Mom still felt bad about my nails, as if she'd failed a major test of mothering. She had a theory that my kindergarten teacher, Ms. Blaine, had pressured me when I didn't make my eights right. I had used two circles and thought that turned out perfectly good eights. Somehow my teacher could tell, and eventually our difference of opinion turned into all-out war. I was more interested in fooling Ms. Blaine than making them right, and she was convinced my future as a student was in jeopardy.

"Well," Mom reasoned as I modeled a black sleeveless top, "at least you don't smoke."

When April came, our outings stopped. Mom stayed mainly in bed with her books and music, but she was dressed when I raced home from work for lunch, and Dolores propped her in the study when scheduled visitors came around.

For me, the most agonizing part of Mom's last months was the relentless sense of waiting. Waiting without knowing what was next or how long it would take. Meanwhile, I was getting postcards from friends with jobs in big cities and news of former classmates now in graduate schools. And I had wistful phone conversations with the more adventurous types, old friends off to the Peace Corps, or Europe, or Nepal. And yet, counting the days felt traitorous. My desire to move on seemed like the worst kind of betrayal.

One afternoon I found Mom resting in bed, and she waved for me to join her. "I saw you outside before," she said, nodding at the

French doors near her bed. Her view looked out past the brick fountain, onto the full expanse of our yard and gardens.

"Dad asked me to clean out the azalea bed," I explained.

"Oh," Mom said. Her jaw moved back and forth, the way it would when she was trying to keep her composure. I lay down next to her. She let her hand drop on my arm and pinned it there.

"So?" she said. "Are you okay?"

I grunted. She wiggled her fingers to stimulate a more specific reply.

"I feel stuck," I confessed. The minute I said it, I ducked my head in shame.

"Me too," Mom replied. She lifted my chin and made me look at her.

"I can't believe you'll actually be *gone*," I blurted. "I mean . . . what am I going to do?"

"I wish I knew," she sighed. "I really wish I could see it."

"Nobody knows me the way you do," I said bitterly. "And nobody ever will."

After a silence, Mom said, "You're right." Looking away, she added, "Keep that."

She didn't want to die in a hospital. Mom made three specific requests of Dad: She wanted to die at home, in their bedroom; no special measures should be taken to save her; and I was not to be in the room when she died, under any circumstances.

Dad agreed to everything. He had a hospital bed installed in their room, and he slept in a twin bed beside her. A yellow legal pad outlined a complex schedule of medications, which he administered night and day. What Mom took for pain caused side effects, which were countered by more pills, which caused their own side effects, resulting in another fleet of countermeasures and, invariably, side effects. The chemical avalanche paralyzed her. She lay still through the hours with Betsy close by, and lost interest in most everything.

Ensconced at home, with no more hospitals on her horizon, she let go of life in chunks. She abandoned food, then reading, then oxygen, and finally she stopped making sense. She confused words, and people, and began humming when she got stuck in a sentence or thought.

"I water of tree," she'd say. If I asked her to clarify, she looked at me as if I were crazy.

I should have known better than to pack my car and shuttle my belongings to an apartment I'd found with Dad's blessing. It was in a Bohemian part of St. Louis, near Washington University, and I had signed the lease before Mom's latest bad turn without telling her. By the time she was showing signs of mental confusion, I was too set on my freedom to surrender before tasting it. So I ignored my conscience and worked all day to unpack new kitchen equipment, furniture, books and records, and, as a final touch, a vase of flowers for my entrance.

I was awash with excitement when I came home for my last load, but Dad looked worried. "Better tell Mom now," he said.

We walked down the hall together, and I felt a growing sense of dread. "It's not your fault," Dad added, putting his hand on my shoulder. "Whatever happens."

I took a seat, facing Mom in bed. She opened her eyes and muttered. Then she waved and said, "In thing the dish for."

"What?" I asked.

"Hi," she replied.

Hoping to slip in quickly while she was making sense, I said, "Mom, I have exciting news."

"What is it?" she asked, clear as a bell.

"I found an apartment. My first apartment—just two seconds away." I looked at Dad.

Mom gripped her blanket. "What? You're leaving?" She looked at Dad.

"Now I'm not going far," I said, "I'm practically next door—I'll be here just as often as ever. Every day for lunch and on weekends—"

"It can't be," Mom moaned. "Fred!" she called. "Fred!"

Madeleine, who was visiting, came running. "What's going on?" she asked.

"I don't want her to go," Mom said anxiously. "She'll be gone, and then she won't be here. Frederick!"

Dad cleared his throat and looked at me.

"I'll stay," I said quickly. "I'll stay, Mom. I'm not going anywhere."

My sister sat down on the edge of Mom's bed and patted her feet.

"Okay," Mom said. "Okay." She squinted at me.

"I want to stay," I added. And then I knew Mom's mind had retreated, because she didn't even spot that open lie.

When she seemed fully appeased, I went to our kitchen and leaned against the wall.

"It's not fair," Madeleine said, following me. "It's really unfair."

"I'm stuck here *forever*," I cried. "I have no life."

Dad came in, looking embarrassed. "It's my fault," he said. "It's my fault, Caroline, I'm sorry."

"Will she get better?" I asked. "How long will she act like this?"

"No," Dad said weakly, taking a seat at the kitchen table. "She won't get better. She's experiencing dementia now. And she's not eating, which will make her worse."

Madeleine nodded, concurring with this forecast. Both of them had trained insights into Mom's illnesses—her depression and the cancer—which I was spared by not having a medical degree. They had always known what was ahead for her, the ugly details of how her body would give in. And sometimes they seemed to take refuge there, behind their experience with watching patients die. But more often, where Mom was concerned, their training seemed like a curse.

. . .

Dad called Grant that day and suggested he fly home. Within moments, it seemed, he was rushing through our door wearing an expression of primal fear.

"Where's Mom?" he asked, dropping his bags. Like a shot he was past us to her room.

"Well," Mom said, "look who's here!"

Grant leaned down to her forehead and kissed her hello.

"Have a good flight?"

"Yes, Mom."

Dad, Madeleine, and I hovered with plastic smiles.

"Did you plan something for dinner, Fred?" she asked Dad. "Grant likes beef."

Dad cleared his throat and nodded.

Mom glanced at each of us and said, "Please stop smiling at me like that. You look like you want to sell me something." Dad's mouth shrank and closed. We followed suit.

That night, Mom joined us at dinner. She listened to us make conversation for a while and then excused herself. When I checked in to say good night, she was asleep. And sometime in the night her brain lost more ground. Because by morning, she wasn't speaking at all.

Some days passed, and as usual, before the sun was up, Dad whistled upstairs for me. It was my job to sit with Mom while he went running before work. I swung my feet over my bed and trotted zombielike down the stairs. Dad was stretching in the hallway. I grunted hello, and we walked together to Mom's bed. Suddenly, I was awake.

"She's not breathing right," I said. "She's breathing different—don't you think?"

"She's been breathing that way all night," Dad said.

"I don't think you should go," I said.

The sound was dreadful, like rocks in her chest.

"I won't be long," Dad said. "It will be all right." And with that he took off.

I took my place on the wooden chair between their beds and watched Mom's arms move in the air, conducting an invisible orchestra. A few minutes later, the rocks turned to boulders, and I became afraid.

"Sit up," I said, propping pillows behind her. She waved her arms frantically. "What is it?" I asked. "What do you want?"

Her eyes were wide, and she pointed in all directions. I mentally ran through the things she had usually asked for and jogged to the bathroom for water. Back at her side, I fought for access to her mouth. I jammed the straw in and she knocked the cup away.

"Catch in does," she said, "deel ker mede."

"What?" I wailed.

She pushed my arm.

"What do you *want?*"

"Edy ree loo," she answered.

I jumped away from her bed and went to the next, if unlikely, possibility—lotion. Running back, I tripped and fell across Dad's bed, dropping the tube. "Shit!" I screamed. "Goddamn motherfucker shit fuck hell." I stared at Mom, panting. Now she was straining for air and not getting it.

"Please," I pleaded. "Please don't." When she gasped again, in a way that seemed final, I screamed. A rush of tears came down her face, as if a switch had been thrown to empty her. I went running to find Grant.

"Help!" I shouted, opening his bedroom door. "It's *Mom*—"

"Where's Dad?" Grant asked, leaping from bed.

"Running," I panted, pulling him through the house.

Grant saw Mom and stopped in his tracks. He heard her wild, broken breaths, and his face fell. "Go look for Dad," he said softly. "Go see if he's coming."

I ran to the kitchen door and saw Dolores pull up in her Lincoln. I sprinted outside and grabbed her. "Hurry," I said, pulling her along. "Something's wrong."

Dolores tumbled after me into the bedroom and exchanged looks with Grant. She touched Mom's head, took her pulse, and said, "She's going now."

Grant wanted me out of the room. He suggested I go look for Dad again.

"But *do* something," I said, looking between them. I reached for the oxygen tubes and Dolores stopped me.

Grant said, "Oh God, I have to call Madeleine," and left.

I squared off with Dolores. "You put those tubes in her nose," I ordered.

"No," she replied.

I grabbed them myself.

"I understand," Dolores said sympathetically. "But no." She stood between me and my mother and crossed her arms.

"Then what?" I asked, dropping the tubes.

"I'm going to call Dr. Owen," Dolores said. "Your mother doesn't want oxygen now, she was very clear."

Mom uttered something random and shut her eyes.

"Then why is she crying?" I asked. "She wants something   "

"Caroline?" Dad said softly. He was dripping with sweat in the doorway. He walked to the wooden chair and took Mom's hand.

"It's a different kind of tears," Dolores whispered, to answer my question.

Dad brushed the wetness from her cheeks and his and asked me to go.

"Stop her," I said weakly.

"You should go," he choked.

I didn't move.

"*Go,*" he said. "Please?"

. . .

I left them, went to the kitchen sink, and stared at the oak trees in our yard. Grant had paged Madeleine and was now on the phone with Aunt Estie. My sister was flying down the highway by then. Dolores sat quietly at the kitchen table, perched at the edge of her chair. Dr. Owen was on his way, too. In the garage, I heard garbage cans being lifted and dumped, which meant it was Tuesday morning. I remember thinking, as Dad's slow steps came down the hall, that the ladies were gathered up the hill, expecting me to show.

My father had never wept in my presence before, but after telling me Mom had just died, he shook like a child in my arms. I remember thinking right then that I should be crying too, or feeling relief that Mom's ordeal was over and life could resume. Instead I felt an avalanche of regret, as though I'd just failed a critical test. As soon as I could, I went down to Sam's grave, and I pondered how to make things right. But I'd let both of them down, it seemed to me, and my apologies were greeted with silence.

Give me a sign, was all I could beg.

I wanted another chance.

Chapter THIRTEEN

"I am here to save your life," Nick said. He hopped up on the backroom counter where I was labeling and handed me a newspaper. An ad was circled. It described an "international house" looking for "artists, scholars, or generally interesting people."

"You're interesting," Nick said, "on a good day."

I had been moaning about my long commute since starting at Sorrell's but had yet to move from moaning to a solution. My co-workers, who had tired of this, suggested I either check out the house or shut up, so I made my appointment, with Nick dialing the phone.

The green ranch-style house was on Waverly Street, a quiet residential area in Palo Alto, with modest yards and palm trees. A shaggy-haired American named Alex greeted me at the door. He blinked a lot, and his face twitched. "You'll have to meet the rest of the group before we decide anything," he said quickly. He raked his fingers through his hair over and over again, flicking a smile, which collapsed into a frown, then became a smile again. I caught him on a smile and smiled back.

Five bedrooms and a kitchen surrounded a tidy brick courtyard with a full-size swimming pool, and then there was a small pool house where Alex lived. He showed me the room that might be mine, but only, again, if the rest of the group liked me.

A bright green wall-to-wall shag rug gave me pause, but otherwise the room was perfect, much bigger than my studio, and one whole wall had floor-to-ceiling built-in bookshelves. There was even a private entrance—tall French doors, opening to a secluded brick path that led to the street. I gasped with desire. Alex looked pleased.

"It's the biggest room in the house," he said. "Do you have a lot of stuff?"

"Oh yeah," I said. "Yep."

"So what do you do?" he asked, leading me through the kitchen. I selected one of my lingering fantasies, hoping to fulfill both the "interesting" and "artist" requirements with one shot, and I said I was a screenwriter. I almost believed myself when I described the pile of scripts I was working on.

Alex perked up. "Have I seen any of your movies?" he asked.

I said they were currently unproduced.

He gave me an understanding nod. Alex, it turned out, was six hundred pages into a book about the origins of human thought.

We walked to the pool house, where the rest of the group was waiting, and Alex introduced me around. There was Peng, a business student from China; Greta, an artist from Holland; Lisette, an archaeologist from Geneva; and Torsten—tall, blond, sleepy-eyed Torsten. He was German, a marine biologist, and his blond, sculpted beauty made me stutter when I said hello.

"Caroline is a screenwriter," Alex announced.

"Unproduced," I added.

Since English did not come easily to anyone but Alex and me, I had to hope that the smiles and nods were a good sign.

Days passed before I was officially accepted into the Waverly Street house. In the meantime I had bought books on screenwriting, signed up for a summer screenwriting workshop at Stanford, and come to believe that my destiny was to marry Torsten and accept Academy Awards.

I didn't waste time getting moved. I worked into the night, shuttling my belongings from foggy Masonic Street to what I hoped was the dawning of a better life. My new housemates observed my coming and going with amused interest, eventually settling into lawn chairs to see what curious belongings would appear next. They drank wine and cheered me on as I lugged one box after another from my Toyota and dropped them on my green shag rug. Applause greeted my television, stereo, books, and VCR. My housemates had traveled far, and light, so their rooms had only bare essentials. It appeared that I was the arrival of entertainment.

By the time I returned with the last load, my stereo and television were up and running and Greta was fighting Peng for the remote. Lisette and Torsten had my field hockey sticks out and were using them like swords. Otis Redding was playing on my turntable. Everyone politely acknowledged my arrival, then returned to their new toys. I made a nest in my pile of clothes and collapsed. Sometime later, Lisette's accented voice penetrated my sleeping head.

"Maybe we should go?" she asked. I felt a hand touch my shoulder. "Caroline?" she whispered. "You are . . . unconscious?"

Before I could answer, I was gently lifted in the air. I opened one eye and saw Torsten's cheek inches from my own. He smelled like wine and soap. He lowered me to my bed, and a blanket came to my chin. The next time I surfaced, the room was dark and quiet.

In the morning, I heard voices in the kitchen and smelled coffee.

I threw back my covers, stood and stretched, and pulled open the French doors, inhaling jasmine and warm air. Then I peeked into the dining room. Lisette was reading a paper and smoking, and Torsten was in the kitchen putting jam on toast. He was wearing red sweatpants with no shirt, and his blond hair stood straight up on his head.

"Good morning," Lisette sang, seeing me.

Torsten pointed me to the table where Lisette was sitting. "Toast," he said. His accent had a quickening effect. "Toast" was a command.

Later, after Torsten and Lisette rode their bikes away to work at Stanford, Greta emerged from her room and went to work on a metal sculpture by the pool. Peng was long gone to the city, where he worked for a mysterious "company." Alex's latest theory was that he worked for the CIA. He kept a close eye on Peng.

I made the most of the morning by my new pool. I put on my bathing suit and sunglasses, stuck my feet in the water, and, using a cordless phone for the first time, called Dad.

"Guess where I am," I said. "Beside my *pool* talking on a *portable phone*, with *palm trees* all around."

"You've moved already?" he asked.

"And I had my first workshop class at Stanford," I said. "My teacher wrote a script for Oliver Stone—for the movie *Salvador*. It got nominated for an Oscar—"

"Classes are good," Dad said confidently.

"And next week I'm going to pick up an application for the real graduate program at Stanford," I said. "Film school, Dad. I mean it."

"Do it today," he said. "Hang up and do it now."

Greta fired up a blowtorch.

"And they're having a party to welcome me," I continued. "Isn't that great?"

"Things are looking up," Dad agreed. "Get that application."

"I'm going to be a screenwriter."

"Great," Dad replied. "As long as they teach that at graduate schools."

"Sunglasses, pools, and portable phones." I sighed. "Can you believe it?"

"And master's degrees," Dad said. "Don't forget."

By lunchtime I was feeling so good that I decided to go directly from Sorrell's to pick up the application at Stanford. When River asked if she could come along, Jane, who was tight on my heels, flat out said *no*, which had me stuttering in the middle of them until River gave us both the finger and Jane disappeared ahead of me. A few minutes later, Jane and I were driving down El Camino in my Celica, and she voiced enthusiasm for my interest in film.

"You could make a film about me," she pointed out.

I asked if it would be a drama or a comedy.

Jane laughed. "Slow down, dammit."

I downshifted, and she shot forward into the dashboard.

"It would be a tragi-drama-action-comedy," she said, grabbing her seat.

"Aha," I said. "A new genre."

"And there will be nudity. And gratuitous sex."

"Oh, a *documentary*."

Jane laughed. "Better change the names or I'll be arrested."

I picked up the application, and then we stopped for a sandwich at the campus deli. Jane perused the requirements for getting into Stanford and seemed unimpressed.

"Screenwriting's great," she said, "but this place will be a waste of time."

"Why?"

"You'll be throwing away Fred's money." She sighed and tossed the application on my plate.

I took the application off my sandwich and cleaned it with my napkin. "But I want to learn about film," I protested. "And I'm going to pay for it myself."

"Really?"

"My father has paid for enough tuitions," I said.

"So where *did* you get all of this money, honey?" Jane took my pickle and pointed it at me.

"My mother left it to us," I said, as if that should have been obvious.

"*Oh*. Well, good for Monny. So you'll be wasting *her* money on this stupid school."

"But I need training if I'm going to make films," I said. "And equipment." I clutched the application.

"Bullshit," Jane said. "Read, watch movies, write a screenplay, buy a camera. Places like Stanford are ridiculous."

"But you went to *Harvard*," I said.

Jane rolled her eyes and shook her head. "Will you get off that? I never went to Harvard, Caroline. Cripes."

"But you told Tom you went to Harvard."

"That's none of your business. And why were you spying on Tom and I?"

"Tom and *me*," I corrected impulsively.

Several students turned toward us. I shot Jane a quieting look, which was the fastest way to make her louder.

"Fucking elitist white-bread patriarchal corridors of *learning!*" she bellowed. "Please. Go ahead, Caroline. Join Stanford University and turn into everyone else."

I chewed my sandwich and kept my eyes on my plate. A part of me already felt Stanford slipping away.

After a few minutes Jane stood up and said, "Let's walk."

We were already late for returning to work, but I didn't care. The anxiety I felt over making Jane angry seemed much more important to resolve, so I decided to tell Tom I'd had car trouble and took off with Jane on our familiar route, past the fancy houses and gated estates. As we walked, Jane asked me what I had felt right after my mother died. I said it was too hard to describe. She demanded adjectives.

"Lonely," I said.

She nodded and took my hand.

"And now?" she asked.

"Lonely."

"Even with me?"

"Not the same," I replied.

"Oh. Monny was taller?"

I kept walking, but a smile leaked out.

"Well, I envy you," Jane said. "I'd rather lose a mother like yours than have one like mine."

"No, you wouldn't."

"You don't know my mother," Jane pointed out.

We stopped in front of a house we'd passed before, a three-story Victorian with gardens, a thick green lawn, and a wraparound porch. Jane and I had taken to imagining we lived in there.

"I'm a lying conniving manipulative bitch," Jane went on, "according to my mother."

"Come on," I said. "Why would she say that?"

"I wonder if the kitchen has a fireplace," she mused, looking at the house.

I looked between Jane and the house, unsure of which direction to go.

"Here," she said, lifting her shorts so I could see her thighs. Long white lines the size of threads crossed her skin. She held out her arms and showed faint lines there, too.

"What happened?" I asked stupidly.

"Number five straight-edged razors," Jane said.

"What?" I asked, struggling to understand.

"Sometimes I cut myself," she said impatiently. "Keep up, honey."

I stepped back and covered my mouth.

She looked away with an embarrassed laugh.

"Because of your mother?" I asked.

"Who knows," Jane said. "It started after I was molested." She paused, waiting for my reaction.

"Oh, God," I said, backing into a tree.

"I've wanted to tell you, but it's kind of hard to slip into conversation."

I picked up a twig and snapped it.

Jane said it had started when she was about five. She had gone to visit an old family friend, Mr. Friedlander, who lived with his wife nearby and whose own children were grown. That day, like always, he invited Jane to his basement. She said she was down the stairs before he finished the sentence, hoping he would unlock the cabinet where the best toys were kept, where they had been stored ever since his children had gone.

Jane said that instead, Mr. Friedlander—who had known her since she was born, had been at her house for dinners, bridge games, Fourth of July parties, and weekend cookouts—unzipped his pants and suggested a different game. She said he asked her to come closer, said that she could trust him, that he had always loved her the most.

Afterward, and for several years, Jane said she walked home from Mr. Friedlander's a little more changed every time. I imagined her passing neighbors and other kids and maybe her mother, working in the house. I imagined that she stayed away from her brothers—maybe they were roughhousing in the backyard—and continued upstairs to her room, where she stayed as long as she could.

Jane said Mr. Friedlander had always let her play with the toys when he was done. That he gave her special, affectionate looks and that his wife often said she was his favorite. Jane turned six, then seven, then nine, and then twelve. She told me that when the Lowells moved away to a nicer town, she finally gathered her nerve to tell her mother. When that didn't help, she said she had tried to erase both betrayals with straight-edge razors drawn across her arms and thighs. By the time Mr. Friedlander died, she said, she was classified as crazy.

"I'd play with the trains when he was done," Jane told me. "Or with the Barbie Camper he kept hidden just for me, or with the remote-control Jeep he bought because my mother had told him how much I wanted it. There I was, pulling out toys while he stuck his dick back in his pants and went upstairs to have tea with his wife."

I looked at her, speechless.

"So as for the cutting," she continued, "that's for the shrinks to figure out. But I imagine it's related."

I felt the corners of my mouth twitch and pull. I was dangerously close to the unwanted smile. "I expect so," I said, regaining facial control. "I expect you could have done worse."

"Don't think I haven't tried," she shot back.

I continued snapping twigs in my hand and said, "Your mother really doesn't believe you?"

"She went to his funeral. Everyone did."

"But why? What did she say when you told her?"

"That I was making it up." Jane shrugged. "I guess that's when the lying conniving manipulative me was born." She nodded toward the house. "And my guess is a granite island, built-in bookcases, and no fireplace. We'll have to build our own fireplace."

I suddenly thought nothing would be better than building a fireplace for Jane. I would build her anything she wanted and repair this crime. I would make her mother believe the truth and stand by Jane Lowell in any court that opposed her.

"We'll have a fireplace with Italian tile," I agreed. "And a mantel for your photographs. We'll have the best goddamn fireplace in the neighborhood."

And Jane looked happy at the thought.

FOURTEEN

Most days I followed Jane home for lunch, and each time she served up tuna. Tuna sandwich, tuna salad, tuna melt. One day, as she stared into space, I browsed the movie section of the local paper. I saw that the Stanford Theater was playing *All About Eve* and circled it.

"The best movie of all time," I said, tapping the paper. "If I could be any movie character, I'd be Margo Channing."

Jane wasn't listening.

"Margo Channing," I repeated.

"Okay," she said.

"Who would you be?"

"Louise," she said. "Off the cliff with my lover."

"*Thelma and Louise* Louise?"

"Is there another Louise who drove off a cliff?"

"But they weren't lovers," I said. "They were fugitives."

"Oh, they were. Both."

"You must have seen the uncut version," I said, joking.

"Idgie Threadgoode," Jane said.

"*Fried Green Tomatoes,*" I answered.

She nodded. "Same thing."

"Come on."

"Idgie was in love with Ruth, and Ruth was in love with Idgie."

"Right. But not *sexually*. Ruth was marri—"

"You're not listening to me. They were in *love*."

"I heard you."

Jane said it again. "We're talking about *love*."

"Yes, we are. There is love, and in love. And *in* love by most definitions is sexual."

"Interesting," Jane said. "Your mouth is moving, but all I hear is blah blah blah."

I squinted at her, then decided to cut bait and go back to my paper.

"Have you ever slept with a woman?" she asked.

I lowered the paper and said, "No." I shook my head for emphasis.

"I have."

I felt warm suddenly. "Oh?"

"Um-hm." Jane took a bite of my sandwich and said, "It's different." She winked. "A whole different thing."

On days when Katherine or Jason was occupying their kitchen, Jane usually followed me to my house, where we ate lunch on the picnic table by the Waverly swimming pool. We watched Lisette there one afternoon, reclined near the water in her swimsuit, looking dreamily into the distance and smoking. She was thin and exotic, with dark curly hair and pale speckled skin. In her delicate hand the cigarette looked sexy—a paper vessel by which deep thoughts might arise, lifting her on a carpet of smoky distractions and novel insights.

"I can't believe you live here." Jane sighed. "It's paradise."

I was especially pleased that my new paradise came complete

with its own Adam. Torsten was stretched out on the opposite side of the pool, half reading and half watching Lisette. While Torsten yawned, Lisette exhaled a long tunnel of smoke. They glanced at each other. Jane and I observed.

"See how the male extends his legs," Jane said in a low voice, sounding like a *National Geographic* narrator. "Opening his mouth in a gesture to the female. Inviting."

"She responds to the male," I continued, "emitting a smoky shield to intrigue him."

"Her technique is good," Jane added. "Cigarette between the lips, slight squint to the eyes, slow inhale, pause, faint *whoosh* to the side."

Torsten smiled at Lisette, and Jane elbowed me.

"The male shows immediate interest," I whispered, "see how he bares his teeth."

"Soon they will mate," Jane said. "And then he will kill her."

I looked at Jane. "Kill her?"

She squirmed. "Or something."

Lisette smiled back at Torsten and called across the pool, "What are you reading?"

"See how the female approaches . . . ," I murmured.

Jane studied her fingers.

"What would happen if another female entered the picture?" I mused. "Say a midwestern species?"

"She'd lose a leg," Jane said quickly.

"It would be worth it." I sighed dreamily.

"Don't," Jane blurted. "I don't want to hear it." She looked decidedly hurt. It hurt to see her hurt.

"What?" I asked.

Suddenly her face turned so severe that I edged away. Her jaw jutted out, with redness spreading across her cheeks. "You are either stupid or toying with me," she muttered.

Then I got it. I didn't want to, but there it was, exploding in my gut. I was being pursued. That afternoon, as Lisette and Torsten flirted by the pool, I slid into a confused quandary. The lines that had been clear all my life started to blur.

"See how she balks," Jane murmured bitterly, watching my body tense beside her. "See how she retreats."

One of the strangest ironies of this period is that while Jane pursued, I took up smoking. If she had lines across her thighs and arms, I seemed just as compelled to scar my lungs. I had circled the idea for weeks before turning to action. Lisette always smoked after dinner, and sometimes Alex came out of his literary seclusion to join her. They smoked and drank wine, with candles lighting the table and pool. One evening, with Torsten, Peng, and Greta, the cigarettes were out, and my housemates were debating their favorite topic—the strangeness of Americans. On previous occasions I had looked to Alex as an ally, but he said he felt more "European" than American, so I was on my own.

"Why do they have so many words," Peng asked me, "that sound the same but mean different?"

"Like 'wait' and 'weight,' " Torsten said.

"Or 'rain' and 'reign,' " Lisette remarked.

"And horses' reins," Alex added.

Instead of coming up with my usual defense (I don't know, I don't care), I stood and said, "Guys, I am going to buy myself some cigarettes."

"You smoke?" Torsten asked indignantly. He had quit in his teens and thought the habit was "dirty."

"Sometimes," I lied.

"Have one of these," Lisette said, passing her pack.

"No," I said. "I smoke a different brand."

Everyone was quiet, looking blankly at me.

"Okay," Alex said slowly. "Thanks for letting us know."

I nodded, felt a surge of anticipation, and got moving.

Lisette shrugged and continued the conversation. "What about 'break'?" she asked everyone. "There's *coffee* break, *automobile* brake—"

"Break a glass," Greta said.

I found my purse and stepped out the front door, still hearing their faint voices. "Breaking *wind*," Alex exclaimed.

As I accelerated down the sidewalk, I heard everyone yell, "Caroline—break a leg!"

I felt completely excited, but also nervous, as if I were about to break a federal law. Had my family been there, my announcement to my housemates would have amounted to: *I am going to buy a loaded gun now and point it at my head.* My cosmic revenge was neither planned nor rational, just an impulse that had grown into need—a persistent desire to smoke, for the same reasons I'd hated it before.

The closest pack of cigarettes was at a café down the block, and as I walked the thrill grew inside me. If there was a train of logical thinking left in me that night, it jumped the tracks when I stood at the counter and pointed.

"A pack of Kents, please."

Gus, the owner, searched behind him. Judging by his expression, Mom's brand was no longer in vogue.

"Kents," I repeated. I pointed to the blue-and-white pack behind him. I drummed my fingers on the counter.

"These?" he asked.

"Right," I said, reaching for the pack. After paying, I ran out the door.

I found a secluded table on the patio and opened the pack. And sick as it sounds, I secretly wished my mother could be watching when I inhaled the first time. After a few tries, the cigarette caught fire. I inhaled, and right away a sharp sting hit my lungs. I inhaled again. The sting was beautiful, like a primal scream.

Lisette and I started smoking together after dinner, and while

Torsten insisted I was crazy, I found that with wine, cigarettes were pleasantly enhanced. Over time, the occasions to smoke grew more frequent and my body more tolerant. Finally, I felt a physical need to light up, wine or no wine, friends or no friends. And I learned to obey, several times a day.

Next came the driving.

It had started as a way to smoke without being seen, since at heart I was an antismoker, the type who used to make loud gagging noises when the smell came my way. So I took long detours on the way home from work that became smoking extravaganzas. Eventually I arrived at the ocean, where I parked, smoked some more, and listened to the sea lions bark at the night. On these drives, I argued with myself over how to respond to Jane. I thought of Idgie Threadgoode, and Thelma and Louise, and kept lighting cigarettes.

"Where have you been disappearing to after work?" Jane finally asked. We were shelving poetry, and I'd been quiet for a while.

"I drive around."

"Where?"

"Wherever."

She was silent. Then she took a book of poems off the shelving cart and opened it. "This is for you," she said. Holding my arm, she read:

> let it go—the
> smashed word broken
> open vow or
> the oath cracked length
> wise—let it go it
> was sworn to
>
> go

let them go—the
truthful liars and
the false fair friends
and the boths and
neithers—you must let them go they
were born
      to go

let all go—the
big small middling
tall bigger really
the biggest and all
things—let all go
dear
      so comes love

"Cummings," Isaac said, coming around the corner. River followed behind him and gave me a suspicious frown. When I spotted Faye through the shelves, rolling her eyes at River, I tucked the book in its place and tried to act cool. It seemed that somewhere along the line Jane and I had started irritating the same people who had previously been under her spell. Jane said this was because they were jealous, and I figured that was true. Later that afternoon I snuck back to the same shelf, thinking to buy the book with the poem Jane had read. River, ever the snoop, caught me in the act.

"Cummings?" she asked sweetly, pretending to straighten a shelf.

"So?" I replied, pulling it down.

"What is *up* with you two?" she asked. "You're like her appendage now—it's creeping me out."

"We're friends," I said. "Good friends."

"I'll say." River chuckled.

"Why does it bother you?" I asked. "Why is everyone acting so strange lately?"

"That's a good one," River laughed. *"We're* acting strange. It would be one thing if you guys were, you know . . ." She waited while I squirmed.

"Two women can't be friends?" I asked. *"Just* friends?"

"If one of them is Jane, I'm not so sure," River replied. "I don't mean to be pushy," she added, walking with me. "We just miss you, that's all."

After work, Jane stood again by my car in the garage. She held up two hot chocolates for the ride and said, "Can I come tonight?"

I said, "Sure." Because as much as I feared the next advance, I wanted her company.

Once we were away from the store, driving up the steep hills toward Woodside, Jane pulled out a pack of Marlboro Lights.

"Okay," she announced, "so I smoke sometimes."

I revealed my pack of Kents, and Jane looked shocked. "Only when I drive," I lied, pushing in the car lighter. Alice's Restaurant receded in my mirror, and my Bob Dylan tape played the song that would become our agreed-upon theme, "Shelter from the Storm."

We smoked and drove, and after a while, as the sun dropped into the ocean, Jane said, "Let's park."

I pulled over and faced us toward the water.

She said, "So, Monny died of lung cancer." She slipped her thumb into her mouth and blinked. I glanced at our cigarettes on the dashboard and hesitated. Jane arched an eyebrow and smiled.

"Never mind," I said.

Over her thumb she whispered conspiratorially, "Carrying the torch there, honey?"

I ignored this. We watched the moon glow against the water. Jane took my hand and held it in her lap. She said, "Relax," and stroked my arm. This did not help me relax.

After a long silence she said, "Did you hear about the whales?"

I was having trouble concentrating. I think I said no.

"In Cape Cod, near my parents' summer house—a whole pack got beached."

"A school," I said. "Whales swim in schools." I thought for a second. "Or is it herds? A herd of whales?"

"Some were dead," Jane said. "Dried out. And rescuers came to save the others. They put a tent over them and kept them wet, and then they rolled the living ones back into the water."

"Pods!" I said. "Whales swim in pods."

Jane said, "They got the healthy ones into deep water, but then they turned around and beached themselves all over again, in the same exact spot. It was right there in the newspapers."

"Oh, yeah?"

"The article said that some whales will do that. They actually go back and beach themselves because they don't want to leave the dead ones."

"I thought whales were supposed to be smart," I said.

"Do you think it has to do with smarts?" she asked. "I mean . . . look at yourself."

I'd walked right into it.

"You're smart," she said. And then she winked.

FIFTEEN

My Waverly housemates were serious about throwing a party, and though originally the celebration had been intended to welcome me, now that I was old news they were more keen on meeting my co-workers. The Sorrell's staff was uniquely "American," according to Peng, and stocked with "beautiful women," Torsten observed. Lisette wanted to meet "the guy with the hair," who was Nick, and Alex thought River had looked interested when she sold him a book on the cognitive meaning of language. Greta had more practical hopes: she wanted to sell some of her poolside sculptures. This left me to make the invitations. To get the word out fast, I mentioned the party to Julian, who was suffering through a rare morning shift, in the back room at the store. I approached him as he nodded along to Neil Young and swiftly labeled a shipment of dictionaries.

"Excellent," he yawned. "I'll bring my guitar." After an interlude in which he seemed to sleep standing up, he blinked himself awake, ambled across the room, pushed the floorwide intercom, and alerted the store. Faint cheers went up, even from customers. Isaac came into the back room and said he'd bring some friends. Faye said she'd bring pot and her yoga class. When I cornered Jane later, she said she'd make sure she was busy. She didn't like parties, and she didn't like Torsten.

The party day started off with great potential. Torsten and I were assigned shopping duty, which meant I'd get to look at him for hours and have him all to myself. He was triply appealing— gorgeous by any standard, a gifted biologist, and endowed with a halting German accent I found endearing. As we drove around Palo Alto to collect food and liquor, we traded dead parent stories, which I always found refreshing. He said his father had died when he was seventeen, and from then on he'd been in charge of his little brother and mother. He said his fellowship at Stanford had been his first break from running his mother's house and from the small town in Germany that he felt had held him back. Torsten's apparent calm acceptance of losing a parent gave me hope. I had never seen him depressed or disorganized in the way that I was, and quite often he was genuinely happy. I asked him if time had been the way to get over losing his dad.

"What do you mean?" he asked, steering us to the Keg Emporium.

"Well, after he died," I said, "you were a mess, right?"

"I had to study," he said. "I had finals."

We went inside the Emporium, and Torsten pushed his sunglasses up on his blond head. A few young girls saw him, then saw me with him, and for a moment I imagined how it must feel to be beautiful.

"Heineken," Torsten announced, proceeding ahead.

I trotted after him, beaming at the girls.

I had thought our conversation was over, but when we stood at the register, Torsten looked at me and said, "My little brother was the mess."

"Oh," I said. "How?"

"He was reckless for a while. And confused. The babies are always confused."

"Great," I muttered.

Torsten rolled the keg onto a cart, and he smiled at my indignance. "But no," he said, "I envied him." He pointed a playful, half-accusing finger at me. "Harold knew I wouldn't let him waste his life. *He* knew there would be a net."

I considered this.

"You don't think it's better not to need a net?" I accused back. Torsten heaved the keg into the car trunk and slammed it shut with authority.

"I think it's better not to talk about it," he said. "Maybe you and Harry can meet someday and talk yourselves unconscious."

I had no response for that.

Torsten's car—a coughing brown Chevy four-door—was sinking low when we pulled in front of the Waverly house, each brooding silently over our argument. Greta had finished placing her sculptures around the house and pool with little tags suggesting a price, Alex was selecting hours of music, and Peng and Lisette were cleaning. As we unloaded bags of food, Torsten asked if any of my female co-workers were "unattached."

"Hook up with River or Angela," I said curtly. "You'll have a big time."

Torsten didn't know what that last figure of speech meant, which I found gratifying as I turned on my heels and left him. But after I closed the door to my room, the feeling disappeared. I paced and worried, thinking it was possible that I'd just delivered Torsten to either River or Angela on a big German platter. Angela was the bigger threat. Maybe if I steered nearsighted Nick in her direction without his specs, he'd inadvertently knock her in the pool.

. . .

Faye arrived first, with two friends from the "east side," Fiona and Gilbert. Torsten, bless his heart, wore swimming trunks the whole time. He served drinks and looked after me, once even putting his arm around my waist.

Faye strolled through the house holding a bottle of whiskey, her round body swaying to the music, eyes half-closed. "This is some pad," she said while I offered her chips. "Some fucking pad, sister." Which was funny, because she'd been born into a family that would have used the Waverly house as a barn.

Julian dispensed little white pills as he passed. He looked at me and said, "Maybe not."

"No," I agreed, watching Faye. She was dancing out of step.

Julian gave me an inexplicable high five and moved along.

For some reason, almost everyone had crowded into my room by the time I realized I'd had too much to drink and got to thinking of going to sleep. Alex's favorite group, the Velvet Underground, had dominated the night, and as I perused my own books to seem busy, two stereo speakers played "Take a Walk on the Wild Side" over my bed, which was in use. Nick came up to me, holding his glasses in his teeth, sweating and swilling brown liquid. "So . . . ," he said, feeling the air near my face.

"So that's my eye," I replied, batting his hand away.

"You and Jane Lowell," he smiled. He giggled into his hand.

"Yes?"

"She watches you like a hawk," Nick slurred. Touching my nose, he added, "And the eyesight of a hawk is eight times better than a human's."

I tipped Nick's hand away from my nose and said, "Go away."

Torsten came striding over with purpose and asked if I needed a "refill," which I understood to mean "help." He eyed Nick with tight lips, then introduced himself. Nick looked at me with surprise and said, "Boyfriend?"

I teetered and considered this. "Are you?" I asked Torsten, certifying that I was drunker than I'd ever thought possible. Angela answered that question fast. She came up from behind him, slipped her hand into his, and said, "Great party!"

"Did you know hawks can see eight times better than humans?" I asked, stepping away. And with that smooth segue, I ran.

Outside I saw the pool was full of people, some clothed, some not. Doors were closed to almost every bedroom, including my own, and Lisette was dancing by the front door with a Spanish-looking man I'd never seen before. I found the only open seat in the living room next to Faye, who was slouched in front of our muted television, asleep. The Scotch bottle on her lap was empty, and her friends had taken her car and left without her. I rested my chin on my knees and contemplated the odds of finding a blanket and a private corner in which to sleep. I had started nodding off right there when Torsten's hand touched my back, and he crouched down, putting his forehead against mine.

"Need a lift?" he joked.

I yawned and nodded. "Or a net."

"You babies . . ." Torsten sighed. "Always looking for the net."

"I'm not a baby," I said.

"No?"

"Nope. Full grown."

"I don't believe you," Torsten said affectionately. He stood up and patted my head. I saw Angela hovering behind him, smiling at me, and inwardly groaned.

"Well," Torsten said, "I'm turning in. Is that how you say it? *Turning in?*"

Angela giggled.

"Something like that," I muttered.

"So," Torsten said briskly. "Good night."

As he and Angela aimed for his bedroom, Peng came over and handed me our phone. I put it to my ear and grunted.

"Nice voice," Jane said. "What are you doing?"

"Having a party. Which you ditched."

"Come over and visit me," she whispered.

I looked at my watch. "You'll be closing any minute."

"Come on. I haven't seen you all day."

I was feeling incrementally better just hearing her voice.

"But the party is for me," I said.

"Honey," Jane said, "they'll live. Get over here, pronto."

I smiled, resurrected. "I'll see you in a minute," I said, and tripped out the door.

I maneuvered the few blocks in an excited haze, stumbling over curbs and weaving around trees. Sorrell's lights appeared, surrounded by the blackness of closed shops and quiet streets. I rounded the last corner and saw Jane leaning in the doorway.

"Wow," she said, looking at her watch. "You ran."

I stepped inside, panting. Bob Dylan was singing "Shelter from the Storm" on the PA. I looked at Jane and smiled, pointing up to the music.

"I bought it," she confessed, showing me the CD we always played, *Blood on the Tracks*.

Otherwise it was quiet in the store and empty except for John, a homeless man who stayed as long as he could. Eric, the other night shift worker, was counting a register drawer. John came over and said hi. He had a young-looking face and thick white hair. He would have been handsome if he didn't look crazy. Ten years before, he'd been a tenured philosophy professor at Stanford.

"What did you read today?" Jane asked John. He held up *The Bridges of Madison County*, which had swept the country like a fever. He shook his head with disappointment.

I slid onto a stool behind Jane's register and put my feet up.

"You are de-runk," she said, waving her hand in front of her nose.

I nodded.

"And have we had a few cartons of cigarettes?" she asked. She looked to John for confirmation that I stank.

John said, "I could have a drink. . . ."

"Oh no, we're closing up soon," Jane said quickly. "And where are you sleeping tonight, John? It's getting cold now. . . ."

He shrugged. "What are you doing here?" he asked me. "You're never here at night."

"Neither is Jane," I pointed out.

"Yeah," John said. "What are *you* doing here?" He pointed at Jane.

"Yeah," I said. "Tell us."

"God knows," she said.

"Avoiding my party," I told John.

Jane said, "Okay, then, tell us about this grand event. What did I miss?"

"Torsten and I—"

"Exactly," she shot back. Even John looked surprised as she went to the stereo, shut off Dylan, and began to hit the lights.

At first I was alarmed and regretted Torsten's mention. Then, in the dark, I felt a rush of nervous joy. The feeling was electric when Jane returned to me and stood close, waiting. John might as well have disappeared when I whispered, "I'm really glad that you called."

"Don't forget who knows you," she whispered back.

"You are in a whole different league from Torsten," I said. And I couldn't have been more sincere. My German crush had become a fleeting fantasy, but Jane, I felt more and more, was permanent.

"As long as he stays in the minors." Jane smiled. "And you goddamn step up to the plate."

Chapter SIXTEEN

As winter approached, and even Palo Alto got chilly, keeping up with Jane's moods became an athletic event. One moment she was giggling and passing me notes, the next she froze me with silence. Sometimes I felt like I was back in St. Louis, retrieving my flowers and cleats from the trash for reasons I couldn't quite grasp.

"You know what I want," Jane said evenly while we packed returns in the back room. She was finishing a fight that had started the day before and run right through the night on the phone.

Isaac's head was already turning our way.

"It's torture," Jane said. "I'm not going to take this forever."

"What does that mean?" I hissed.

"It means I'm about to cut you loose," she said. "For my own sanity."

I closed the box and started taping it shut. Jane filled out the return slip. Barbara watched us over her bifocals from across the room.

"I'm with you every day," I whispered. "What more do you want?"

"More."

Feeling way too close to what had become a terrifying and magnetic edge, I stepped back. That afternoon, I asked Nick out on a date.

He had been undergoing a fascinating metamorphosis, beginning with new contact lenses and an inflated, muscular body, which had been morphing steadily from the skinny frame I had loved. I decided I had to catch him quick, before he turned completely into someone else's ideal. My invitation surprised Nick, and it took him several stuttering tries before he said yes.

What I liked most about Nick was his complete lack of worry. The movie is sold out? No problem (I pouted and cursed). An hour wait to be seated at dinner? More time to chat and drink vodka (I elected coffee and watched the clock). Nick was planning to go to college but in no hurry. He was stone broke and enjoying it. This, I told him, was because he grew up in Southern California, where, like the Bay Area, the norm was not the norm. The way I saw it, worries worked backward in the Bay Area—the overtly rich were suspect, education was a euphemism for "living," and speed was found only in pills. Nick said I thought too much. He ordered me a vodka.

"So is Jane Lowell seeing anyone?" he asked.

"Not that I know of," I said. "Why?"

"She's so hard to figure out. She digs *you*, though. She's always writing you notes at work."

"Jealous?" I asked.

"A little." He smiled.

Well, that was honest. I buried my disappointment in the menu.

Jane and I had been writing a lot of notes for a while because one of Tom's schemes had been to separate "the twins" by having Jane work in the back while I worked on the floor, or vice versa. On our first day apart, Jane had passed me at the info desk and handed me a fat, folded letter, in which she described what was going on in the back—how Faye was in a bad mood, and Angela was reading horoscopes out loud, but you couldn't hear her over Julian's music (and didn't the Grateful Dead sound like a high school band? And didn't anybody notice?). She wrote about meeting her friend Debbie in the city and how their conversation had seemed terribly dull compared to the way we always talked. After a series of general philosophical musings, she wrapped up by confessing that she'd recently been jolted awake while dreaming about me. *You were hanging from a kite*, she wrote, *and every time I reached to unhook you, the wind pulled you away. Finally, you hit a tree and fell to the ground. And then I woke up. (It's a cliff-hanger.)*

After reading her letter, I enjoyed the excited endorphin rush that always followed Jane's exclusive attention, then ducked behind the card rack to write back right away. Since I was there, I selected a card, one with a photograph of a young couple by their trailer, and I dubbed them Ed and Marlene. I tried hard to rise to Jane's standard of witty prose, offering my own random observations and small confessions with the pain and care of a doctoral thesis. I summed up my piece with *I miss you out here. The whole place seems as dull as Debbie. And Carla is picking her nose at the register. And someone put the Carpenters on the PA, which is worse than a high school band. And River is singing along about Mondays getting her down. And did I say I missed you?*

Now, with Nick, I was trying for once not to focus on Jane. I asked him to tell me about his family.

"Why?" he asked.

"Aren't they interesting?"

He shrugged.

Our table was finally ready, and we transferred ourselves to a corner next to a young couple who also looked to be on a date. I felt exceptionally normal as Nick pulled out my chair.

"What do they do?" I asked, sitting down.

"Who?"

"Your parents."

"Oh." Nick squinted at the menu, pulling it close to his nose. Turned out he'd lost a contact on his way to fetch me, so now he could only see with one eye. "Mom died when I was eight," he said blandly. "I have a stepmother. Dad—"

I sat forward, alert. "My mother died, too," I said eagerly.

"Really?" He glanced at me, then returned to the menu.

"Go on," I said. "Tell me about your mother."

"Is this a date or a survey?" he asked.

"How did she die?" I asked.

"Car accident." His jaw tightened. "I was in the car."

I sat back, horrified. When a smile came tugging at my cheeks, I ducked my head. If ever there was a time not to laugh, this was one. In desperation, I hit my forehead on the table. The silverware jingled and my water glass splashed over. I did it again and looked up, refreshed.

"Are you okay?" Nick asked.

"Fine," I said. "That's awful. I'm sorry."

"You just slammed your head against the table."

"I know. It's okay." I went back to the menu.

After that, I didn't ask any more personal questions. We talked about the bookstore and Faye's sick cat, Aggie, who was coming with her to work and scaring the customers. Nick told me he'd taken up the drums so he could jam with Julian, and he sounded almost poetic when he described the spiritual epiphany he'd experienced while surfing in Bodega Bay. Over dessert we segued to my favorite subject, movies. We debated the best decades (me, 1970s; him, 1980s), and I asked him who he thought was the better reviewer, Andrew Sarris or Pauline Kael. When he said he'd never heard of either, I realized we were doomed. I called for the check.

We ended our date on the curb in front of my house, with Nick scuffing his boots deep into the yard. Along with his new body, he had started wearing leather and swearing a lot.

"Fuck," he said about nothing in particular.

"Well, that was fun," I said.

He looked tense, as if he might explode. "Thanks," he said quietly.

We parted, and I felt pretty sure he'd crossed me off his list of possible girlfriends, if I had ever been on it to begin with.

I realized, as I undressed for bed, that despite my determination to feel "normal" with Nick, I had been missing Jane all night. I briefly circled the phone, wanting to call her, then took refuge under my covers instead. I moved between feeling guilty about my secret date and rising irritation over this unwarranted guilt. If I could just put Jane in Nick's body, I thought, I would live happily ever after.

Then, in the middle of the night, my phone rang.

"Hi," Nick said.

"Hi," I said back.

"I think I should come over."

"Now?"

"Right now."

I squinted at the time. I had unshaven legs and bad breath. I would have to work fast. "Okay," I said. When the line went dead, I shot out of bed.

Nick must have run every light. He was at my door before I'd finished brushing my teeth, and I was still in my pajamas when he stormed through my private French doors into my room. By his expression, I half expected him to just rip off his clothes and point to the bed. I motioned for him to hold the thought, then dashed back to the bathroom, spat out the toothpaste, and switched into a silky nightgown. When I returned, Nick was standing in the middle of the room naked, except for his glasses and leather jacket. This was no kind of turn-on, so I got them both off fast and prayed that from there on, he knew what he was doing.

He wasn't half-bad. I had to count back to college—junior year, even—to my last time. Nick was patient as I relearned my technique, and up close he seemed to be seeing my face clearly for the first time. He touched me with his nose, lightly circling my mouth and chin. I gripped his new muscles, moved my hand down to his groin, and kissed him hard. He didn't need to be asked twice.

"Oh, Caroline," he said into my ear. "Sweet Caroline." He released with a great *whoosh* of breath and collapsed on my chest. He was instantly asleep, which amazed me. I slid from beneath him. Looking out my French doors at the new light seeping in, I imagined Jane there, watching me.

Idiot, she said. *Look what you've done now.*

At eight A.M., my phone rang again.

"What are you doing?" Jane asked.

I rolled over to look beside me. Nick was gone. No note. I stalled with a yawn.

"Something is up," she said. "You left with Egghead after work. You didn't say good-bye."

"Nick was here," I admitted. "*Just* here," I added, frowning at his empty spot.

Sunlight trailed through my doors, spotlighting Nick's jacket, still crumpled in the middle of my room. I peered at the phone, awaiting Jane's reply.

"You are so disappointing," she said bitterly.

I took my punishment quietly.

"Well. Was he good?"

"He was . . . eager," I said.

The phone went dead.

I flew into Sorrell's on the late side and dumped Nick's jacket on his chair. Jane skidded in front of me.

"Traitor," she said.

"Hi," I replied.

Nick walked in through the back, and Jane watched him. "Good God, honey," she sighed. "A skinny half-blind surfer nerd?"

If only Nick knew how he'd blown his chances, that by sleeping with me, Jane's Cowardly Lion had just tarnished his sexy golden mane. He pulled off his bike helmet, leaving his hair sticking up at all angles, and made his way over. When he saw Jane, he smiled.

"Ladies," he said.

"Hey," I said sheepishly.

Jane muttered, *"Cripes,"* and walked away.

I lost track of Nick over the course of the afternoon, and then Jane, and then it was time to go home. Walking to the parking garage, I stopped on the stairs and heard them.

Nick: "One drink?"

Jane: "Are you kidding?"

Nick: "You should give me another chance."

Jane: "I'm waiting for Caroline. Remember Caroline?"

Nick: "Come on."

Jane: "Did you or did you not just fuck her?"

Nick: "Shit. Yes. Okay, yes. But I didn't plan to. It just sort of . . . well, I knew she wanted to. She asked *me* out—it was her idea."

Jane: "Whatever."

Enter Caroline (clearing throat loudly). I walked past them to my car and carefully inserted the key.

Nick said, "Fuck," and then, *"Fuck."* He raised his arms in surrender. "I didn't mean to get in the *way* here."

Jane gave me her *I told you so* face, which turned into alarm as I took off in my car.

While I went driving, Jane slipped into my room and left a copy of *Bartlett's Quotations* on my bed. When I arrived home, I saw it and found an inscription that read, "See page 429." The quote was by Emerson:

> Give all to love;
> Obey thy heart;
> Friends, kindred, days,
> Estate, good fame,
> Plans, credit, and the Muse,
> Nothing refuse.

The phone rang as I was midway through reading it. "Jesus," Jane said instead of hello. "Don't take off like that again—I was *defending* you."

"Thanks."

"Do you like the book?"

"I was just reading page 429."

"Well, finish."

I finished.

"Honey . . . ," Jane said.

"Yes?"

"He's just a boy."

A tear hit the page, and I made a trail with my finger, wetting the words.

Jane said, "You should have listened to me."

"Yeah."

"*I* love you."

"Yeah?"

"Oh yeah."

"I'm going crazy," I said, watching more tears hit the page. "Literally."

"Swa-ha," Jane said, dismissing my quandary. "I'm already crazy. Join me."

After we got off the phone, I answered that invitation by starting an official box in her name. I printed *"JRL"* on the top and put Jane's letters inside, along with poems she'd written and pictures of her striding across the cliffs at Point Reyes. In went the Cummings, and *Bartlett's Quotations*, and a handful of stones that she'd given me. When I was done I put the box in my closet, next to Maggie's, and Sam's, and my mother's.

When Jane tapped on my French doors late that night and walked in, I knew why she was coming. She dropped an overnight bag on my floor, and I sat up in bed. Jane removed her khakis and handed them to me. "There's a hole," she said, pointing to the knee. "Can you fix it?"

Mechanically, I opened my mother's big green sewing kit and worked on threading a needle.

Jane watched me fumble to thread the needle and then said, "I want to kiss you."

I brought the needle closer to my nose.

"I really, really do."

I pinched together the hole and started sewing.

Jane was sitting close. I could smell that she'd just showered. I covered my face with her pants and took a deep breath. This was one line I never thought I'd cross.

And yet.

Jane's voice was soft and inviting. I heard myself say, "Okay."

She whispered, *"Really?"*

I released an exasperated whimper and started sewing again.

"Wait wait wait," she said.

I lowered the pants, poised to either laugh or cry, I wasn't sure.

"It will be different," she cautioned.

I was seconds from running.

"You might not like—"

"Jesus, Jane, just do it," I barked.

She took a deep breath, then moved her hand up my leg. She leaned into my mouth and kissed me. I hesitated. She edged closer and then straddled my hips. She leaned in for another kiss, this one deeper.

It was different.

I felt Jane's lightness, her smooth softness, arcing above me. Two blue eyes absorbed me, reeled me in, and then closed. She smelled of shampoo, faint perfume, and soaps. She was pure emotion. As her long hair came down, shaping a thick tent around us, I closed my eyes, in free fall. The sameness of Jane's body was all over me, thick with need. It took my breath away.

She eased me back, her hands under my pajama top, and stroked my body. She moved across, over, and around me, her mouth brushing lightly over my skin. When she kissed my mouth again, I kissed her back. I let her hands travel wherever they wanted and was silent, except for an involuntary moan that escaped when she entered me.

Jane stayed all night, and as she slept I lay still, eyes wide. Everything I'd been sure of was exploding in my head, so of course I quietly laughed.

As if my life weren't confused enough, now I had a naked woman in my bed. And as far as I could tell, I loved her. It was bewildering. And very different from how I'd loved the few men who had taken me that far—much more intense and much less physical. I felt completely unshielded and bare, as though someone had just browsed my genetic code for pleasure. And deep down, I felt doomed. Jane and I had erased the last boundary between us; there were no barriers left to keep me separate, no gender walls behind which to hide or regroup. This was a vast, strange-looking territory. Already the familiar landmarks were receding, and wherever we were, Jane was my only companion there, my only guide.

When morning came, she opened an eye, squealed, and buried her head. She popped her head up for air and squinted at me.

"Still here," I said.

In went her thumb. Jane watched me, thinking. For my part, I'd done too much thinking and felt hung over from too many unsolved dilemmas. The sun was up, and I was finally ready to sleep.

"You and me," Jane said.

"Us," I agreed.

"Wow."

"Yep."

I saw Jane completely differently, as though I knew all of her best and worst secrets, and she knew I knew. I wondered if the same was true for her.

"Honey," she said, "I always want to know you. I want to know you when we're old."

"We'll buy our walkers together," I promised.

"And take trips," Jane said dreamily. "Those old people tours."

"Folks might wonder about that," I said in a hick voice.

"To hell with folks," Jane replied. "And where are you from all of a sudden, the Ozarks?"

"Well, not a cruise," I said, switching to British English. "No cruises."

Jane kicked the sheets and laughed. "We'll be two old biddies, bickering all the time."

"I can see that," I admitted.

"But first we'll be famous," she said with certainty.

"For doing what?"

"You'll make films, and I'll star in them."

"Ah. Of course. Like Woody Allen and Diane Keaton. Scorsese and De Niro. Truffaut and—"

Jane threw her hand across my mouth. "I've got my Oscar speech ready," she said. "So get busy."

I heard Torsten in the kitchen and then Greta joining him. Breakfast smells made their way into the room. Slowly reality penetrated our fantasy, and I realized Jane would be hard to explain. If Torsten knocked as usual, bringing me coffee, things would get awkward.

"I'll go out the side door," Jane said. "We've got the staff meeting in an hour, anyway."

She swung her legs over the bed, pulled on my shirt and her pants.

"Honey?" she said sweetly, putting her hair up in a ponytail.

"Yes?"

"Don't tell anyone about us."

That caught me by surprise.

"This is private," Jane said seriously. "Our business. Okay?"

"Well, I'm not taking out any ads," I said.

Jane kissed my forehead, said, "Good," then grabbed her bag and walked out my door.

And in my dizzy exit from reality, I didn't think to wonder—is that what the old man had made Jane promise, after he pointed to the toys, and zipped up his pants?

SEVENTEEN

Stella Reinhardt was the first person I met who had known Jane before I did. She appeared around Christmastime, when she took a break from medical fellowship in Texas to see her sister Katherine, brother-in-law Jason, and their baby, Emma, in the house where Jane had a room. More to the point, Stella came to see Jane, because as far as she knew, they were still in love.

Jane had been vague about Stella. She said they had lived together, briefly, until Stella had to take the fellowship. She said that compared to me, Stella was a bore, but to keep things smooth with Katherine and Jason, she had to pay her dues and spend time with her. She said the time away from me would be agony. That I should just hold on, she'd be back.

At work, Jane was extra affectionate, if that was possible, and careful to assure me that we were a team. In return, my senses stayed heightened, my mind racing in circles. Nerves jumped when she came near, and we thrived in the subtext of our secret. Jane's hands and eyes had known me. And I knew her in ways I could feel but not explain. With men, I had been secure in our differences. With Jane, I felt gone, swallowed, subsumed. Lost and found at the same time.

It was this chemistry that Stella observed when approaching Jane and me in the history aisle at Sorrell's. Jane had jumped at the sight of her and then turned mean.

"What are you doing here?" she snapped.

Stella froze, looking between us. She was so sweet looking, so lovely, that I immediately felt for her. She had pale straight hair and light skin turning pink with embarrassment. I was drawn into her soft brown eyes.

"Hi," I said.

"I'm s-sorry," Stella stuttered, looking at Jane. "I just came by to see you."

Jane took Stella's arm and guided her away.

"I told you not to come," she muttered in her ear. "Jesus, honey."

The next time I saw Stella was at my front door, the morning I left for Christmas in St. Louis. Jane had come over early in the morning and asked Stella to kill time while we exchanged gifts.

While we sat on my bed, drinking tea, Jane made one last case for me to stay.

"I have to go home," I said.

"You don't *have* to do anything," she replied.

"You're busy with Stella anyway," I pointed out.

"I still want you to stay."

"But I have to go home for Christmas."

"Why? Monny's not there. You've got a brother and sister who don't get you at all, and your father is in love with that Jaguar-driving Gayle woman."

When she put it that way, it was a depressing picture.

"*I* am your family now," Jane said.

"I know, but I'm still going home."

She sighed and handed me my present. "It's a blue teapot," she said.

It was a gorgeous blue teapot, the same shade of blue that Jane collected in glass. Inside there was a poem she wrote. About water, and sand, and bodies joined, and drowning.

I blushed and handed her my box. "It's a bear," I said.

I had hunted all over the Bay Area for the right gift, the perfect object to show my devotion. I settled on an Indian luck charm—a brown bear made of marbled stone, with jade eyes. It was small enough to fit in a pocket.

"It's Native American," I said as she pulled it from the box. "It guards you. For while I'm away."

I had copied a description of the bear's powers from a book on Zuni objects:

> The Bear is the Guardian of the West and has the power to heal and transform human passions into true wisdom. Zunis believe that the Bear is invaluable whenever you are faced with change and transition and that it can be your ally when you are attempting to resolve conflict, forgive yourself or others for errors of the past, or when you are faced with new challenges in your spiritual path. There is a particular kind of depression of the spirit sometimes associated with the deep introspective stage of transition and change. When this occurs, the Bear is a reminder that there is a parallel between depression and the natural state known as hibernation, when involvement with the outer world is minimized in order to focus more energy on the inner processes necessary for a successful transition.

Had I been more aware, or separate from Jane in my mind, I would have slipped that little bear into my own pocket. But I was always confusing Jane with me in that way.

The doorbell rang, and Jane grabbed me before I could stand, kissing me on the mouth and holding me down. "I hate that you're going," she sputtered.

The doorbell rang again, and I rolled out from under her to let Stella in.

"Am I too early?" Stella asked. She looked worried, deathly worried.

"Not at all," I said. "My cab will be here any minute."

"Okay," Jane said, punching my arm as she walked past. She continued on to Stella's car without looking back.

Stella paused at the door, unsure. I liked her already. I wished all the formalities were behind us, so that I could call her a friend. "So you're an ER doctor?" I asked.

"Yes," Stella said nervously.

"My dad and sister are doctors," I ventured. "Pathologists."

Stella paused for a second, looked genuinely interested and about to speak, then seemed to remember who was waiting in her car. She said, "Neat," then smiled warmly, backed up, and turned with a wave to join Jane.

As I sat on the airplane taking me back to St. Louis, I felt the same old twinges that used to shadow me when I was young and homesick at camp. It was no secret that I had a poor record when it came to separating. But I don't think anyone ever fully understood the terror I felt when I was little and leaving home.

I was ten the first time, when after years of hearing about the amazing exploits of my brother and sister at summer camps, I begged my parents to send me along with my sister to High Trails in Colorado. Madeleine had described riding horses, camping out, and nights around bonfires singing John Denver songs. I expected this would be a big improvement on my own scouting attempts in the woods by our house and envisioned myself a modern-day Davy

Crockett as I boarded a plane for the first time alone. At the gate, Mom gave me a tight squeeze and promised that Madeleine would be on the other side, already in her second week of pioneering.

During the three-hour flight, things disintegrated fast. First, it dawned on me that I would not be sleeping in my bed for a long time, or playing under my oak tree, or scooting around the kitchen asking questions while my mother turned summer berries into jam or worked on the details of yet another dinner. It occurred to me that I was alone, completely alone, and without any independent means of returning home. A terrible hole started to open in my chest, and I knew I had made a big mistake. By the time the camp bus had brought me to the Welcome Office, I was in a panic and held my tears just long enough to demand a phone. Noting my frantic expression, the welcome staff quickly responded. When Mom answered, her voice provoked in me such a longing that I started to cry.

"I want to come home," I said.

"But you've only just arrived," she answered.

"Well, I don't like it. Can you get your money back?"

"Unpack your things and have dinner," Mom said. "We can talk after dinner."

Fine. I would pretend to unpack and then sit through dinner. I would be on the next plane home after that.

Later that evening, Mom called as promised. I was waiting by the phone, and Robin, the head counselor, looked very concerned. My sister was apparently off in a tent somewhere, so Robin was on her own.

"I want to come home," I said again into the phone.

"Hold on," Mom said. "What did you have for dinner? What's your cabin like? Is Madeleine there?"

"I *can* come home, can't I?"

I heard her cover the phone and say something to Dad.

"Can't I come home?" I asked.

"Honey," she sighed. "Come on. You haven't even spent one night."

So I spent one night, and then Robin and I were sitting by the phone again.

"Is it really so awful here?" she asked. She gestured toward a big picture window, where clear blue sky framed green hills and snow-capped mountains. There were probably even horses running in the distance.

I wanted to puke.

When I dialed home, Dad answered. "Look, I'm sick," I said breathlessly. "I'm sick and I need to come home."

He handed the phone to Mom. She asked me to pass the phone to Robin, who verified that I was in fact *not* sick. There was a string of yeps, yeses, and sure sure sures, and then a final, "Absolutely, Mrs. Kraus, I understand," before Robin hung up.

She looked at me sympathetically. "I'm sorry, kiddo," she said. "The word is you're here for the duration."

She might as well have said a firing squad was meeting me at dawn.

After that, I was the talk of camp. I was sullen and teary and sometimes so frustrated that I actually screamed spontaneously into the air. Even I would have stayed away from me. When my sister came back from her camping trip, she was quickly escorted to me by three worried counselors. Madeleine missed her afternoon campfire-building demonstration and a chance to build a tepee out of real cow hide, but she didn't hesitate to take my hand. As we walked through groves of birch trees, she tried in vain to get at the source of my distress.

"What if Mom is dead or something?" I asked. "I wouldn't even know."

"Why would Mom be dead?" Madeleine asked.

"That's not the point."

"Are you worried about Dad, too?" she wondered. "How are you imagining they died?" She seemed genuinely curious, which only fueled my paranoia.

"And what if I forget what they look like?" I continued.

"Come on," Madeleine said. "They look the same as when you left them."

I folded my arms across my chest and wondered how my sister could be so calm, so confident that our parents hadn't slid off some embankment in their car, or been burgled and stabbed, or just died of random asphyxiation. It was a real possibility in my mind that we were orphaned.

I spotted my first chance to escape when a quiet redhead named Regina broke her wrist playing the camper classic Red Rover. She hadn't wanted to play because she was small, and she swore she'd just flip over the arms and land on her back. But Dawn, the hippie counselor in charge of games and recreation, encouraged Regina to give it a try.

"Experimentation," Dawn told us, "is necessary for progress."

Regina was feeling singled out by then and must have figured that flipping over locked arms was better than public humiliation, so off she ran, eyes wide, right at our human chain.

She picked the two smallest girls on our team and did a fast flip over their arms, just as she predicted. When she landed on her arm we all heard the snap, and Dawn came running.

"Uh-oh," she said, biting a nail.

At dinner I heard that Regina was going to be sent home the very next morning, and I set my alarm so I could witness her liberation from my bunk bed. At seven A.M., I saw the camp van take her to freedom, and right then I began plotting my own injury. Maybe a sprained ankle or a wrist. If I had to, I was ready to break my own leg. I could almost taste my first dinner at home.

. . .

Unfortunately, hurting oneself is not as easy as people might think. Humans, I discovered, are designed to avoid injury. Our bodies will instinctively counter any move that might result in pain. The first thing I tried was falling off a low ledge by the tennis courts, with a mind to sprain my ankle, but at the last minute my legs tucked under me and I rolled into a safe landing, arms wrapped around my head.

"What are you doing?" asked a heavyset girl named Jessica. She looked at me through the tennis court fence, all precious and clean in her spiffy whites.

I looked away and cursed.

Next I tried accidentally placing my ankle between my bed and the frame, planning to slip off and scream bloody murder. The cabin was full of witnesses, and I gathered my nerve.

"You look like you're going to take a dump, right in your bed," Leslie said loudly behind me. A towel was wrapped around her head turban-style, and she smelled like pine.

I looked at her and thought I might.

"Why is your foot like that?" asked Alexis, joining Leslie. Alexis was perfect down to her painted toenails.

I cleared my throat. "Just had an itch," I said. I rubbed my foot up and down under the steel to demonstrate how I was about to scratch my foot.

Before long, I had gained a reputation for not only hysterics, but astonishing clumsiness, which was hard for the athlete in me to stomach. I decided my next attempt would have to be colossal. No more playing around.

I spent days scouting locations. I gazed at roofs, ledges, passing cars, and horses, developing elaborate schemes for my undoing. Finally my chance came when we were assembled for our Jumping Juniper West cabin picture. Being on the tall side, I was directed to the top row of a set of bleachers. I estimated the distance and thought surely something would break, twist, or bruise if I just happened to tumble. The girls filed in below me, and with everybody smiling, I said a prayer before letting my shoes slip off the edge. The shutter clicked as I took my plunge, and I was forever frozen in time tilting backward, looking wall-eyed at the ground.

Again my young body tucked and curled, bouncing me back into the standing position as if I were a rubber ball. All eyes peered down at me, and counselors came running. Out of sheer humiliation, after that, I gave up.

After I returned home I refused to talk about High Trails, and I barred its mention in my presence. When the cabin picture arrived, with my swan dive recorded for all to see, I shredded it right in front of my shocked and disappointed mother.

You'd think that by twenty-four I'd have mastered the art of leaving, but as soon as my plane took off from San Francisco, I felt that same sinking sensation. Which was odd, because I was heading home. It dawned on me, as I rose through the clouds, that a sneaky switch had occurred. Now my home was not in St. Louis. Now home was Jane.

EIGHTEEN

We were all muted that Christmas, the second one without Mom. Madeleine and Dad kept busy with cooking, and Grant took charge of placing Christmas wreaths and ornaments around the house. I felt detached as soon as I stepped in the door, seeing them with Jane's eyes, imagining what she'd say. My father was pleased that I was there but distracted by Gayle and too many presents to buy all on his own. My brother teased me about the "California experience," where he envisioned yoga and hippie culture converting me into something hilarious. The Birkenstocks Jane had assured me were cute had been Grant's first piece of evidence. I did not see the humor.

My sister, whose bedroom was adjacent to mine, tried to connect in her way, which was to probe like a scientist with questions. How large is your room? What toothpaste do you use now? Do you write at your desk or in cafés? Whom do you like better, Dustin Hoffman or Al Pacino? When that failed, she invited me to help her bake Christmas treats, or we sat together flipping channels on TV.

Often I found myself using Jane's language, which I'd absorbed without knowing it. She had two frequent expressions, "Swa-ha," which was a verbal shrug, as in "The register just blew up before our summer sale? Swa-ha." And the other was "Cripes." That one I liked especially, since I was more apt to be cursing than shrugging.

During dinner on my first night home, I let Dad know I was through with Episcopalian religion and favoring Buddhism, which of course was more evidence for Grant. I told my brother that he should think twice about using his law degree to defend greedy corporations, where, as Jane had explained, corruption was the rule. And Madeleine found it hard not to take the bait when I suggested that health care was a joke.

A few nights later, having alienated my immediate family, I moved on to Gayle. There was nothing to dislike about her, which irritated me. She was perceptive and patient, and she never let me see it if she was hurt. So I offered her nothing, no provocations, no arguments. I ignored her. I locked her out and snuck cigarettes and wondered what Jane was doing back at home.

When Christmas dinner was over, nobody ran for the Swiss bell Dad used to ring to pretend Santa had just come. There was no screen in front of the living room as before and no Mom rushing to get desserts and tea on silver trays. We took our time getting to the presents, laid in the usual generous piles around living room chairs. Grant built a fire, and when it roared to life, Gayle, Dad, and Madeleine stood with him to admire it. They turned in unison, hearing me tear open a gift.

"That's exchangeable, of course," Dad said as I produced a cashmere sweater. Gayle looked nervous, so I suspected she'd picked it out. Of course, it was splendid.

"I hope I didn't give you that last year," Dad added when I

opened a set of monogrammed Cross pens. I thanked him, reached for the next box, and then the next.

Madeleine and I each opened a card from Dad as our last present. In it he wrote that we'd have an afternoon to divide Mom's jewelry. He said he couldn't choose who got what, except that Grant got Mom's wedding ring. Earlier in the evening I had already watched the ring pass from Dad to Grant and swallowed my scream. I had assumed it was buried with Mom, and in my most selfish moments, I had thought Dad's interest in remarrying was buried there, too.

The next afternoon, as a thick snow fell all around us, my sister and I set up a card table by the fireplace and Dad brought out the jewelry. He spread out the pieces, some old and familiar, some expensive, some cheap. He shared some anecdotes about a few of them, remembering that a gold pin had belonged to Grandmother and the silver charm bracelet had been Mom's as a child. Then he stepped away and let my sister and me begin.

"Do you want this?" Madeleine asked, holding a thick gold bracelet. On the inside it was engraved with a date and Mom's many names. "I always loved this," she added.

"Take it," I said, eyeing one of Mom's favorites, a colorful scarab watch.

"You take her watch," Madeleine said, observing me. She reached across the table and selected a smaller gold bracelet. I took a gold coin Mom had made into a long necklace. Madeleine picked a brooch with ivory insets. I took a funny-looking brass frog pin. And so it went.

Of all the gifts that Christmas, the best find I stumbled upon while secretly prowling the house for hidden Mom treasures. I thought I'd covered every corner before leaving in the spring, but tucked below Mom's hanging files, in her big oak desk, were pages of loose lined paper, rolled into a scroll and tied with string. When I opened it I found a journal, written in pencil while she was in the hospital with depression. As I began to read, I saw vividly how terrifying the experience had been.

I once saw a medieval painting, she wrote, *where the damned were being flung into space, forever separated from God. Their faces were filled with agony and fear, their mouths opened in screams. That's just how I look and feel. I have lost the path. I cannot find the old familiar signs to guide me. Why can't I find them?*

I felt a sad rush reading my mother's thoughts, the same way I did after dreaming of her—as if we had just had a real visit, in the flesh.

I certainly did cry today, she wrote in another entry. *Cried with Dr. Singer and cried after activity. Ellie sat with me . . . I don't feel well. I have pain in my chest, but I know there really isn't any pain there. . . . Why have I always needed to keep busy?—knitting, needlepointing, weeding—I'm not a very peaceful person. . . . Isn't it odd that I like structure and control and my cigarette smoking was totally out of control for thirty years—I finally got control over that and I have lost control again. I am a mote in God's eye.*

Suddenly I was too sad to go on. I started to roll the pages back up, then caught sight of my name and looked closer. *It was good to feel Caroline today,* she wrote, and though I looked for more, that was all. Those words shook me. Though I hadn't the insight to understand it yet, they described what I'd craved since she died—to have such closeness as to be *felt*.

I rolled up the pages and took them directly upstairs, planting them deep in my still-packed suitcase. Someday I would tell Madeleine and Grant what I'd found and ask my dad if he'd ever read the journal. But for the moment I stole it to keep for myself and silently promised to guard her confessions.

After Christmas I went straight from the San Francisco Airport to Sorrell's, where I knew Jane was finishing an evening shift. She was at the information desk with River, and I dropped my bag and galloped over. When she spotted me her face went flat.

"Hi!" I said breathlessly.

"Hi!" River said. "Welcome back!"

Jane said, "What are you doing here?"

River's smile faded.

"I just got in," I said.

"I'll finish shelving," Jane told River. She took off, and I trailed behind like a puppy.

I tugged at her sleeve and said, "Hey, what's wrong?"

She shook off my hand. Just then Susan—a stocky Sorrell's employee who was deathly shy and filled notebooks with agonized poetry—walked by. She and Jane exchanged covert looks that sent a knife through my heart.

My phone didn't ring at eight A.M. the next morning, and at lunch Jane said she was busy. When I approached her in a group, everybody got quiet. Her puzzled "Have we met?" expression left me stuttering.

After work, I paid her a visit. Jason and Katherine Marks's nanny waved me through, pointing to Jane's room. She was in bed, reading a book called *Trauma and Recovery*.

"Hi," I said.

She glanced at me, then returned to her book. I took a step closer. She reached for a mug of tea and sipped at it. "You're upset," I said.

"I'm fine."

"Look, I'm sorry," I said.

After a silence she said, "Why?"

"I don't know," I admitted.

She couldn't look at me. She pointed to the door.

"But what's wrong?" I asked. "What did I do?"

Jane's expression was so ambivalent and detached that she seemed like an entirely different person. Too politely, she said, "Go home, Caroline."

I walked out, muttering. I didn't want to cry so much as explode. That evening I skipped dinner with my housemates and must have looked unusually stressed, because each of them came to ask what was wrong, in separate visits to my room. But the threat of betraying my Jane secret silenced me, and one by one I realized I could not confess or explain. On other occasions, I'd always been able to find comfort by confiding in Jane or my friends in the house. Now I dismissed Lisette with vague excuses and told Torsten I might have the flu. I let Greta believe there were boy troubles afoot and assured Steve I was just really tired. Only Peng seemed doubtful when I told him I'd had a really bad day at work.

After he left, I lay in bed and stared at the ceiling, with anxiety flooding my body and warping my thoughts. Secrets are toxic, as Jane knew well. And mine was already infecting me.

I could remember feeling this way before, though on a smaller, more rational scale. When I was little, and I had done something wrong— maybe all the cookies had disappeared from the tin on the highest shelf of our highest cupboard—my mother always came looking for me. My brother, the future lawyer, was never a suspect, and my sister was much too crafty to be caught. Madeleine was a professional at keeping secrets. When questioned by Mom, whose interrogation skills rivaled those of the FBI, Madeleine could lie with a perfectly calm, thoughtful expression. For extra effect she would appear surprised, even offended, by the accusation. She had alibis and witnesses, and she knew when and how to dispose of the evidence.

So if cookies were missing, or a school report card hadn't shown up, or there was a dent in the car door, or the back of the television was warm when my parents came home at night, Mom always started with me because she knew that if I'd done it, she'd get a fast confession. First she called, searching me out, challenging me to show myself. Then I'd march from my bedroom with a heavy heart and drooped head to the top of the stairs.

"I did it," I would say quickly. And I would be relieved right away, because the secret was always worse than the crime.

Stealing cookies was a minor, if irritating, offense. I could apologize my way out of that. Sneaking television after hours was worse; that caused lengthy monologues about Trust and My Future. But some crimes had catastrophic consequences—for instance, the five speeding tickets I hid when I was sixteen, pocketed within one month of my having a license. As they had accrued, I'd kept each ticket a secret. Eventually I sat on my bed and stared at a letter requesting my appearance in court. According to the letter, a parent or guardian had to join me before the judge, and since I was fresh out of guardians, I handed my mother the letter. She became very still while she read it, and then she froze. By her expression you would have thought I'd robbed a bank and shot six old people on my way out the door.

"Think of this," I'd said as she glared at me. "I am not pregnant, terminally ill, or on drugs of any kind." Her eyes sharpened and cut a hole in my hopeful smile. Those were not good images to have brought to her mind.

That evening, instead of going to an event with Dad, my mother found herself standing beside me before a silver-haired judge, fighting to preserve my "record," which I was learning was "important" and also separated the "good citizens" from the "bad citizens." She stood beside me and argued, one hand locked on my shoulder, until the judge finally became so exhausted that he agreed I could be forgiven this time, as long as Mom kept my license and I didn't drive alone. He was visibly weakened by their exchange, and we traded sympathetic waves as I exited the court.

"I cannot talk to you for a while," Mom said as we left court, and sure enough, she was silent the rest of the way home. Later I trailed her through the house, making up questions just to cause her to speak, but she had departed from me. I was irreparably, and horribly, invisible.

Maybe my mother's anger was so great that she feared losing control in my presence. Maybe she thought I might kill myself driving so fast or kill someone else. But I would have welcomed her rage. After several days and nights of silence, my anguish grew beyond the limits of my control, and suddenly I found myself shrieking and throwing my head against my bedroom wall. Mom came running. I had never seen her so profoundly stunned.

"Honey, stop!" she yelled. "I *love* you."

Separated from Jane, I paced and fretted. On my lunch breaks I drove home, climbed into bed, and lay there. I wished I could explain my personality change to my puzzled friends at work, or my housemates, but along with my vow of secrecy, I was too confused and embarrassed to admit it to myself. When Lisette and Torsten caught me pacing around the pool, they cornered me by the diving board and demanded an explanation. I told them I didn't know what was wrong with me, which was at least partially true.

"But a light has gone out in you," Lisette fretted. "Your face is so dark."

On the spot I made up a boy. "There's a guy," I admitted.

"*Oh,*" Lisette said, touching my arm. "Okay."

"What guy?" asked Torsten.

"A guy I like, who won't talk to me," I said. "His name is Henry."

"Well, why didn't you say something?" Lisette asked. "Of course you're miserable."

As Henry became my accepted excuse—an older man, I'd decided, whom I'd met at Stanford the past summer during my screenwriting workshop—I slipped cards into Jane's coat and watched her from a distance, laughing and talking with River or Faye as she'd never done before. And, increasingly, she had emotional, intimate exchanges with Susan, who, while in the throes of Jane's seduction, seemed more and more nervous, confused with customers, and generally unhinged.

When I finally called in sick to work, in a full-blown paralyzing depression, Jane called me at her old time, eight A.M.

"Honey?" she said brightly.

I rubbed my eyes and sat straight up in bed.

"What are you doing?" she asked.

I blinked and sputtered. "I'm right here in bed," I said.

"Why aren't you *here?*"

"What?"

"At work, why aren't you at work?"

"I don't feel well."

"You are so stubborn."

I clutched the phone. "I'm stubborn? *I'm* stubborn?"

"Meet me at the bench at noon," she said. "And bring a good mood, dammit."

Jane was waiting on the bench, bundled in a coat and scarf. I sat down and stubbed out a cigarette. We watched a woman drop her purse across the street at the bus stop. The contents tumbled out onto the pavement.

"Well, that sucks," Jane said, looking at the woman.

I didn't bite.

"So. Do you miss me?" she asked.

"What is going *on?*" I blurted.

"Now you know how it feels."

I stared at her.

"Right?" she asked.

"Jesus Christ, Jane."

"I thought you should know."

"What is wrong with you? I can't leave town?"

"You can do whatever you want."

"Oh. And come home to this?"

"It's your choice."

"That's sick."

Jane said, "So I have a little trouble with reentry, I can't help it."

"It was Christmas," I said. "I had a round-trip ticket."

"You don't *understand*," Jane seethed.

"Then explain," I seethed back.

"Do you think I like feeling this way? How do *you* like it?"

"I don't like it," I said.

"Right. And it kills me when people leave. Because, in my experience, the people I count on don't come back."

"I came back, Jane."

"This time."

"I'll always come back."

Jane's lips swelled and quivered. "Prove it," she said.

"How?"

"Take me with you next time," she said. "Or don't go."

I had to catch my breath. It was thrilling to be the object of such intense need. To be desired so much that leaving town was banned. I set aside all rational thinking as I pulled my coat tight around me and said, "Okay."

Days later, when Jane marched into the back room of Sorrell's, distraught, my antennae were up. I had been waiting for the next crisis to prove myself.

"I'm homeless!" she cried. "Fucking Katherine and Jason, they kicked me out!"

She came to Susan, took a seat in her lap, and snuck a quick thumb fix. "That's awful," Susan said. "What happened?"

"Fucking people," Jane muttered.

She put her head on Susan's shoulder and looked at me.

"They want you out right away?" I asked.

Jane nodded.

"Why?"

"Because they are assholes. Cripes. What am I going to do?"

Susan looked worried but stumped.

"You can stay with me," I offered.

Susan's eyes got big. She looked at Jane.

Jane smiled and said, "You mean it?"

She moved in that night. I carried her bags and boxes and made room on my shelves and in my dresser for her things. "Home at last," Jane said, throwing a mattress on the floor. She set up a little reading lamp on a stack of books and put her hands on her hips.

"Home," I agreed happily.

Jane said, "Honey?"

"Yes?"

"We need to change a few things."

"Already?"

"Let's get past this fast," she said nervously.

"Past what?"

"Past the fact that you and I ever slept together."

Had I been a thumb sucker, my thumb would have gone right in my mouth.

Jane said, "We have to pretend that never happened, okay?"

It was a little late.

"Because I love you," she said. "Nobody knows me the way you do—"

"Susan might disagree," I said.

Jane gave me a quick punch to the arm. "You don't get it at all," she said. "Who I fuck has nothing to do with us. You are untouchable—my first and only actual friend. I need a *friend*, honey, not another lover."

I backed down quickly.

"I love you completely," she continued. "As far as I'm concerned, we're married."

That both perplexed and reassured me. Then I got it. "Oh," I said, "Thelma and Louise?"

"Exactly." Jane smiled. She gripped my wrists excitedly. "We're at the beginning of something great, honey. Something rare, that only you and I can have."

I was more than willing to accept that fantasy. And if our future was tied to a movie, well, that was a bonus. So I got excited, too. Jane and I would have something new, untested. We were pioneers, fugitives from reality. We were Thelma and Louise.

"Okay," I said, grinning, "I'm yours."

Jane hugged me. She kissed me on the mouth.

"I know you are," she said. "And *God*, I love you for it."

Jane was so gifted in moments like these. In the space of one conversation, she had simultaneously broken my heart and married me.

Shakespeare would have been proud.

Jane had one more thing to say before she unpacked and we started our new life. "And remember," she said. "Don't tell anyone about us. Not anyone, not ever. I don't want people knowing the details of our lives. We'll keep us between us. All of it. Okay?"

Satisfied by my obedient nod, she turned her attention to my bed. She had named it the *Titanic* because of the big sinkhole in the middle. "Anyway," she said, "you were never quite there, were you, honey? I mean, let's face it, you never even *moved.*"

While I pondered this last comment, Jane got busy putting clothes in my drawers and hanging her shirts and pants in the closet. She put on music and lit candles. I liked how my room was transformed, made womblike by Jane's veiled lamps. When she was satisfied, she tapped my shoulder and said, "The other thing is, I'm in sort of a pickle."

I was still worried about the "not moving" in bed comment, feeling that I wanted another shot if I'd been such a failure.

"It's embarrassing," Jane went on, "but I'm broke. Jason and Katherine let me stay for free."

In a clearer mind, this would have cast their "asshole" status in a different light. Missing the point, I said, "Oh, of course you can stay here for free."

"Well, no. I mean, I can't make some bills," Jane confessed. Her thumb slipped into her mouth and rested there. She blinked at me.

"So you need help?" I asked.

"Car loan," she said, and extracted a payment book from her back pocket. "Three hundred a month, can you believe that? Highway *robbery*."

I fetched my checkbook as Jane produced an accordion file full of bill statements. "And I owe the credit card assholes," she said. "And my therapist is going to cancel me if I don't pay back sessions, which could be bad for both of us."

I handed her check after check, and it felt fabulous. I finally had one leg up on Jane. Until then I had been on the receiving end of her agenda, but when I finally took action—made real problems go away just by signing my name—I had the feeling we were partners.

"Are you sure?" she asked, holding the checks.

"I have more money than I know what to do with," I said confidently.

"Must be nice," she said with a sigh.

"It's yours," I assured her. "No paying me back."

I realize now that, like Jane, I was hiding my real agenda with that first transaction. It wasn't charity. Not purely noble. I was looking for a return on my investment, was paying for permanence. When Jane hugged me, and I promised to help her as long as she needed, a deal was struck. And it seemed such an easy route to love. It never occurred to me that I'd just signed away my entire inheritance with that one little sentence.

As we lay in our respective beds that night, Jane proclaimed us Lucy and Ethel. I was Ethel. I noticed that beside Jane's pillow there was a large crumpled paper sack and wondered about it as I fell asleep. The next morning, while Jane was in the shower, I peeked inside.

The sack was full of sterling silver, piles of it. Later I asked her where it came from. "Oh, I just carry it around," she said vaguely. Then with a grin she said, "Let's call it my dowry."

Meanwhile, several blocks away, a nice young couple had just moved baby Emma into Jane's old room, as had always been the plan. Some months later, Katherine and Jason would open a drawer and discover that all of their family silver had mysteriously disappeared.

Chapter NINETEEN

When a customer started coming around the store for repeat visits to see Jane, I figured out where she had been disappearing to several nights a week. I had suspected Susan, but apparently Jane had put her on hold. The customer's name was Garrett, and he looked like a Garrett. He had short dark hair and a square, confident jaw, and when not saving lives in his ambulance, he obviously worked out at a gym. His love for Jane was so obvious, it was embarrassing.

I mentioned him one evening when Jane and I were in our beds, hoping to hide my worry. Jane immediately kicked off her covers and started pacing around my room, naked. She found one of my cigarettes and cracked the French door, puffing into the moonlight. "What I do is my business," she said hotly.

I pouted. Eventually Jane came over and sat next to me. "Honey?" she asked. "Do you think the girls look swollen?" She glanced down at her breasts. I had often been called on to inspect regions of Jane's body that most people restrict to doctors, but this time I looked away and shrugged.

"Garrett has a beautiful body," she said. "When we fucked—"

I turned my head back slowly and stared Jane into silence.

"Oh, get *over* it," she said. "What are you worried about? It's just sex, for God's sake. You are in a completely different category. *You* are my wife."

"Whatever," I said. Truth be told, I had no good argument for why I cared.

"Sometimes you are a totally unenlightened thinker," Jane said, taking my hand. "I *love* you. And reassuring you all the time is getting old. Just accept that I will always love you the most, and let's move on. If I ever get married, we'll all live together, okay?"

Somehow, that was not reassuring.

At work, Susan was looking gloomier and gloomier. She brightened only when Jane was near, and when they disappeared she came back glowing. While they were on one of their outings, Garrett came into the store and right up to my register. "Is Jane Lowell here?" he asked.

"She is working today," I said, "but out for a while."

"Ah. Do you know when she might be back?"

Just then I saw Jane and Susan coming in behind him. When Garrett followed my eyes, he caught Jane ducking, and his face went white. When Jane popped her guilty head up, she saw that she'd been made.

"Surprise!" she said weakly. Then it was Susan's turn to blanch when Jane galloped over to Garrett and gave him a movie star kiss. He fell back from her, profoundly confused.

"Were you hiding? From me?" he stammered. "You didn't want me to see you?"

Jane's smile faltered, and then she turned cold. "Don't corner me," she snapped.

"Well, it's pretty humiliating," he said. "I'd like to know why—"

"No, you wouldn't," Jane said evenly. When Garrett didn't move she said, "Swa-ha," and disappeared into the back room.

He stood for a long time in front of my register as customers came and went. I kept an eye on him, and also Susan, who patrolled the stacks like a discarded pet. If I had worried about Garrett coming between Jane and me, that disappeared as quickly as his spirit drained, right there, by the postcard rack. He watched the backroom door for a while, then left.

At first, Jane's residence in my room had been sanctioned. But as time went on, it was clear that everyone was wary of Jane, for reasons I didn't understand. Lisette felt that we were secretive, always giggling in my room. The movie nights I'd started when I came to the house had been abandoned, and, Torsten commented, I never spoke for myself anymore.

"When you open your mouth," he told me, "she stands there and speaks." He patted my back and said, "Where is Caroline? Eh?"

Alex was more concerned that Jane was not paying rent. Greta thought she was creepy, and Peng remarked that two adult unrelated women should never sleep so close.

I had promised my housemates that Jane's stay would be brief, and Jane had tried to stay out of the way, but the weeks passed, and sometimes there was a line at the shower, with all the housemates, myself included, accounted for. Her car sometimes took the last spot near the house, and too often the refrigerator was low, as Alex said, "on essentials."

Had Jane tried her magic to win any one of them over, things might have been different. But she couldn't be bothered, and by February a meeting was called to discuss her immediate eviction. Jane wasn't allowed to come. My housemates and I sat around our dinner table, a circle of glum faces.

"She's not paying rent," Alex said for the hundredth time. "She's been here how long? A month?"

"She's broke," I said. "That's why she's here."

"That's not our problem," Peng interjected. "She's an adult."

I looked to Lisette for support.

"She has a strange power over you," Lisette said ominously. "Why can't you tell her to go? We want you to stay."

Greta nodded in agreement. "We want you to stay."

"Just tell her to find her own place," Torsten said with exasperation. "What is so hard about that?"

"I can't just put her on the street," I said. "She's really, really broke."

"You underestimate Jane," Torsten said, as if he'd known her for years. "She'll find another keeper."

"I'm not her keeper," I shot back. "And it's my room, so I don't understand the problem." I pointed at Alex and said, "Your girlfriend stays over all the time."

"Is Jane your girlfriend?" he asked.

I clenched my teeth.

"What *is* up with you two?" Greta asked. "It's a little weird. And whatever happened to Henry?"

"She has to go, period," Torsten said. "She doesn't pay rent. She uses our shower. She's taking over your brain."

"She's out, Caroline," Alex agreed, lowering his fist like a gavel. "Tell her to go."

Jane was reading in the back room at the bookstore when I went to deliver the news. "Why?" she demanded. "What did I do?"

I chewed on my fingernail.

"They really want me out? Right away?"

"Yesterday," I admitted.

"Well, well," she said bitterly.

"They just want everybody paying rent," I explained. "They don't want extra roommates."

"Generous people, your friends," Jane commented. She picked up her book and resumed reading.

"They're pissing me off," I assured her.

"Oh, I can tell," she said. "That's why you told them that your room is your business, and to shove it."

"I did, I did," I said. "Well, not to *shove* it, exactly—"

Jane said, "Forget it, honey. Just go back to your life and I'll go back to mine."

"What does that mean?"

"It's my problem," Jane said a little too agreeably. "Anyway, I never liked that bunch you live with—they never made me feel welcome."

"I can loan you some money to help you move," I said.

"No, I'll stay at Susan's. You go play with your friends."

"Jane—"

"Honey," she interrupted, "I'm bored now. Don't you have work to do?"

When Jane didn't come home that night, I tracked her to Susan's in the morning and found her eating breakfast in her kitchen, watching television. Susan welcomed me in.

"Honey?" Jane called as I entered.

Susan and I responded in unison.

"Susan," Jane specified. "Do we get the Discovery Channel?"

"Channel twenty-seven," she said. Jane pointed the remote and smiled.

Of course I did not have the Discovery Channel, or any cable television at all. Susan asked if I wanted some food.

I said, "No thanks."

Jane looked happy. Relaxed. Which made me more nervous.

Susan grabbed her coat and Jane caught her by the wrist, saying, "I don't want you to go—honey, *stay.*" Susan took a seat.

"I've been thinking—" I began.

"Caroline," Jane interrupted, "Susan said I can stay here, isn't that great? We'll move my stuff today."

"Oh," I said. "Well."

Jane took a bite of eggs and said, "Listen, if those blockheads on Waverly Street are your kind of people, that's great. Susan is my kind of people." She smiled at Susan.

"Well, I was thinking—"

"You know what you should do?" Jane said. "Give old Torsten a try. What you need is a good old-fashioned lay, Torsten style. Maybe this is your big chance—I think he really digs you." Jane turned to Susan and said, "Torsten is a big German guy in her house. He looks like he was made in a factory."

"Jane," I said firmly.

She went back to the eggs and television.

"I was going to *say* that I'm moving out. I don't like what they did, so I'm leaving." Even as the word sprang from my mouth, I couldn't believe it.

"Oh yeah?" she asked. "Leaving paradise?"

"I am."

Jane put down her fork and considered this. She put her thumb in her mouth, shifted in her chair, put her feet in Susan's lap, and waited.

"And I'm going to have a *fireplace*," I added, standing to go.

Jane cocked her head. She smiled over her thumb.

"With *Italian* tile," I continued.

"And a big mantel?" Jane asked, straightening.

"For your art," I finished.

Susan's eyes darted between us, and Jane grinned in her knowing way, which always made me feel home again. We figuratively shook hands as Susan looked baffled, and I signed on then, for more Jane, with relief.

Everyone at Waverly house was shocked by my announcement. As they ate together and relaxed by the pool, I packed and planned and kept my checkbook open. Jane's car payments kept coming, as did her credit card bills. She was out of tampons or shampoo, or her dry cleaning was ready and she was short on cash. New CDs needed getting, along with blank tapes. There were the shoes she admired, a warm coat, and groceries to get, phone bills that broke records, and tires that blew. Then came the big rent on our new place, a bigger deposit, and the shopping spree to decorate our new pad.

When I said good-bye, only Torsten and Lisette were there to see me off. My car was loaded for the short drive to our new studio, on Emerson Street. Torsten gave me some hand-painted dishes as a housewarming. Lisette sent me off with a worried hug.

Chapter TWENTY

Not long after taking the new place, Jane decided we needed to make a trip to her parents' home back east. We took the red-eye on a happy mission, to pack up the remainder of Jane's belongings—especially her art—because, Jane had said, with me she had finally found a permanent home.

Mr. Lowell picked us up at a train station near their house. He was younger than I expected, with thick blond hair and gentle eyes. He was an artist but had built a fortune for his family as an engineer.

The Lowells' house was magnificent: a bright yellow clapboard three stories tall with white trim. Their kitchen sparkled, with granite tops, a spacious sitting area, and a professional oven that her mother, Linda, showed off right away. Jane and I put our bags in her old bedroom and then bumped into Jane's little sister, Annie, on our way downstairs. Annie and Jane hugged and squealed. Then I got a big hug, along with another squeal.

"Well, Caroline," Annie said. "We are all amazed by you. Every time Jane opens her mouth, it's Caroline, Caroline, Caroline."

Annie was another beautiful Lowell, with short curly hair, big white teeth, and the spontaneous effervescence of an untroubled mind. Jane had marveled at her sister's luck, to have been born last, after the Lowells had moved away from the low-rent district and Mr. Friedlander to the gentrified wealth of their safe coastal town.

Jane and I were to stay for five days. The first two went smoothly, with relaxed dinners, movies, long lunches, and longer shopping trips. Linda was big on discount shopping—the lean days were never far from her mind—and she was devoted to movies. Jane liked hearing us discuss everything from *Citizen Kane* to *Star Wars* as we exited their local theater. I bought Linda a book of reviews written by Pauline Kael, and she gave me a booklet of coupons to a national cineplex.

On the third day, Jane said she wanted to show me around town. We rented a car, and I drove while she pointed to landmarks from her past and remembered.

"That was my high school," she said, waving toward a line of low buildings overlooking playing fields. "I played field hockey there," she added.

We drove over bridges, through woods, and past shops that Jane had frequented.

"And that's Gullies," she said, pointing to a sad-looking dance club on the outskirts of town. As we drove farther out, Jane got alert. We paused near the gates of a place for kids with antisocial, psychiatric, or behavioral problems.

"The loony bin," Jane said. "Fuck."

"How long were you there?" I asked.

"I don't know."

"How old were you?"

"I don't remember."

Jane squinted at the building, then she stuck her arm out the window and said, "That's my window, there on the corner. See it? Second floor."

Before I could look, she said, "Forget it," and waved at me to keep driving.

We drove on to a spot where a big waterwheel churned into a pond, and got out. Jane squatted next to the water, fished under a log, and found a pack of old razors. "I love the sound of the wheel," she said, replacing the pack. "Don't you? Like a heartbeat."

We ate lunch there, deli sandwiches. "There are things I love about this town," Jane said. "I miss the East. I miss taking the train to New York, thunderstorms, driving to the Cape. We used to go sailing and deep-sea fishing. Mom took us to all the exhibits in the city."

I nodded, envious. That was the life I had imagined for Jane. Cultured, privileged, elite. Glamorous young parents, precocious children. Temperamental, of course. That was part of the allure. A little madness seemed always the price.

For our final stop, Jane guided us to a modest-looking town, where we stopped in front of a plain one-story house.

"*He* lived there," Jane said, nodding at the house.

I saw a wreath on the door and potted plants lining the front walk. It was a friendly-looking house, cared for.

"The wife still lives there," Jane said.

I had a bad feeling then, confirmed when Jane said, "I'm going in."

"Whoa. What will you say?" I asked.

"I'm going to say what happened. I want her to know what he did to me. I want her to know she was right there, every time."

"Oh, geeze," I said. It seemed like a brave idea, and doomed. But Jane was out of the car before I could put my worry into words.

When she knocked on the door, an elderly woman answered. She threw up her hands in surprise, smiled, and welcomed Jane inside.

I sat in the car, waiting. So often it seemed as if I were either escorting Jane somewhere or waiting for her. To kill time, I found an alley between houses and smoked, peeking around the corner to make sure Jane didn't come skidding out on her ear.

I wondered what Jane might have been like had Mr. Friedlander never been born. It was so tempting to think that I could reconnect the pieces that were broken by him, that I could single-handedly return her to the girl she might have been. Because then I could know it was possible. Then maybe my own pieces could reconnect, too.

Jane was quiet on our drive back. She only said, "I think she knew," when I asked how it had gone. I felt a little sick when we walked into the Lowells' house, sensing that Jane was primed to blow. At dinner, she pulled the pin.

"I saw Mrs. Friedlander," she said casually, placing potatoes on her plate. Linda frowned and Annie froze. Mr. Lowell sighed and kept his head down.

"Did Jane show you the botanical gardens?" Linda asked me. "The hyacinths are featured in *Home and Garden*—"

"I think she knew," Jane continued. "She knew all along."

I sipped iced tea and prayed.

"Don't do this," Linda said firmly.

"How do you suppose she knew, if it never happened?" Jane asked.

Mr. Lowell asked Annie to pass the asparagus. She was paralyzed, so I passed it myself.

"Don't do this now," Linda said. "If you want to dig it all up again here in front of Caroline—"

Jane smashed her fists against the table. "Shut up!" she shouted. "Shut up! Shut up! Shut up!" The table shook and rattled.

Alarmed, I said, "Hang on—"

Annie groaned and gave a silent plea for me to keep quiet. Mr. Lowell pushed his chair back.

"Stay out of it," Jane said to me. Her crosshairs were fixed on her mother.

Linda folded her arms.

"You don't believe me!" Jane shouted. She pointed at me. "I wish I had *her* mother, and she's dead!"

Annie and Mr. Lowell evacuated their chairs. Jane stood up, too, and said we were leaving.

In haste, we packed boxes with Jane's art and keepsakes, her books and old clothes. As we shuttled them through the house, Jane shouted, "You want to know the truth about these charming rooms, Caroline?"

I said I didn't.

We marched out the door and dropped the last load into the car. Jane turned and shouted at the front door, *"You* guys are crazy!" And with that we drove away.

She was still twitching when I asked, "Where are we going?"

"We'll go to Nelle's," she said, biting a nail. "My real mother."

Nelle was a name I'd heard periodically in California, whenever Jane was homesick. I knew her as a mysterious ideal, a voice at the other end of our phone who had always managed to calm Jane just by saying hello.

Nelle lived near the water in a neighboring town. She was the very image of a Yankee artist, with flowing slacks, a practical handmade sweater, salt-and-pepper hair, and noble features upon an expressive, very intense face.

Nelle flew out her door when she saw us pull in. "Jane!" she cried. "I didn't know you were in town. It's like Christmas!"

Jane kicked the ground with a bashful grin and introduced me. "We're a little fried," she explained. "Caroline just witnessed the wrath of Linda."

"Uh-oh," Nelle said. "You could use some liquor."

Nelle's house was cozy, a two-story shingled cottage with a big, sloppy painting studio in the back. "Your room is waiting," she told Jane, who bounded up the wooden stairs like a kid home from camp. "And here's a room for you, too," Nelle said to me. I plopped my bag down on a day bed and must have looked scared, because out of the blue Nelle hugged me. "It will be all right," she said, patting my back. "Deep breath."

Downstairs, she opened a bottle of wine, and we sat in front of a fire.

"Nelle almost adopted me," Jane said.

"Almost," she agreed.

"Have you got any shows up?" Jane asked her.

"I do. A little exhibit at Yale. Landscapes. With a twist."

"Always with a twist." Jane smiled. To me she added, "You are in the presence of greatness, honey. Nelle is why I love art."

"*You're* the one," Nelle said. "You should be famous by now, Jane."

"I wish I could paint," I volunteered. "I never had the knack."

"It's genetic, honey," Jane said sympathetically. "You should see my mother's watercolors—did you see? In the kitchen?"

"Those were hers?"

Jane nodded. "She had something in the local museum once. There was a reception. I think David broke one of the pieces." She giggled.

"Wow. Who knew someone like Linda could paint like that?" I asked, hoping to assure Jane that I was on her side.

A silence followed.

Nelle sent me a warning look, not so different from Annie's a few hours before, but it was too late. Jane's eyes were narrowed into daggers. "Don't ever speak of my mother that way," she said in a low voice.

I froze with a mouthful of wine.

Later, Nelle and I were cleaning dishes in her kitchen. Jane had gone up to bed.

"A word of advice?" Nelle offered.

"Please."

"Don't go near the subject of Linda Lowell. You can't win, either way."

"I don't think I'll make that mistake again," I said.

"Jane is complicated," Nelle explained. "It's not easy being her friend. We're all on probation, you know."

"But Jane loves you," I said. "She has your art up everywhere."

Nelle smiled. "Jane loves me when she needs me."

I sat on a stool while Nelle scrubbed the counters.

"Was I on your itinerary before Linda blew a gasket?" she asked. When I didn't answer, she said, "Exactly."

"I don't know why it is," I said, "but the worse Jane's trouble is, the more I love her. Do you know what I mean?"

"I could introduce you to a lot of people who know what you mean," Nelle said. "Everyone falls in love with Jane. She's a goddamn phenomenon."

Outside it was dark, and I could hear the ocean in the distance. Nelle motioned me over to her studio and a box of photographs and paintings.

She held up a photograph of a little boy in a swimsuit, leaping into the air near the ocean. There was an old man alone in a chair, photographs of African villagers, deserted American streets. The images had a child's perspective, pointed up at the tall world. "Jane did these," Nelle said.

"I love her because she keeps trying," she added. "And, it's a cliché, but I love her because she's broken. You can't help but want to fix someone who sees things this way." She handed me another photograph.

I nodded.

Nelle said, "But I fear her, too, sometimes. Because she spares no one." She spread more pictures on the table and said, "Jane has no boundaries left. It's survival, survival, survival."

I said, "I think she can make it."

Nelle sighed.

"What?" I asked.

"Oh, I'm not surprised she found you, that's all."

She looked at me with soft eyes and said, "If I'm right, you've got lots of money, lots of time, and an open wound."

I went white.

"She finds us, but we find her, too," Nelle mused. "We all have our reasons. There are always two sides."

TWENTY-ONE

Back in Palo Alto, Jane's art went up on our blank walls, and we chalked the visit up to one more example of why we choose our own families. I suppose I should have predicted trouble when Linda Lowell called soon after and declared she was coming to visit us in the studio as soon as we were settled.

Our new building on Emerson Street was six floors high, and we were in the middle, on the third. It had a slightly ratty but still historic ambiance, with an oak-paneled elevator and red velvet on the walls. Jane called it quaint.

"New ground rule," she said as we unloaded supplies from my car. "No more smoking."

I blinked at her, cigarette in hand. I had already imagined myself smoking out our quaint windows.

"I'm serious," Jane said. She pulled boxes from my car and headed inside. "If I don't need them, you don't need them. It's filthy, and you are not allowed to die."

I tossed the cigarette under my shoe and followed her in.

The studio was tiny, one main room and a walk-in closet, with a galley kitchen. My books, desk, enormous futon bed, and old wooden dresser dwarfed the space, but Jane was excited about living in the walk-in closet. She won it with the argument that she was the only one having sex, and as such she needed a door.

Jane's experience on sailboats came in handy as she organized books and art supplies in tight order around the perimeter of her closet floor, with stacked sweaters and shirts up high on built-in shelves. Her twin box spring covered the rest, with just enough room for a reading table and lamp beside her head.

It galled me that our new place was so expensive. I had gone from a five-bedroom house and pool to sleeping in a living room.

Our first order of business was to acquire *things*, to create instant completeness, a fortress of culinary gadgets and wares, of candles, baskets, vases, flowers, and cupboards spilling with mysterious, organic-only food. Susan was put on hold while Jane and I nested, negotiating where pictures went, how a desk would fit, where the television sat, who cooked, and who provided.

"We can have a party," Jane called from the bathroom. She was grunting with effort, scrubbing our new bathtub. Bathrooms, I would soon find out, were like an office to Jane—where she schemed and dreamed and had all her meltdowns naked, in soapy, lavender-scented water. As I hung pictures by my dresser, she shined it up with gusto. Maybe she was already envisioning me there on the toilet lid, holding her towel, lifeguarding while she bathed.

"Who would come?" I called back, not meaning to sound so pessimistic. But truthfully, we had pretty much amputated the gang at Sorrell's. Jane had literally attached herself to me in the store, popping up whenever I was talking to someone else and quickly presenting a reason why I was needed elsewhere. People who had been dizzy under her spell now found themselves banished if they showed passing interest in me. When I saw the looks between co-workers as I trotted around with Jane, I felt a mixture of embarrassment and pride—sure, I was hooked, but hooked to a star. Gradually I had noticed that people were leaving me alone. And they avoided Jane as if she carried a gun. At the end of a shift, even on movie nights, they passed me without saying good-bye. As an appendage of Jane's, I was carefully quarantined.

As for Jane's relationships, Garrett was on hold along with Susan, and Stella was on double hold two towns over, having returned to the Bay Area for good from her residency.

I stopped arranging my CDs, went to the bathroom door, and caught Jane wiping her eyes.

"What's wrong?" I asked.

"I'm so happy," she said. "We're home. Finally home."

When all our new toys were in place, and beds were made, with sinks, floors, and counters cleaned and readied by Jane's hand, she twirled with pleasure, as if we'd landed in a palace. She said it would take her a while to believe it was real. She said maybe I'd withdraw my money or change my mind and leave her. Of course, I said she was crazy. That was always my line to say. Promises fell from my lips like seeds in spring.

And Jane was a good gardener. She helped me plant my promises on schedule—promises that would bloom and silence me down the road. If the day came that I had to withdraw, I think she knew I'd be stuck. I would have to admit to being a filthy, traitorous liar, like all the rest.

My family recalls a distressing sequence of events here, when I became a certified mouthpiece for Jane and receded fully from my own familiar nature. Dad describes a phone call he received in which I suggested he might send funds for *two* graduate school tuitions—

Jane's and mine. Apparently I wasn't specific about either of our academic plans, and certainly neither of us had applied anywhere that I know of, but nevertheless I lobbied for cash.

"We can discuss tuition for *you*," Dad said. "But I'm not sure why you'd ask me to sponsor someone I don't even know."

"But she's had it hard all her life," I replied. "Jane has never had the kind of love and support from her family like I do, and she deserves a break." Which was exactly how I felt—from Mr. Friedlander, through the razors and loony bin, and then her disbelieving parents, I felt soiled and guilty for having had it so comparatively easy all my life. I wanted Jane to feel the security I had, with money, love, and hope for a future. My mission was also a perfect foil at the time, a bottomless distraction from getting on with my own life or saving myself.

"It's the first time I can remember easily saying no to you," Dad says now. "The request was so bizarre, so unlike you. Of course, I wondered what was going on over there. For sure, I worried about this Jane."

My brother got his phone call in Washington, D.C., around this time, from a high school friend of mine who lived near him. Mary was one of the few old friends who had kept track of me after high school, and we talked on the phone sometimes. Apparently I had mentioned casually to Mary that Jane said my mother would have wanted me to take care of her. And I had said that I felt Jane knew Mom, somehow channeled her, even though they never met. Mary was alarmed. She relayed my condition to Grant, and he was quickly on the phone to me.

It was evening when he called, and Jane was cooking while I sat on my futon, chewing my nails. "I'm coming out," my brother said brightly. "I've got some work in the Bay Area, so let's get together."

"Really?" I said, trying to sound happy. "Where are you staying?"

"Oh. Well, I could find a hotel . . . If you don't have any room."

We barely had room to walk, and the idea of adding my brother to our strange arrangement made me giggle. "It's just the one room here," I said. "Otherwise—"

"That's fine," Grant interrupted. He had slipped into his parental tone. "So where does Jane sleep?" he asked.

"Walk-in closet," I replied, as if that made perfect sense.

"Uh-huh." He exhaled loudly.

Jane came around the corner, asking who was on the phone. "Grant," I answered, covering the receiver. "Coming out here," I added, rolling my eyes.

Jane came closer, curious. "When?" she asked. Grant was talking in my ear, so I raised a finger and said, "Sorry, what?" to him.

"I was *saying*," he continued, "if you want, I can take you and Jane out to dinner when I come. I'd like to meet her."

"He wants to meet you," I said to Jane.

She said, "Let me talk to him."

"No," Grant said hurriedly. "Just make a reservation somewhere. I'll be in town next week."

It was Jane's smart idea to get a reservation at Chez Panisse, possibly the most expensive restaurant in all of Northern California. We picked Grant up at his Holiday Inn, and he sat in the backseat while Jane and I giggled in front. Periodically she glanced back at my brother and made conversation. I heard her subtle digs about his heartless job, amusement at his interests, and side comments about the suit he wore. All the while I felt giddy in my tight alliance with her.

At dinner, Grant recalls, we sat across from him in a booth and drifted for long stretches into private jokes and coded language.

"I loathed her," Grant admitted later. "She had the strangest control over you, to the point of answering when I asked *you* questions. And there was nothing I could do—you were so stuck in this woman, and seemed to love it. All I could do was pay the massive bill and go back home."

Meanwhile, Jane had started bringing Susan over to our studio after work. They drank wine and read poems to each other on my bed while I paced. Susan rubbed Jane's feet, and Jane gazed at her with devoted eyes.

"I'm going out," I would say.

"No, you're not," Jane would return.

"I'll be back in a while."

"Why?"

"I have nowhere to sit," I would try.

Jane would point to the kitchen chair, crowded against a wall. "Sit there," she'd command. "Talk to us."

My desire to flee at these times was overwhelming, but conflict was worse. So I sat down and tried not to look where Jane's hands went while I conversed about the weather.

At night, Jane's walk-in closet was singing with sex. Shrieks and giggles poured under the door as I smoked out the window, dangling by my waist.

"What are you *doing?*" Jane shrieked, catching me halfway to a bloody death.

I dropped the cigarette and watched it swish to the sidewalk. She pulled my heels and reeled me in.

When I stood in front of her, dizzy and reeking of smoke, she tried not to laugh. Then she got mad. "You are embarrassing me," she hissed, motioning toward Susan, who was peeking at us from the closet. "Stop with the fucking cigarettes." She let me have a swift knuckle punch to the arm.

"*Ow.*"

"That's nothing compared with what you'll feel if you don't cut it out," Jane said. "Cut it out, okay?"

I knew I should quit. My lungs were giving me trouble, and my coughing kept both of us up some nights. I felt weak willed. Weak and embarrassed that Susan had witnessed it.

"I'm sorry," I said. "I know. I have to stop."

For that Jane hugged me. Into my ear she whispered that she wished Susan would go away so we could stay up and talk. I never needed more than that.

It's the mark of a true pro that Jane could turn such agonizing events as Susan's sleep-overs into convincing arguments that I was unwell.

"You know what's wrong with you?" she asked after Susan had left. She stood at the kitchen counter, breaking my cigarettes into little pieces. "It's grief."

The tobacco spilled onto the floor.

"Lungs are where grief is stored," she explained. "You have to let your grief breathe, honey, not poison it."

There are actually people who would agree with that—smart people, in the business of lungs and grief. And this was the tricky thing about Jane: sometimes she stepped into pools of clarity, of insight, and not only sincerely cared about someone else, but cared about herself. And in these times, if I listened hard, I heard little confessions. Sometimes I thought I heard remorse.

I wanted to smoke more than ever when Jane chopped up my cigarettes, which became a regular ceremony. I wanted to torch the remains and inhale. Jane had tried to scare me out of smoking, tried hitting, crying, hiding them, and shredding. But I'd done that and more with my mother, so I was way ahead of her. One day, she brushed the tobacco mess into a trash can, placed a bottle in front of me, and said, "Garlic pills."

I drew a blank.

"Take these every time you get the urge. No more smoking, or I'll kill you."

"You're kidding," I said, holding the bottle.

"Garlic," Jane said. "Or death."

So when my body was racked with anxiety, when I was trapped on my bed, listening to Jane have sex, or forced to entertain Jane's lovers with witty repartee, I was supposed to take a garlic pill.

And *I* was sick.

So I became crafty. I learned better ways to sneak. I disappeared with mints, hand lotion, and my Kents, making sure all traces were gone when Jane found me next. I got good at lying, saying I'd been in the bookstore bathroom or forgotten something in my car. I always volunteered to empty the trash at home and gladly ran out for the ice cream, pizza, movies, or suddenly essential bath oils needed to soothe Jane's worried heart. I was handy. On the way back I smoked in alleys, behind trees, up on the roof, and on fire escapes. And for months I ate garlic pills by the gross.

When a studious-looking man started visiting me at Sorrell's, I was taken by surprise but delighted. He said he was a photojournalist. I had helped him find books about Diane Arbus, and we'd gotten to talking about my favorites, Margaret Bourke-White and Walker Evans. His name was Stewart, and my stomach flipped when one day he asked me out on a date.

"He's, like, thirty years old," Jane carped. "He *says* he's a photojournalist, but he's probably a checkout clerk at Walgreens."

I primped in front of my mirror and said, "Well, he's coming in an hour."

Jane ran a bath and called me in for lifeguard duty. I came around the corner, holding lipstick. "Talk to me," she said, pointing to the toilet.

"I don't have time," I said. "I haven't picked out what I'm going to wear."

Jane said, "Cripes," and rolled her eyes.

After trying on every piece of clothing I owned, and even some of Jane's, I settled on the first skirt and button-down shirt I'd selected to begin with. Then I watched out the window until I saw my date coming down the sidewalk. He was actually whistling.

Jane was on the phone having an extra-animated conversation with Milo, a new guy at work. She'd taken a fast interest in him, ever since his first day. "I'm going downstairs," I told her, waving good-bye. Jane didn't react or seem to hear.

Stewart was checking his tie in a shop window when I came down. He wore a handsome suit and the kind of sunglasses that can transform an ordinary-looking man into Mel Gibson. He blushed when I caught him.

"I thought Il Fornio," he said, touching my back. "And I don't know if you're interested, but the Stanford Theater is playing *All About Eve* again. . . ."

I hopped in the air. "I know," I smiled. "Yes. Perfect."

As we crossed the street, I glanced over my shoulder at our third-floor apartment. Jane was at the open window, watching. Seeing me turn, she stepped away.

"You look great," Stewart said.

I cleared the lump forming in my throat and thanked him.

I thought about Jane on and off during dinner and simultaneously thought how nice it would be to lie in bed with Stewart. To feel the weight of maleness again, in and on me, to feel the way I used to about love.

"What kinds of stories have you photographed?" I asked as we walked to the theater.

"Mostly overseas," he said. "Political pieces." He paused by a magazine rack, opened *Life* magazine, and said, "Here's one." I looked at his three photos, saw his byline, and then bought the magazine. A Walgreens clerk he was not.

The next day, Jane was in a grisly mood. She stayed in bed while I dressed, her door partly closed. When I peeked in, she told me by her expression that I should go away.

But I was still giddy about my night and undeterred. Anyway, I knew the remedy.

"I'm going shopping," I said, brushing my hair. "Anything you want?"

Jane's door creaked open just a bit.

"I was thinking J. Crew," I added, "Pottery Barn . . ."

"Shoes?" Jane asked, pushing the door a little more. "I need shoes."

She softened during breakfast, had enough eggs, toast, home fries, and coffee for both of us, and even went so far as to say it was a pretty day. A good day.

By the time we were trolling the third shoe store, Jane was back to her chatty, witty self. "Honey, you have to get these shoes," she said, holding up a pair. I backed away, shaking my head. They were dull brown and orthopedic looking. Possibly they were the ugliest shoes I'd ever seen.

"Try them on," she directed.

"No. No way." I shook my head and pointed down to a pair of fantastic knee-high boots, already on my feet. They were soft black leather. They zipped up the back with a thin braid finishing the top. Sleek and stylish, I thought, with a good heel. "I like these," I said, wobbling toward her.

Jane said, "Boots? You? In those?"

"No?" I asked. She was my fashion guru, so her approval was critical.

"Honey. You are . . . easy to wear—reliable, comfortable, dependable." She handed me the ugly brown shoes. "*These* are you."

I folded my arms and sighed.

"Try them on," she barked.

"I'll take an eight," I said quickly, to the clerk.

"Eight and a half," Jane corrected.

"Eight and a half," I agreed.

"I'll try these," she said, handing the clerk a pair of Gore-Tex-lined all-terrain boots. "Six and a half."

I sniffed as the clerk took away my boots, and I slipped my feet into the orthopedic shoes. They were comfortable, really comfortable, but besides being ugly, the toes were extra wide, so it looked like I had duck feet.

"Fantastic," Jane said.

"Really?" It was hard to believe, but if Jane said they were cool, I had every reason to believe they were.

Having settled that I would take my shoes, Jane pranced before a mirror in hers, looking to me for judgment. "They're great," I said. They were indeed. And the most expensive shoe in the store.

When we stepped out the door my old shoes were in a bag, the ugly shoes were on my feet, and I was several hundred dollars poorer.

"Onward," Jane said as we hit the sidewalk. Tower Records awaited.

I had never refused Jane a purchase, not until our next stop, a little store just a few doors down from where we lived, where Jane held up a $300 cashmere blanket.

"We have blankets," I said. "No blanket is worth three hundred dollars."

She said, "But it's so soft—can you imagine napping under this?"

I looked at an overpriced trash bin. "How about this?" I suggested.

Jane sighed loudly and turned to a rack of Stussy shirts, which were apparently all the rage.

I couldn't find her when I brought the trash can to the counter. Then I heard my name, called from the sidewalk outside. She was waving at me to come join her.

"Look what I got," she said, as we walked together down the street. She unbuttoned the top of her shirt and showed me a cotton Stussy underneath.

"You bought it?" I asked.

"Are you kidding? For sixty dollars?"

I stopped in my tracks. "You *stole* it?"

Jane shrugged.

"How did you—"

"I'll show you sometime." She smiled. "It's easy."

I could have wagged a finger at her then, or marched her back to the store, the way my mother had done when I'd once pinched Wint-O-Green Life Savers from Annie's Market in St. Louis. The humiliation of that moment in front of Annie had been very effective. But after Jane's endearing wink, and her joyful bounce forward, tugging me to the next shop for us to browse, I couldn't help but think she'd pulled off a great stunt and saved us $60 in the package. I giggled with amusement and followed her happily down the street.

When it came to stealing, ever since my Wint-O-Green debacle, I had always possessed a highly preventive fear of getting caught. But it turned out that I was even more averse to disappointing Jane, which became an expected outcome if I wasn't genuinely cheerful about her spoils. And Jane, I gradually realized, had also begun taking books from Sorrell's without paying for them. Working from the inside, I supposed, it wasn't hard to get them out, unless you had a conscience.

"We're paid nothing," Jane reasoned. "The store won't collapse because a few books are gone." And she proceeded to take home books she fancied, with my blessing.

I think Jane did believe that her thefts were righteous. I think she felt she'd already been robbed on such a colossal level that the world owed her whatever she took. And I readily joined her on that planet of thought. We made such a perfect pair—Jane felt the world owed her, and I felt I owed the world.

Meanwhile, one of my daily jobs at work was to apprehend shoplifters, of which there were many, and some were pretty clever. The most unlikely people would do it—men in business suits exiting with erotica tucked in their pants, competent-looking mothers hiding dictionaries and toys beneath their babies in strollers. Alarms would sound as they walked through our gates, and if I was closest to the door, I would apprehend them. They seemed such unlikely suspects, but so did Jane, on the surface. As I took Polaroids of the shoplifters to hang in the back room, I silently cringed at the irony.

Like so many of the mental lines I'd already crossed, this moral lapse seemed to slip past me at the time like one more crack on the highway. But it was an important crack. So far, I was only an accomplice. But how long would it take before the next crack crossed under my wheels? And how fast would I be going?

Chapter
TWENTY-TWO

"My mother likes to keep busy," Jane warned me on the day Linda was set to arrive. "No time to think." In preparation, Jane had made detailed plans, outlining every minute of her three-day visit. There was a special breakfast at Alice's Restaurant in the Woodside Hills, a stop at the ocean to watch the sea lions, then lunch, shopping, and, after dinner, a trip to a hip new circus called Cirque du Soleil.

After taking the red-eye flight, Linda entered our studio looking stressed, in a polite sort of way. I reached for her hand. She pulled me in for a hug.

"Hey," Jane said.

Linda ruffled her hair and said, "Hiya, Jane."

She stepped into our one room and said, "Yep, it's small." She looked at me and added, "Where do you sleep?"

I turned sideways to include Jane. "Jane has the walk-in closet," I explained.

Jane pointed. "My cave," she said. "It's yours while you're here."

Linda looked at me again and asked, "Where do *you* sleep?" I pointed to my futon, which was folded up into a sofa.

"We call it the *Titanic.*" Jane giggled. "Because it sinks."

Linda laughed politely.

Our first stop was breakfast, and because I had to go to work, I tailed Jane and her mom in my car. Linda was excited for the long drive, which took us through hills and past big mansions. Afterward, they planned to watch the sea lions in Half Moon Bay.

As we drove, I could see Linda's bare feet propped out the window the way Jane liked to do, and they were chatting back and forth in what looked to be a happy exchange. Then Jane rolled through a stop sign, and revolving lights cut in front of me and chased her to the side of the road.

I thought it was funny. Parked behind them, I took my camera, which I'd brought to record Linda's visit, and I pointed it at Jane's side mirror. I could see her speaking to the officer, not hiding her anger. I groaned, seeing hostile words come spitting from Jane's mouth. When she gave the officer the finger, I pivoted my lens to see what Linda was doing. She was shouting at Jane. Zooming in on the policeman, I could see him call for backup.

Jane started to open her door, and the policeman pushed it shut with his foot, causing her to shout, "Motherfucker!" so loud that I heard it clearly over passing traffic. The policeman yelled something back. Jane opened her door again and stepped out, fists in the air. Then Linda shot out of *her* door and yelled at Jane to get back in and shut up. The policeman radioed again for help.

Once she was faced with two blue uniforms, Jane finally signed a ticket that admitted her guilt.

Weeks later, when we went together to pay the ticket, after waiting in two wrong lines, Jane stepped up to the desk at City Hall, ready for a fight.

"I'm not paying this," she informed the officer.

"License plate number?" he asked.

Jane slammed the ticket down on the counter. The man eyed her, then typed the number into his computer. He couldn't hide his surprise.

"Wow. Looks like you have a few other parking tickets to settle. Four hundred eighty dollars in parking tickets." He smiled.

My jaw dropped.

"What?" Jane said. "I'm not here for that."

He looked at the new ticket. "For this you can pay now or elect to appear in court."

Jane looked at me, steaming.

"Do we have to pay *everything* now?" I inquired.

"Or her car will be booted and towed," he finished. "And every day it costs more."

Jane stared at the officer. "You should be ashamed," she said.

"Excuse me?"

"This is a hideous racket—provide no parking, then ticket everybody? And this one"—she held up the new ticket—"that cop abused me. He should be fired."

I pulled out my checkbook. "I'll pay," I said.

"Driver's license?" the officer asked me. I produced it.

"Well, well, well," he said moments later. "*You* owe three hundred sixteen dollars, Ms. Kraus. You are *also* on our list of cars to boot and tow." He suppressed a laugh.

"*Motherfucker!*" Jane exclaimed.

The officer pointed a finger at her and said, "I can put you in jail."

"Whoa!" I interjected. "Everybody simmer down." I put Jane behind me, switched from my checkbook to a credit card, and asked the officer, "So what's the grand total, then?"

We were late for work after that, which caused Tom to request our presence in his office. We were on thin ice, he said. Get in on time or get out for good. I promised we'd improve.

When Jane and I manned the registers, she said, "I'm really sorry about the tickets."

"Yeah," I said. "Well, we've single-handedly improved the roads and schools in San Francisco. That's something for the résumé."

When a woman approached and handed Jane a book and some cash, Jane pretended to make a sale on the register, then handed the woman her book and some change, leaving the cash beside the register. When the woman turned away, Jane pocketed the cash.

I didn't even blink.

After the incident with the policeman, breakfast with Jane and her mother had been quiet, but Linda tried hard to be pleasant. She laughed that the policeman had sure met his match, and Jane relaxed a little. That evening we readied ourselves for the Cirque du Soleil. Jane had done her homework with that choice; the idea was a big hit with Linda, and Jane resurrected Garrett from the archives to join us. Amazingly, he came.

Once we found our seats at the circus, I excused myself. After puffing behind the concessions stand and eating a pack of mints, I returned to my seat just as the show was starting.

"Ohmygod. You *smoked?*" Jane asked loudly.

Garrett leaned across Jane, and Linda leaned across Garrett. "What?" they said in unison.

"She smoked," Jane said.

"*You* smoke?" Linda asked me.

"No, no," I said. "I must have just passed someone who smoked."

"And sucked on their skin?" Jane asked.

Garrett excused himself. Linda moved over.

"But why would you smoke?" Linda asked. "Your mother—"

I groaned.

"Died from it," Jane finished. "Sometimes I don't know why I care."

Right in front of us, a man balanced a woman on each shoulder while he sang and lassoed a little boy. And yet, they continued to be more interested in me.

"It's not like I chain-smoke," I said. "I hardly smoke at all."

Linda muttered something about the burden of children.

Jane said, "Your promises mean nothing."

I sulked through the rest of the show and felt Jane's anger as we walked to our cars.

"Do you think it's serious with Garrett?" Linda whispered as he and Jane trailed behind us. She locked arms with me and glanced over her shoulder at the happy couple.

The sheer weight of what I couldn't say rendered me mute.

"He seems nice." She sighed. "My guess is Jane will drive him away within a month."

I glanced at Linda, surprised.

"I'm realistic," she shrugged. "I'm not getting my hopes up."

Back at home, Jane, Linda, and I sat with mugs of tea on the *Titanic*.

"I think I could marry him," Jane blurted after a silence. She looked at my puzzled expression and said, *"Garrett."*

Linda pursed her lips.

"He likes me," Jane said, looking at her mother defensively.

I was wondering how Susan fit into all of this or, for that matter, how I fit into all of this.

"I like Garrett," Linda said.

Jane's jaw tightened. "We'll have to get a big house," she said to me. "One wing for you, one wing for me and Garrett."

"Oh, for God's sake," Linda said. "That's not normal."

Jane said, "I'm not aiming for normal, Mom."

"Well, bull's-eye," Linda shot back.

I offered my usual, "Hey now."

Jane seethed.

"Okay, I'm going to bed," Linda said. "In a closet."

Jane paced while her mother slept, and I lay in bed, looking out the window.

"Fine," I said, "I smoked. I'm sorry."

Jane said, "Whatever, Caroline, they're your lungs."

That made me worry. I never got off the hook that easily.

"Okay. I'm going out," she said.

"What? Where are you going?"

Jane grabbed her coat and went out the door.

The next morning, Linda was anxious. We were sitting on my bed, which had been turned back into a sofa, waiting. I checked my watch. Linda stared at the clock on my dresser. "I don't like sitting here waiting for the queen," she said. "Jane doesn't realize that the world turns without her."

"I'm sure she'll be here soon," I said.

"It's not like I visit every day," Linda huffed. "It cost me three hundred dollars to come here—*with* frequent flier miles."

"She's really glad you came," I said. "She was excited about it all week. She got her hair done—did you notice?"

"She's got nice hair," Linda admitted. "Gets it from her father."

The phone rang.

"Hey," Jane yawned when I picked up.

"Where are you?" I hissed.

"Susan's. Is Mom up?"

"We've been up for a while. . . ."

"Why don't you take her to the city, honey, and show her the sights."

"Oh no, I think you should get over here," I said.

"Let's just go," Linda said flatly.

"I heard that," said Jane. In the background Susan said something about coffee.

Linda found her purse, stood by the door, and waited.

"Go for a ride on the trolley car," Jane suggested. "Mom will love that. Please, honey?"

I could tell that saying yes would earn me big points, and Linda was growing on me anyway, so I said sure and told Jane not to worry.

We both loved the trolley. We caught one on Hyde Street and hung off the edge the way they did in the commercials. We had been enjoying each other's company all morning, but as we clanged our way up and down the steep hills, Linda seemed to fade in spirit. She muttered through clenched teeth, "Typical," and shook her head at me. I knew she was thinking of Jane.

We stopped for lunch and sat across from each other with a big salad between us. I could tell that Linda wanted to talk about her daughter, and she began on the defensive.

"I've tried everything," she said after apologizing about the explosion at their dinner table. "But Jane has always been wild, and I never know what's going to happen. I keep hoping things will get normal with her, but they never do for long."

Cautiously, I ventured to tell Linda what I'd been suppressing for a long time. "It would help if you let her know you believed her," I said. "About the abuse."

Linda stiffened. She said, "But Caroline, that *didn't* happen. I was there, trust me. It's not the kind of thing a mother misses, and it's exactly the kind of manipulative tactic Jane has used all her life. I would have known. I would have known if he'd done that to her."

"Well, I don't think she *invented* it," I said hotly.

Linda pointed her fork at me. "Don't fall for this. Please. Jane is always hoping someone will."

"Linda," I said, "it happened."

"Oh my," she said. "No wonder Jane likes you so much. You're perfect for her."

"But how can you be so sure it didn't happen? I mean, sometimes parents don't know."

"You have no idea what went on," Linda said. "You have only what Jane tells you, and my guess is she's been pretty selective. I mean, *Caroline*, she still sucks her thumb. At her age."

"But doesn't that suggest that something is *wrong?*" I cried. "That something might have *happened?*"

"Yes, something happened," Linda said bitterly. "She has an evil streak. From the day she was born."

My eyes widened.

"I don't understand why smart girls like you are so easily taken in," Linda continued. "Once again I thought Jane was straightening out, having a normal friend like you. But now I see she's just taking you for a ride, like everybody else."

I couldn't believe what I was hearing. Any mother, I thought, should support her child no matter what. It never occurred to me that Linda could be right. In retrospect, I should have listened closer to Linda. Maybe I would have realized that whatever was true, her apparent desire to see her daughter thrive instead of self-destruct showed that she sincerely believed what she was telling me. But instead of considering her point of view, I thought of Jane, wherever she was, and felt renewed solidarity. If her mother wouldn't step up, then I vowed that I would. I asked for the check.

Linda leaned across the table and looked at me, deflated. "You can say I'm cruel," she sighed, "but you have no understanding of what it was like to raise Jane. You can't step in now and think that you have a better handle on what makes my daughter tick."

We stared at each other in stubborn silence.

Linda said, "I do love her. Of course I do. I'm here, aren't I? But honestly, sometimes I don't like her very much. But every time I think I've given up hope, or that I'm finally too tired of the havoc she wreaks on our family, Jane says or does something that makes me try again. She's mine, and I love her. I'll always hope, and I'll always worry about her. I do want her to be safe and productive in the world. But Jane ruins everything—you've seen it yourself. She ruined this day, she's ruined this trip, and I'm beginning to think she might ruin your life, if you don't open your eyes. You can believe she was molested, or whatever you want. But don't ask me to. I won't participate. Never."

As Linda paid our tab, I told her that I did, and would always, believe Jane. I said that I believed her because nothing short of the trauma she described could explain the woman I knew. Looking back, Linda was at the very least partly right—my determination to fix Jane was a hopeless, wrongheaded mission. But no one could argue there wasn't something there to fix. And I wanted to make it right. I wanted to make it right for all of us.

Before we left the table—never to revisit the subject again—I asked Linda, rhetorically, which was more risky: believing a lie or not believing the truth.

She replied, with a sigh that spoke volumes, "Worse for *whom?*"

TWENTY-THREE

After Linda left, Jane must have rediscovered that Garrett was boring, because he was formally excused, again. She resumed spending nights with Susan, but more and more I also encountered Milo in our studio, the new guy from the store. Suddenly *they* were rolling around in the walk-in closet, with him periodically opening the door for air and Jane winking over his shoulder. Jane was on a bender, gone for days, staying with Milo or Susan, I wasn't sure.

This left me at loose ends, although I did welcome the free time to smoke. I smoked and worried and periodically urged myself to get my life together. Wasn't there a career I had wanted once? A life? But then Jane would return just in time—wooing me back with her affection and company, with the happy ordinariness that had always glued us between crises: simple trips to get groceries, regular nights at the movies, serene breakfasts and *The New York Times*—right before I remembered the answer.

The details of these calm periods have faded in my memory, in comparison with the cascade of calamities that Jane and I either produced or endured. But in terms of dissecting our bond, they were equally revealing. The calm periods were evidence that, given other backgrounds or circumstances, Jane and I might have made good friends in the best sense of the word. Jane wasn't always scheming, and I wasn't always unhinged, desperate, or smoking. It might have been easier for me to unhook or escape had only trauma filled our days. But sometimes all of that receded, and normal life seemed just within our reach. With Jane, it was like seeing the wizard drop his curtain, revealing an old man who'd been faking as best as he could. With me, it was like waking from a dream.

But the calm periods were fleeting, and before long, at work, I could hardly speak to Milo. I knew too many personal details about him, like the high whimper that escaped when he released into Jane, or the paleness of his naked backside racing past my half-open eyes to the bathroom, or the Snoopy boxers he wore, which Jane liked to throw from the closet onto my lap. After he left, I sat on the toilet seat for long stretches, hearing about Milo's sexual technique ("anemic") in comparison with Susan's ("naive"). Eventually Susan suspected something and came to me at work for advice.

"I don't know what I did," she said, pulling me aside. "Did I do something?"

"Jane works in mysterious ways," I replied cryptically.

"She always talks about you," Susan said. "Like you hung the moon. Every trail ends at Caroline, so I figured you might have some insight . . . ?"

"Oh."

"Is it Milo?" she whispered. "I see them together, all the time."

I kept quiet.

"It's so confusing," she said.

I nodded. "Yes."

She pulled me deeper into the stacks and whispered, "You know, I never slept with a woman before Jane."

I tried not to smile.

"She's like . . . all-powerful or something," Susan said, twisting her hair.

Suddenly I envied her. When all her misery cleared, she would be free. For the first time, I said something helpful.

"I think you should give up," I said.

Susan's eyes got big. "Why? What do you know?"

I gave her a stare, as if that were communicating something.

"Milo?" she asked.

"Just go. Run. Before she changes her mind."

Susan turned white. Crushed. I saw Jane searching the store for me, standing on a chair at the information desk. I added, "And don't look back."

Days later, Jane had me back on the toilet lid, playing therapist while she took a bath. The expensive candles were lit, which meant the session was serious.

"I can't believe it," she said. Her jaw was quivering, and she held her knees to her chest, rocking in the water. "She won't return my calls, and she didn't open her door when I went over." She stared at her toes. "And I know she was there. I could hear her breathing."

As a rule, my job while on the toilet was to agree with Jane. I made the mistake of stepping out of character when I said, "You *are* sleeping with Milo, though."

Jane turned her head slowly, like a bird. "But Susan doesn't know that," she said.

"Oh," I said. "Right."

Jane started soaping up, and she asked me to scrub her back. I took the sea sponge and started scrubbing. "Does she?" she asked.

"No, I guess not."

"Then will you talk to her?" she asked. "Explain that I'm devastated, and all I want to do is talk."

I imagined how strange that conversation would be, given my warning to Susan. "But don't you like Milo?" I said. "Maybe you should focus on him. He's nice."

"Just talk to Susan," Jane said. "Make her understand."

I was feeling pretty silly as I walked to Susan's house, bearing a chocolate cake that Jane had baked and a book of Anne Sexton poetry. I knocked on her door and smiled like an idiot when she opened it.

"Hi, Caroline," she said, looking at the cake.

"Jane asked me to bring this over," I said, handing it to her. "And she said you like Anne Sexton, so here's this. It's out of print, I think. Jane wants you to have it."

Susan looked at me, confused. "What's going on?"

"That's all," I said.

She looked doubtful. "Do you want to come in?"

"No, that's all," I said, backing away.

Susan grabbed my arm. "Oh no, you don't," she said. "You have to explain this."

I stepped inside. Books lined her walls and lay stacked on the floor. Classical music was playing—Bach, I thought. I saw a row of books by Pauline Kael and went right over to see if her collection was bigger than mine.

"Do you like Kael?" she asked. She opened the cake box and looked in. "What the hell," she said. "Let's eat the damn cake."

"I do," I said, touching the spines of each title. My finger landed on *When the Lights Go Down*. Out of print. I didn't have that one.

Susan handed me a piece of cake. "I better not," I said.

"Why?" She smiled. "You've earned it."

It struck me that she was on to something. I took a bite.

"So why are you here, *really?*" Susan asked. "Not that it's not good to see you."

My mouth was full when I gave up and replied, "To win you back for Jane."

"Oh. Geeze. Don't you have anything better to do?" she asked. "And weren't you the one who said, 'Run and don't look back'?"

"Yes on both."

"Well, you're not doing a very good job of winning me back," Susan said.

I said, "Oh well," and stood to go.

"Hold on," she said. "Sit down."

I sat.

"I'm worried about you," she said.

"*You* look good, though," I redirected. "Happy."

Susan nodded. "Honestly? I think you saved my life. I feel like I've been through some kind of intervention and come out sober on the other side. It's like I have my whole life back."

"That's great," I said.

"Tell me something," she said. "Have you and Jane slept together?"

"Oh no," I said quickly. I shook my head for emphasis. "Nope."

Susan squinted at me. Then she said, "Well, that's good. Because I think she captures people that way."

"Hmm." I chewed my fingernail and scanned the ceiling.

"I mean, have you seen Milo lately? He's like a walking catatonic."

"Yeah, he doesn't look good," I admitted.

"And you were dating a really cute guy for a while—Stan or something?"

"Stewart." I looked at the door. "He . . . gave up."

"Oh," Susan said sympathetically.

That wasn't completely accurate. Lots of little crises had flared up after our few dates, I couldn't remember them all specifically. Jane's wallet might have been lost, and we had to scour the shops to find it, or my car had been towed, or I had bronchitis again, or I was caught smoking and in trouble. Circumstances seemed endlessly to intervene. It might have looked as though I'd lost interest.

"I'm leaving for Peru," Stewart had told me the last time I saw him. We were taking a walk during my lunch break at work, and I was pretty sure he wanted off the hook.

"How long?" I asked.

"I don't know," he said. "A few months."

"I'll look for your photographs," I said cheerfully.

Everything about us felt awkward, and we were passing the same fancy house that Jane and I had claimed as our own. I remember thinking how happy Jane would be when I told her it was over with Stewart, pretty much before it had begun. In my heart of hearts, I was relieved that he was going; one less thing to hide or lie about at home.

Susan delivered some parting instructions when I stood at her door. "Tell Jane I said no," she said firmly. "Tell her you tried your best, but I was definite."

I nodded and thanked her. I was at the elevator when she dashed out her door, calling for me to wait. "Here," she said, handing me the Kael book I'd lingered over. "Now we're even."

Jane disintegrated after Susan's rejection. She stayed in her closet reading and refused to go to work. In the evening, I came home and heard her in the bath.

I grabbed a towel and took my seat.

"Everything okay?" I asked.

"Sure," she said. She moved a loofah up and down her arms.

"Did you eat today?"

"No. I don't know. Yeah."

Jane's knees broke the water and then her thighs. Fresh razor cuts peeked at me through the soap and then disappeared.

"Jane . . ." I stood up.

"Mmmm." She smiled.

"Oh no." I crouched at the edge of the tub. *"Why?"*

She raised her legs again and pressed the welts, wincing with pleasure.

"Jane is on *really* thin ice now," Tom told me at work some days later. "She hasn't even called in."

"She's under the weather," I explained.

"It's not just the skipping work," he said. "Tell her we need to meet. Soon."

I called Jane right away.

"What," she grumbled. That's how she answered our phone.

"You'd better come in. Tom seems pretty steamed."

"That's news?"

"He says you're on thin ice."

"Okay, then," Jane said. "Tell old Tom cat I quit."

"What?"

"Better yet, I'll do it myself." Then she hung up.

A while later Tom came to find me. I was helping a man in battle fatigues find the *Anarchist Cookbook*. Tom caught my arm and led me away.

"What is the *Anarchist Cookbook?*" I whispered.

"It shows you how to build bombs, nuclear devices, that sort of thing," he said. "How to fire weapons, break into laboratories, steal, and such."

I looked back at the man in his big camouflage coat. "Should we be selling that?" I asked.

"Probably not," Tom remarked. "People always steal it."

I kept an eye on the anarchist as Tom said, "So Jane quit."

"She didn't mean it," I said quickly.

"She probably wasn't going to last here anyway," he said.

"Can you give her another chance?" I asked. "One more chance."

The anarchist walked away, holding the book.

"Frankly," Tom said, "it would be better for you if she's not here."

"Why?"

"Because you don't work when she's around," he said. "You've completely dropped off the planet. I never see you at Julian's or River's anymore. You are the ghost of Caroline past." He looked sternly into my face. "Maybe now you can rematerialize?"

"We're moving to Berkeley," Jane informed me when I got home.

"What?"

She pulled pictures off her closet wall and said, "Fuck 'em. Palo Alto is a boring middle-class wasteland. We're dying here, anyway."

"Berkeley?"

"Moby's books," Jane said. "We can get jobs there."

"But our apartment—money . . ."

"That's your department."

"I'll lose the deposit. And really, money is running out."

"Welcome to my world," she said.

When the wall was empty, she collapsed on her bed. She put her thumb in her mouth and looked at me. "I got us each interviews at Moby's books. It's up to you. Stella says I can stay with her, so whatever."

"Stella?"

"Um-hm. Stella."

"Didn't you have a huge fight?"

"Did we?" Jane asked. "Well, it's over if we did."

Stella had returned from her fellowship a few months before and scored a job at a hospital in the city. She'd called our place periodically, her voice more worried each time, and when Jane listened to her voice on our machine, she either made wisecracks or simply rolled her eyes.

"That's good," I said doubtfully. I had a strange affection for Stella, which seemed to grow even though we'd hardly had any contact. Increasingly, I felt a cosmic kinship with her, knowing she had an affliction similar to mine.

"But I thought you couldn't stand her anymore," I said, wanting to understand.

"Honey," Jane said sternly, "Stella is my business. We go way back, and I'll always have her in my life."

Jane got the job, no references needed. She wanted to get moved and start right away. I was also offered a spot, on Jane's recommendation. "I'm going to stay with Stella while you make up your mind," she told me.

If I had been looking for an out, a chance to break free from Jane, this would have been it. But maybe Jane knew I was so far gone that she didn't need to worry. She saw my fear as she packed her things and my tears when she drove away for Stella's. And she probably knew there was nothing left for me in Palo Alto after she was gone.

The consequences of moving were steep—I'd be broke, in a place with no friends other than Jane, and far from Stanford University, where I'd still harbored hopes of studying. While Jane set up at Stella's, I continued at Sorrell's alone.

River, I discovered, was dating a new guy. They were a full-blown item. Julian had turned nocturnal, and switched completely to the night shift. I didn't see him anymore. I approached Angela to see if she wanted to go to the movies.

"What? No Jane?" she quipped. "How will you survive?"

"Do you want to go to a movie or not?" I asked.

Angela's eyes turned into sleepy slits. "Just like that? You and your twin act like I'm shit, and then I'm supposed to baby-sit you while she's gone?"

I resorted to Faye. She was game right away, even excited to go out. She didn't go to movies, though, only bars, so I joined her at an East Palo Alto dive, and we started drinking.

"Tell me," Faye said with an oily grin, "are you and Lowell a couple or what?"

"We're a *what*."

I couldn't take my eyes off Faye's hair. It was coarse, unwashed, and grayer than I remembered. Her body smelled like sour milk.

"Because you *act* like lovers," she continued. She asked the bartender for a third vodka tonic. "Hold the tonic," she added.

I ordered another Rolling Rock.

Faye started looking at me weird. I leaned away and said, "What are you doing?"

"Sorry," she said. "I'm high as a fucking . . . tree."

We had more drinks, way past my limit. We smoked too much. The air was stale and hot, and I stood up to go home.

Faye teetered off her stool and fumbled for her purse. The bar was empty, except for an old guy reading in the corner. I saw Faye coming at me, I thought for a kiss, but was too drunk to dodge in time. The next thing I knew, I was on the floor looking up.

"She's coming around," the bartender said as he knelt beside me. Faye came into focus above him, puzzled. A glass of water was put to my lips and inadvertently poured down my front. I gagged and rolled to my feet.

"Shit," I mumbled. "What happened?"

Faye kept back, stunned.

After that, I didn't even try to reconnect with my Waverly friends. I had driven past the house a few times and seen Lisette riding with the new girl on her moped. They looked happy. Torsten had a girlfriend—I'd seen them holding hands in town. And Alex just scared me to death. I called Jane and said I was giving notice.

"Don't do it on my account," she said merrily. "Everything is great here, I'm fine."

"Are you going to stay there?" I asked.

"Depends on you," she said. Then I heard Stella in the

background, suggesting Jane invite me over. "Want to come over?" she asked. "We're having rat-tat-tooi." Stella laughed.

"Where should we look for a place?" I asked.

"Honey, you decide. I'm no good at that. And I have to work."

Suddenly Jane's life looked all in order, and mine was a disaster. It was like having the music stop with no chair left for me.

"Are you sure you still want to?" I peeped.

"Honey," Jane said, her voice full of affection. "You shouldn't have to ask."

I got right to apartment hunting. There was nothing in Berkeley, so I searched in San Francisco. Rent was double there, and places were scarce. Jane had said we needed two bedrooms this time and something with charm. Eventually I signed a lease on a big, airy apartment with crisp white walls and fine wood floors. The appointments were old but still elegant—detailed moldings, brass light fixtures, and a kitchen stove that looked like it could drive. My bedroom had a view onto Dolores Park, and Jane's room faced the bay, which we could also see from the roof garden. After covering our first month's rent and deposit, I became acquainted for the first time with insurmountable debt. But I was clever at creating money, at shuffling credit card funds and selling off my belongings, to move us to our next theater of operation. A new bookstore awaited, and a new home, on Hancock Street.

TWENTY-FOUR

Stella and I were knee-deep in moving boxes when Dad called the Hancock apartment. Jane had taken sick, and while Stella and I worked, she lay on her mattress, listening to Enya. I gripped the phone as Dad said, "I've just gotten word from my doctor."

"Doctor?" I said. "What doctor?" I hadn't heard about any damn doctor.

"It's okay," Dad said quickly. "It's just my back."

The last time I'd heard that, Mom's cancer had swallowed her spine.

"What about your back?" I demanded. Jane's head appeared in the hall.

"Well, it turns out there's an infection," Dad said. "I had surgery last week—I'm sure I left you a message about it—and now an abscess has formed. The wound didn't heal like it was supposed to. It's not that serious."

Then I remembered. I had gotten the message and promptly let it escape my mind as I'd raced through the details of moving. "Is it cancer?" I asked.

"Oh no. No, Caroline. It's just an infection. But I've got an intracardiac line in my chest now, for IV antibiotics. And a drain in my back to clear the abscess."

Jane motioned at me about the cancer. I shook my head. Stella staggered in the door, dropping Jane's big duffel bag with a thump. Jane hissed at her to be more careful.

"There's a *drain* in your back?" I asked. "Does it hurt?"

Dad cleared his throat. "Anyway," he said, "I was wondering if you could come home for a while. Just a little while. It's tricky getting the antibiotics in myself—the dosing is every six hours—and at night . . . I'm not walking as well. . . ."

He waited. I didn't say anything.

"It's okay if you can't," he said. But his voice was getting sadder and lonelier by the second.

"What about Gayle?" I asked.

"I'm asking you," he replied.

I bit my lip. Leaving Jane had severe consequences, and as far as I knew, the Void still lived at my father's address.

Jane watched me. "Sure," I said. "I'll come."

He exhaled with a little squeak and said, "Oh, good. Thank you." Jane's head disappeared. I suddenly wondered how I would afford the plane ticket. As far as Dad knew, I still had the money from Mom. I'd have to open another credit card.

"Did you start your new job yet?" Dad asked.

"Yes."

"Do you like it there?"

"It's okay."

"And is Jane working there, too?" he asked.

"Yep."

"You're moved in, then? To this new address?" He was searching for conversation.

I looked at the mounds of boxes. Stella appeared again, sweating and swearing. Jane's portfolio case slapped to the ground. "Getting there," I said. Jane came around the corner, hands on her hips. "I should go, Dad," I added.

"Jane's there, I guess," he said.

"Sure she's here, she lives here."

Dad cleared his throat again. "You just sound different when she's around, that's all."

I didn't touch that.

After we hung up Jane said, "So?"

Stella panted and looked at me, worried.

I said, "I guess my dad's got an infection. He's got a drain . . . in his back. So I need to go home."

Jane said, "What? Why can't your brother do something for once? Or Madeleine? Or Gayle? Why are you always the one?"

"Madeleine and Grant have real jobs," I replied. "And Dad asked me. Maybe Gayle is busy, I don't know."

"What's wrong with his back?" Stella asked. "Is there an abscess?"

"Exactly," I said, impressed.

Jane looked irritated. "What do you know?" she snapped at Stella.

Stella was momentarily stunned. "Well, I *am* a doctor," she replied. Then she turned and went to retrieve another of Jane's bags.

"Cripes, honey. When will you be back?" Jane asked me.

"I don't know," I admitted. "When Dad is better."

"But we have to move in, decorate." She pointed to the blank walls around us. "You can't go. Call him back."

Stella returned, saw us poised for battle, and quickly left for the next load.

"He's my *father*," I said evenly.

"You're an *adult*," she countered.

"And I'm going," I told her. Then I ran after Stella.

.   .   .

Aunt Estie met me at the gate in St. Louis, and as we drove from the airport, she asked me how I was. I thought of the cigarettes hidden in my bag, of my newfound poverty, and of Jane's tantrum before I left, and I said, "Fine." She said I looked thin but that Dad had my favorite beef stew cooking for dinner. The closer we got to home, the more I hoped I could get it down without throwing up.

When we turned onto Price Road I got nervous, the same way I had felt coming home at Christmas. The shady, quiet street was a trigger for memories, with its secret entrances to serene wooded paths, the trails I had explored with Sam bounding ahead.

Aunt Estie pulled into our narrow lane, with Mom's daffodils still waving beneath our mailbox, and we glided past the Reeses' tennis court. The memory of Mom, crouched at that net and denying my forehand, followed me into the garage.

Dad was waiting in the kitchen. He looked older than I remembered, and tired. I reached to kiss him and bumped into a plastic globe around his neck.

"The antibiotics," he explained sheepishly.

"Oh," I said, patting his arm. I looked at his back, and he raised his shirt, revealing a bandage, seeping pink liquid. "Is it working?" I asked.

Aunt Estie got busy at the kitchen sink, clearing a small pile of dishes.

"It's working fine," Dad said. His voice was quiet and thin, the only sign he ever gave of pain.

As soon as I gracefully could, I excused myself to my old room, leaving Aunt Estie and Dad in the kitchen.

Upstairs it was just as I'd left it, only cleaner. Mom had always put flowers in our rooms when we came home, and when I saw a vase of irises sitting on my bureau, I jumped a little, as if seeing a ghost.

The tall bulletin board she'd made was still on my wall, wood covered with yellow burlap. The words *Caroline's Corner*, which had run across the top in white felt, now read *Caroline's Corn*. My old books sat like neglected friends on white plastic stackable shelves that must have been fashionable in the seventies. I ran my fingers across their spines: *The Chronicles of Narnia*, *The Wind in the Willows*, *Peter Rabbit*, *All Things Bright and Beautiful*, *Danny the Champion of the World*. Dad had been a formidable Mr. McGregor and Toad, and Mom a very wise Aslan, a headstrong Peter Rabbit.

I pulled out *Walter the Lazy Mouse* by Marjorie Flack and opened it. Mom had liked to point out that Walter and I had a few things in common. He was "never quite dressed" by the time his family finished breakfast. And when his older brothers and sisters went off to school, he was still eating his cereal. Like me, Walter ran all the way to school, but somehow he would always be late. He was slow to answer in class and even slower around the house. I had always worried about Walter. In the story his family forgets him when they move away (since he was always a step behind), and he takes off to find them. But he gets lost in a forest that, by Mom's description, sounded exactly like the woods around our house.

Now the chapter names seemed all too salient: "How Walter Mouse Lost His Home"; "How Walter Finds a New Home"; "How Walter Does Nothing"; "Danger in the Woods." I flipped to "Danger in the Woods," to the part where Mom's voice always got especially low and ominous.

"Could it be an owl hovering overhead?" she had whispered, pulling me close in her lap. "Could it be a snake, a snake creeping, slipping through the grass? Walter did not know. He dared not call Turtle, he dared not leave the rock, so he stayed there waiting, waiting for he knew not what."

When Dad called upstairs announcing dinner, I jumped, slapping the book closed. I came downstairs cautiously, steeling myself for beef stew, and watched Dad stirring pots through the kitchen doorway. He wore Mom's green-and-white-striped apron and drank a glass of white wine while he stirred. The plastic globe was tossed over his shoulder, swirling with the liquid medicine. The house seemed immense around us and too quiet. I went to put on some music, quick.

At dinner Dad talked about Gayle, how she had gone to Smith College like Mom and rode horses. He said she had a Ph.D. in political science, and she ran her own business, which was remarkable. I poured myself a second glass of wine. All I could think about was how every unmarried woman in town had started calling after Mom died, as if an ad had gone out in the *Post-Dispatch: Now Available! Widowed Doctor, In Good Condition. Wealthy.*

Dad's dental hygienist had called. Society women had sent invitations, and CEOs circled. Women who knew someone who knew someone who knew a friend of Dad's barber had called. I had written down all of their names and numbers, cursing.

Dad and Gayle had met at church, which was in his eyes a point in her favor. The fact that Mom had introduced them added another point, throwing her way ahead of the competition. I was still living at home when Gayle started coming around, and I could see right away that she didn't scare my father like the rest. She was striking, impeccably dressed, smart, patient, and gentle. I saw Dad laugh with her and return from their walks with a lightness to his step. But when he started giving Gayle and Mom similar qualities, that's where I drew the line. That was all I needed to reject poor Gayle.

The more Dad pointed out their likeness, the more I emphasized their differences. Gayle was very tall, she was from a whole different—which was to say *younger*—generation. She hadn't had children and drove a sleek green Jaguar with wood interior. When she had started coming to dinner, I made a habit of dropping Mom's name gratuitously, and I sighed like an old woman whenever she opened her mouth.

In the end, though, I think Dad wasn't so far off. Mom may have directed carpools instead of companies and chauffeured a station wagon instead of Jaguar, but she had had the same drive, talent, and ambition that Gayle embodied. Mom had been a generation short of converting her education into the intellectual dream that rose and fell inside her. She had been a generation short of seizing the chance but still proud that her crowd had, in all their unrest, helped open doors for the Gayles who followed. Mom had liked Gayle very much, which was why they had been standing together that morning after church when Dad came walking over, coffees in hand.

In the long months in St. Louis after Mom died, just before I set my sights on California, what I had dreaded finally happened when my father and Gayle began dating in earnest. In March, on the night before my birthday, he didn't come home. In the wee hours of dawn, I found myself standing with tight lips and crossed arms at our screen door, watching him glide his Lexus into our garage. He looked sleepy, his hair was rumpled, and he came past me with a sheepish smile.

I had launched into loud, rhetorical questions: *Where* had he been? *Why* hadn't he called? And didn't he know I would *worry?* All I needed was a soiled apron and a frying pan wagging in my hand to fully look the part. Dad had practically run to his bedroom. By the time he came out showered and fresh, I was mentally half gone to the West Coast. I sat on his bed as he knotted his tie and told him I was going, as soon as possible. His expression grew sadder and sadder as I explained what I'd read about Joan Baez, Stanford's film program, and Sorrell's bookstore. Finally he sat down, the wind whisked from his sails. When his eyes met mine, they were as scared as I felt.

Now, after four glasses of wine and not enough beef stew, I was ready to tell Dad that I wanted nothing to do with Gayle, so he should just keep her away from me. I was ready to tell him that for me, moving on felt like betrayal, and while I was at it, I didn't care about graduate school anymore. I was ready to look Dad in the eye and say that flowers on a dresser do not make a home. But I didn't get my chance. The music I'd put on changed, and Glenn Miller came piping into the kitchen, silencing us both.

" 'String of Pearls,' " Dad said. We both looked to the spot by the refrigerator where Mom had hiked up her skirt and danced the Charleston, hauling both of us up to join her.

Jane called me regularly from Stella's, where she was sleeping while I was with Dad. The first call was all business—she was using my computer and couldn't make it work. There was some anxiety because Jane—who had started attending a Baptist church in San Francisco—had become inspired by the charismatic minister there and was now applying to divinity school. Time was short, she said. The application was due.

I had supported Jane's sudden calling, mainly because supporting her was mine, but I also had faith in her faith. By then I knew that Jane's behavior was defined by conflicting moods, missions, and motivations. Nothing she did could surprise me. But in light of her darker side, the irony of this particular goal was hard to avoid.

"I can't write the essay," she wailed. "You've got to come back and write this."

"What's the essay on?" I asked.

"Me," she groaned. "And I can't get your computer to *print*."

"Well . . . what have you got to print," I asked, "if you haven't written anything?"

"That's not the point!" Jane shouted.

Which I knew. "I'll work on the essay," I said. "It will give me something to do while Dad's asleep anyway. It's a personal statement, then?"

Jane read from the application, "Please describe, in five hundred words or less, why you feel called to the course of study provided by our divinity school, and what in your life experience or background supports your qualification for admission."

I tapped a pencil against one of Dad's legal pads. "Why *do* you feel called?" I asked.

"Because I can't bear what's going on in the world," she said. "I see what's happening in Bosnia, what's happening right here in the Tenderloin, and I can't stand the misery. You know what I mean, honey—write something. You know me better than I do."

"There's the background part," I said cautiously.

"I know." Jane groaned again. "We have to explain why I have weird transcripts. But I'm spiritually qualified—we can stress that, right?"

"Your work at the church is good," I agreed. Jane had been volunteering at St. Marks several times a week, not to mention Sundays. She had made a number of friends at the church, all of whom were the hip kind of Christians. They wore jeans to church and sang their hearts out while they danced in the aisles. In particular, Jane was powerfully drawn to a bald woman in the choir who walked with a cane. I wasn't to tell Stella that they had been dating.

"Exactly," Jane said. "And I just joined the AIDS project there yesterday—don't forget to put that down. I'm going to get assigned someone with AIDS and be her helper."

I made the note and said, "So . . . you really want to be a priest?"

"It's my calling, honey," Jane said with certainty.

So between cleaning the drain in Dad's back every few hours and helping him switch the antibiotics in the little plastic globe, I started writing Jane's application to divinity school. I ignored the additional obvious irony, that I was helping a potential priest cheat her way into the fold. The challenge was diverting, and Jane's gratitude on the phone reassured me that I might not be punished this time when I came home.

For the next two weeks, in the middle hours of the night, I felt my way into Dad's darkened room with medical supplies in hand. Whereas Mom had let out little screams when I moved her, Dad only tightened his lips and exhaled as he pushed his legs over the side of his bed and let me get to work.

I had carried my mother when she couldn't walk, but Dad was six foot three. Sometimes he leaned on me as we made our way from bed to bathroom and back, and more than once we almost went down. Had he landed on top of me, I imagined we'd have been discovered days later, expired, on the floor. Dad sat on the edge of his bed while I raised his pajama top to change the bandage on his back. I had never gotten used to seeing my mother that way. The scar where her lung had been removed had made a thin white line across her chest and along her shoulder blade. She always crossed her arms over her breasts while I changed or cleaned her.

"You're seeing too much," she would mumble through the Darvocet.

"I don't see anything," I would assure her.

When I changed Dad's bandage, and touched his freckled back, and saw the years encroaching on his skin, I felt the same way—like I had pulled the cape off Superman and found a mortal underneath.

Dad slept most of the time, and time passed. I became engrossed in the divinity school application, going on long spiritual tangents based on books I'd read in college. I felt I was channeling Jane when I described her life and background; the devotion she felt for people in need, and her education in art as a means for connecting with God. Jane had checked in every day for the first week, asking when I was coming home, but then the calls stopped and I couldn't reach her at all. While Dad slept, or when Gayle came over to visit, I worried upstairs, smoking out the bathroom window. A few times Dad asked about the smell.

"I was at Blueberry Hill last night," I'd tell him, referring to the bar I used to go to after college. "Bars are smoky."

And Dad would believe me, because the daughter he remembered had never lied very well, though I'd tried plenty growing up. And because I had been the athlete, and the only child who had so flamboyantly flushed Mom's cigarettes down the toilet, I was probably the last person he'd expect to start smoking.

But I had hidden everything from Dad, from the moment I drove from the desert and Elmer's clutches. His only clue had been my silence and a vague uneasiness he sometimes expressed that Jane was somewhere behind it.

After three weeks, when Dad's infection was resolved and he was walking well, he bought me my ticket back to San Francisco. He took me to the airport and sent me off with the best advice he could. "Try to make a plan," he said. "Don't drift too long."

I wish I'd confided in him then, told him how long I had been drifting already, that I felt trapped, out of control, caught under Jane's wave of need. But he had no idea, when we said good-bye, that I was returning to where undertows awaited and shores could not be seen.

Jane was supposed to pick me up at the airport, but she didn't show. When I got home to Hancock Street, the boxes were still stacked in the hall, and Stella came around the corner as I dropped my keys.

"She's in here," she said, and her expression told me to be afraid.

Jane sat cross-legged on the floor of her room, sucking her thumb. She rocked back and forth, and fresh red cuts lined her arms and legs. I dropped my bag and covered my mouth.

"She's back now," Stella said to Jane. "See?"

Jane's eyes were fixed on my feet. I crouched next to her, terrified.

"I finished the application," I said, pulling pages from my bag.

Jane nodded glumly.

"I'm back for good."

There was a flicker of relief on Jane's face. "I'm a mess," she said in a hoarse voice. She looked at Stella and me, and for the first time in a long time I glimpsed naked fear in Jane's expression. *That*, I remember thinking, was the Jane I was fighting for.

But that Jane didn't stay around long or return very often. After the application went out, there was another crisis, and then, after being accepted into divinity school, she took an about-face interest in law. My credit card debts mounted, and daily the walls closed in.

I had one refuge, though—a friend at Moby's named Piper, who was smart and unaffected, balanced in every way. She had a practical, midwestern way about her, though she had actually grown up in the South. Talking with Piper was unbelievably comforting. Everything she said seemed reasonable, her words were always thoughtful, and on the occasions when I ventured past formality and confessed to feeling out of sorts, she'd listened intently to my vague attempts to elaborate without implicating Jane and made some sound, if puzzled, suggestions.

One afternoon, after a day shift at Moby's, I joined Piper at a café. I found out that she was a graduate student at Berkeley, in literature. My suspicions that Piper had it together were confirmed when she said she already had a teaching job lined up for the coming fall and was midway through her first novel. She was younger than I was by a year and already way ahead. My conversation skills were rusty, because I was used to talking shorthand with Jane about more intimate or volatile subjects, and I knew that wouldn't be right with Piper. So I let her tell me about the books they were teaching in modern American lit, and what her novel was about, and what it was like to grow up on an herb farm in Atlanta. She sensed I was envious and lonely, but when she asked about my future plans, I suddenly remembered that I was due at home, with take-out dinner.

"Jesus," Piper said, "you look like you're going to be sick."

I ran to a phone and shoved coins in, dialing Jane. She was silent when she heard my voice.

"I lost track of time," I said. "I met Piper after work. I'm on my way—"

"Fuck it," Jane said. "Have fun with *Piper.*"

"No, I'm coming—"

The line went dead. I grabbed my bag and handed Piper some money. "I'm in trouble," I said, "I'll see you later." I flew out the door and ran to my car.

The traffic conspired against me. I crept through Berkeley, cursing and throwing my fists against the steering wheel. On the way I picked up the bacon pizza that Jane liked and double-parked to buy the cheesecake I'd promised.

I gunned my car down Hancock Street, pulled onto the median, and jumped out of my car. After gathering the food and my bag, I turned to see Jane coming out of our building with keys in her hand. She climbed in her car as I called across the street and jogged over. The pizza flew from my hands as Jane peeled out, just missing my feet. After her car screamed up the hill and out of sight, I left the pizza in the street and hurled the cheesecake at a tree.

I went into our apartment, then proceeded down the long hall to my room, passing Jane's open door. A new mural was up on her wall, a combination of Matisse-like cutouts, oil pastels, and photographs. The theme was world poverty, genocide, and hunger, recent preoccupations of Jane's. I wondered if she was telling me something.

I continued down the hall and reached my bedroom. I slammed the door behind me, then, unsatisfied, I opened it and slammed it again. Something toxic was boiling in me, trying to spill out my ears and eyes and mouth, something that stung and tasted like acid. I kicked the wall, then pounded it. I threw what I could find and screamed. Then, behind my door, I spotted my field hockey stick.

Bracing myself with one hand against the wall, I held my breath and threw it against my forehead, right at the hairline, over and over again, until I felt the birth of a small contusion, the size of a walnut. I stood dazed for a moment, then the acid came out of me. Time passed. My thoughts slowed and then stopped. A trickle of blood headed for my eye, and I blocked it with my finger.

Sweet relief.

TWENTY-FIVE

When I was little, the kids in our neighborhood gathered in the evenings to play a game we called Escape, O Prisoner! The game had been created by one of the older boys who no longer played with us, but the tradition lived on.

I was the youngest of the group that formed two teams on a cool fall night, after dinners had been had, dishes done, and parents were retired to books, bills, or televisions. We each had flashlights, an important instrument in this game, and a lanky boy named Odin recited the rules and positions, as was the ritual.

"Alex, you'll be the blue team guard on the dirt mound right there." He pointed to the spot behind our house where an addition was under construction. There was a big square pit and a mound of earth beside it, about ten feet tall.

"Michael guards the red team prison, at the creek bridge over there." He gestured at the woods, where the bridge was about two hundred yards away. "If someone on the opposite team tags you, you are in prison," Odin said. "And once you're in prison, a member of your team has to tag you—without getting tagged by the guard—to get you out." He looked seriously at our faces, glowing under flashlights, to make sure all was understood.

My brother and sister were the oldest on my blue team. Then there was Stephen, then Dexter, then me. Odin led the red team, with all older boys. I thought the teams were stacked against us and said so.

"Then go home to Mommy," Odin whined. "You shouldn't be out here anyway. This game is for boys."

My sister was taller than Odin, and she stepped close to him, emphasizing that fact. Grant said not to listen. I decided I would tag Odin if my life depended on it.

A loud whistle echoed across our lawn, signaling the start of the game. Everyone took off like rabbits, flashlights on, scampering to hide. I trailed Odin, hiding my light under my shirt.

Right away I felt a thump on my back, and one of the Ellis twins yelled, "Tag!" I spun around, already a prisoner. I couldn't tell if it was Carter or Randy Ellis, but whoever it was, he said, "You hid your light. That's cheating."

I removed it from my shirt and waved it around. "Madeleine!" I yelled. "Grant!"

The twin yanked me along to the creek bridge prison, where Michael stood guard, with an air gun slung over his shoulder. "Stand there," Michael said to me. He strung a rope loosely around my wrists, attaching me to the bridge railing.

I didn't like being a prisoner, but I loved watching the flashlights zip around the woods like giant fireflies. Low whistles mixed with shouts, and it seemed real, as if lives were on the line. Michael's back was to me, nose in the air, listening. I saw a flashlight streak by, accompanied by a familiar whistle. My brother and sister were near, circling to get me out. Michael crossed the bridge behind me, alert to the Kraus signals. "I hear you," he said, pointing his rifle at the darkness.

"Tag!" rang out in the distance. An Ellis boy shouted for help. One for us.

My sister sprinted toward me, reaching out a hand, and Odin cut her off, missing her shirt by inches. He fired his gun, which made a convincing sound. I hit the deck. Madeleine gave me a quick call of solidarity before she stumbled back into the woods, safe.

Grant tried next, and I was holding my leg out over the bridge to help. Again Michael intervened, sending my brother diving off across the creek, splashing as he went.

More calls of "Tag!" sounded, and soon I had company in the form of Dexter. He grew anxious right away and started to cry. When Michael untied him and sent him home, Dexter leapt away without so much as a good-bye and howled into the dark woods.

Lashed to the bridge, I waited. The dozen lights turned to a few, and then there were none. Michael paced beside me, and I began to worry.

"What if everyone on my team is prisoner?" I asked him.

"Then we win," Michael said.

"I think you win," I said, showing him my wrists. "Untie me."

"No-ho-*ho*," Michael said. "Not until Odin gives the word."

I yelled for my brother and sister and cocked an ear to the silence. Michael pointed his gun at me and pretended to shoot. "Bah!" he said. "You're dead."

I looked at him, stunned. "No, I'm not," I said.

"Yes, you are, I killed you."

I wanted to go home and told him so.

"Too bad," he said, twirling his gun, "the dead can't go home."

Now this was a game, and I knew that full well. I knew that my house was on the other side of the trees and that my brother and sister could come get me at any time. But it was one of the liabilities of my particular imagination to forget these things and believe.

"You let Dexter go," I whimpered. "Let me go."

"Dexter was *alive*," Michael sneered.

I called for my mother. Michael started giggling.

I could have shaken the rope loose and run for it. I was perfectly alive. But I didn't. I started shaking.

The triangle bell Mom used to retrieve us rang, and then I heard her voice calling me. Michael shook his head. "I'll come to your funeral," he said, and then he stepped into the woods.

Mom would have been waiting by the bell, eyes cast toward the woods, watching to see me appear. She called my name again, and then my brother appeared, out of breath.

"What are you doing?" he asked, untying my wrists. "The game is over—Odin broke his arm."

Grant led me back over the creek and through the woods, out into our yard. Mom was halfway to us, holding a flashlight.

"Where were you?" she asked. She had a jacket in her hand and wrapped it around my shoulders.

"Prison," I muttered. "Dead."

"It was just a fake prison," Grant said.

We scaled the small slope before our back door, and Mom trotted ahead, saying something about calling Odin's mother.

"It was just a game, Caroline," Grant said. "Are you okay?"

I couldn't explain why I wasn't.

Later, I watched the woods from our upstairs hall and thought about my prison. In the morning I took the long way to school, avoiding the bridge, and from then on I took the long way back home. I never played there again, not without supervision.

And looking back, I have wondered, if my brother hadn't come, how long would I have waited there that night, believing I was dead?

A lifetime later I was in a different woods, bound to a more remote bridge, when I arrived for my second visit with Francine.

"Come on in," she said cheerfully. I stood at her door, bundled in two coats, a wool hat, scarf, and big mittens. It was early December when I stepped in, happy to see another fire to sit beside. I handed her my topcoat, unzipped the next one, gave it to her, and put the mittens and scarf on top. She teetered under the mound of clothes and said, "Hat?"

"I'll keep it for now," I said. As a final effect, I coughed.

We took our seats by the fire. "So. How are you doing today?" Francine asked.

"Oh, fine," I said.

"Do you have a cold?"

"Oh no." I coughed again.

"Have you seen a doctor?"

"No."

"Hmn."

"I was thinking maybe this is a waste of time," I said. "Really it's Jane's idea, not mine."

"You don't need to come on my account," Francine said. "Or Jane's."

I dug out my pen. "As long as I'm here . . ."

"All right. Then what would you like to talk about?"

"Oh, couldn't you start?"

"How's it going with Jane?" Francine suggested. "Since you mentioned her."

I fished out my props, the two pictures of "good Jane" and "bad Jane," and threw them on the table. "She's in love with a bald woman now," I said, sneezing. "At her church. She's bald, and she limps. She has fake teeth."

"Sounds like that bothers you," Francine said.

"Well. It's different," I said.

"*Jane* looks different," Francine observed. "Different in each picture."

"Her moods can be suspenseful," I agreed.

"Interesting," Francine said. She returned the photos.

I clicked a few times and then said, "We're in a fight."

She said, "Elaborate."

I hesitated. "It's an old fight. I'm not supposed to talk about it."

"Says who?"

I didn't answer.

Francine said, "Everything is private here. By law, if that makes you feel better."

Tempting. Tempting. I gathered my nerve and said, "Remember when you asked if Jane and I were . . . you know, a couple?"

She nodded.

"Well, like I said, we're *not*. But . . ."

"Have you and Jane been intimate? Sexually?"

I nodded, relieved. She'd said it, not me.

"Well, that's significant, Caroline. And why aren't you supposed to tell anyone?"

"But we're not that way," I said quickly. "Mainly, there was just the one time. . . ."

"And why aren't you supposed to tell anyone?" she repeated.

"Because I promised I wouldn't. And it's not like I want to publicize it . . ."

"But keeping a secret like that can be devastating," Francine acknowledged.

I nodded, realizing she was right. Maybe that explained the anxiety.

"Why did you tell me?" Francine asked.

"Because it's the same problem I have with everyone. People can't understand why I'm so hooked on Jane. And worried about her. Regular friendship doesn't make sense, and I end up looking ridiculous. I'm like her trained puppy or something, that's what people say. I guess I wanted to explain to you part of why I'm . . . confused. But it's embarrassing. Either way it's embarrassing."

"Do you think you're in love with her?"

"See, that's an embarrassing question."

"Why?"

"Because she's a woman. And I don't feel that way about women. My whole life I've loved men, and as far as I know, I still do. But the topic is moot anyway, because from Jane's perspective it never happened. It was a big mistake."

"Well, perspectives don't always follow the facts," Francine said.

"I'll say."

"So. Are you in love with Jane?" she asked again.

"I thought we just reviewed that."

"No. We evaded it."

"Cripes—read between the lines."

"How about if *you* read between the lines. Aloud."

Click click click. I set my jaw. "Well, I'm in *something*," I said. "If it's love, then love isn't what I want or expected. I'm in something I can't have. I don't know what it is."

Francine listened closely. I stretched my arms out, relieved that someone finally knew my secret. Someone knew I had crossed the line with Jane Lowell. With a *woman*. And I was still breathing.

"Jane compares us to Thelma and Louise," I said. "Do you know that movie?"

"Oh. No."

"Well, it's about two women who are friends, and they go on a car trip together. When Susan Sarandon shoots a bad guy outside a bar to save Thelma, they become fugitives."

Francine seemed interested, so I continued. "Jane claims that by the end, they were in love. That theirs was the purest love, because there was no sex."

Francine said, "Okay."

"Then they drove off a cliff," I said. "The Grand Canyon, I think."

"Oh."

We sat back in our chairs, each thinking.

"That would be a hard landing," Francine commented.

I nodded absently.

"What are you thinking just now?" Francine asked.

"This definition of love. I don't feel in love, exactly, but the strange thing is, every time Jane takes another lover—man or woman—I feel like I'm dying. I'm stuck. Worse than alone. And then they always have sex so close to me. Before it was the walk-in closet, and now it's on the other side of my bedroom wall. And I hear it all night long. I have nowhere to go. But then, when I'm lying there really cracking, it's like Jane knows. Sometimes she leaves whomever she's with and climbs into bed with me. She says just the right things, and I'm so relieved not to be alone. And she sort of glues me back together. In the morning we all have pancakes, and then it starts all over again."

"Sounds like a vicious cycle."

"Vicious. Yes."

Francine got up to stoke the fire. Sherry got up too and watched sparks hit the carpet. "Well, it makes sense to me that you'd feel uncomfortable," Francine said.

"But if we're not a couple . . . ," I reminded her.

"Then Jane climbing into your bed after sex is odd," Francine returned.

"Naked," I added, chewing a nail.

"Extremely odd," Francine said, returning to her seat.

We looked at each other for a while, and Francine let me be quiet. She propped her little feet on a stool near her chair and patted Sherry.

"Do you believe in past lives?" I asked.

"I don't rule it out."

"Jane says we knew each other in a past life. She thinks we were married. Or sisters."

"Ah."

"It's a nice thought, anyway."

Francine smiled.

"And it would explain a few things," I added.

"Like what?"

"Why we're so attached to each other. Abnormally attached."

"There might be other reasons, besides past lives, for attachment," Francine reasoned.

"Jane says she's an old soul, and I'm a new soul."

"What do you think about that?"

"Old soul sounds better."

"Well, apparently you're old enough to have a past life," she observed.

That made me laugh.

"Getting back to attachment," Francine said. "Can you describe it? How it feels?"

"Oh. Boy."

"Throw out some adjectives."

"Intense . . . protective. Responsible. Worried. Permanent."

"Permanent," Francine repeated.

I wanted to take that one back.

She said, "Caroline, what about other friends? Are you with Jane *all* the time?"

My throat tightened. I clicked twice.

"Or your family," Francine said. "Do you see your family?"

A worse question. The only person I confided in there was dead.

"It's strange," I said. "I came here to talk about my mother— about her dying, right? I mean, that's what I came planning to talk about. And I keep getting stuck on Jane. Should we talk about my mother?"

"Oh," Francine said, "but I think we are talking about her. All the time." She leaned toward me and added, "Don't you?"

Chapter TWENTY-SIX

Living in San Francisco had a strange effect on Jane, as if the switch from Palo Alto to an urban environment had awakened yet another dormant side of her, one that must have thrived on the nightclub scenes long before we met. Jane seemed restless, and when things turned bleak with the bald woman at her church, she went fishing for dates. Most often we went to a place called Club 80, a San Francisco dance club. For this, we had uniforms. I wore blue jeans and a big turtleneck sweater. Jane wore a tight black shirt and stone khakis. Her hair was unfurled. We usually got a little drunk before leaving, and when we arrived I was witness to Jane's most astonishing hidden talent. The girl could dance.

At Club 80, you could throw a bottle in any direction and likely hit someone who had either known Jane intimately or wanted to be next on her list. Upon entering, she transformed into sharp-tongued urban Jane, rough talking and sexy. The first time she took me along, I saw her surrounded by welcoming cries. I held her drink and stepped back while women kissed her on the mouth and men hugged her close. People watched from a balcony and shouted down their hellos, and Jane waved back, like a queen.

That first night, when a particularly fast and intense dance song came on, Jane seemed to recognize that the DJ had selected it for her. People clapped as Jane parted the crowd and spun onto the floor.

"*You're* with Jane?" a voice asked me. I looked up at a man wearing a woman's face, complete with mascara and lipstick.

"She's my roommate," I said, yelling over the music.

"I'm Max," he said. He watched Jane and added, "God we've missed her."

I noticed people slipping her phone numbers as she danced, most of which hit the ground.

"So where's she been?" Max asked, shouting into my ear. "I heard Palo stuffy Alto."

I ignored him and gazed around. Women danced with women, men with men, and straight couples watched from the perimeter, like tourists. There were some women who had crew cuts, spoke in deep voices, and walked as though something thick were between their legs. There were beautiful women who looked like models and shy women who looked like me. I spotted fraternity boys, men in business suits, and drag queens. A cornucopia of humanity. The women especially fascinated me; their open desire was mesmerizing. A finger tapped my shoulder.

"Want to dance?" a prime example asked. A smiling woman had taken Max's spot.

"Oh," I said, grinning stupidly. I shook my head. The music had changed to Annie Lennox, and Jane was down to her bra in a giant birdcage, swinging around a pole.

The woman tucked a strand of long black hair behind her ear, leaned into me, and said, "Why?" She had green eyes and olive skin. Her eyebrows were arched in anticipation. Were I to make comparisons, I would have said, honest to God, that she looked like early Elizabeth Taylor, without makeup. If I was going to be attracted to women, I could have looked no further.

"I don't really know how," I confessed, shouting into her ear. Except for the box step in the seventh grade, that was pretty much the truth.

She stepped back, then she took my hand, and before I knew it I was dancing.

"I'm Jane," she said, moving her body into mine. I stumbled when she said it, and she caught my arm, laughing.

"Caroline," I shouted back.

She danced so well, so gracefully, that I did okay just by following her. Jane—my Jane—had said I really shouldn't dance, because I had been so "dead" in bed. "Good lovers are good dancers," she had explained. "You'd better stay off the dance floor, honey."

This new Jane was happy, free. She didn't seem to mind my dancing at all. And I liked the sensation of being swallowed by music. My limbs couldn't help but react, it was instinct—like treading water. Around us, bodies were pressed against each other and people kissed. This Jane gave me space, circling in periodically, brushing past my hand.

Behind me, someone grabbed my rear, hard. It was my Jane, fearless and grinning in her bra. She looked from me to the other Jane and yelled, "What are you doing?" into my ear.

I stood still, disoriented. My Jane slid past me, right into the other Jane's receptive groin. The next morning I found them both in our kitchen, making toast and eggs.

On subsequent nights at Club 80, I learned to drink more and dance less.

"Where's Wonderwoman?" Max asked me one night. He was dancing like a gypsy, snapping his fingers in the air.

I pointed to Jane, down to her bra and khakis again, swinging in the go-go cage. A disco version of "Sympathy for the Devil" had everyone in a frenzy.

Max looked me up and down. "This isn't a ski slope, honey," he said, touching my sweater. Then he twirled away.

Except for Max, people rarely approached me at the club. Jane said it was because I looked queasy, but I think I was invisible. Straight blond hair, Gap clothes, glasses. A sexless tourist. Which is why I was surprised when a tall man in a track suit tapped me on the shoulder and asked if he could buy me a drink.

"I bet you drink Chardonnay," he said.

Because he was right, I asked for Scotch. "Johnnie Walker Red."

I watched Jane surrender the go-go stage and cross the dance floor. Heads turned as she passed and disappeared into the disc jockey booth. Gina was spinning that night. I expected I'd probably see her at breakfast.

"Scotch for the lady," said the track-suited man. "Are you here alone?"

"Yes and no," I said. My words slurred. I swayed.

His eyes darted around my head. "You are awfully cute to be here alone."

"Well . . . ," I said.

He looked over, around, and behind me.

Jane came out of the booth and scanned the sea of heads. I raised my arm, and she jumped down the stairs. The sea parted as she made her way to me and the track suit.

"Honey, we're leaving," she said.

I put down my drink, relieved.

Jane wiped her face on my sweater. "Gina will give me a ride home tomorrow."

Oh. *They* were leaving.

Jane squeezed my hand, kissed me full on the mouth, and said, "Don't worry."

Gina waited by the exit, looking lovely in a black cocktail dress, red lipstick, and expensive hair. I admired her cool smile as she locked arms with Jane and they stepped into the night.

"I said, who is she?" Track Suit asked, poking my arm.

I started to answer, then shut my mouth. The room was spinning. I needed air.

"What's wrong?" he asked.

Suddenly all the bodies seemed too close and the music too loud. I heard the words *Let's get high* float above my head. Track Suit was smiling again.

"Sure," I said. "Why not."

Outside it was cold, but I welcomed the fresh air.

"Have you got a car?" he asked.

I pointed to a gas station lot, and he looked pleased.

We got in, and right away I smelled his strong cologne. I also got a good look at him. He was black, clean-cut, and handsome with a tiny goatee. Under his blue track suit he wore a white tennis shirt.

The Scotch was hitting me hard, and mixed with the cologne, I felt dizzy. I started to crank down my window.

"Don't do that," he said. He was rolling something in white paper. "Cops," he added, nodding outside. I put the window back up.

"So what do you do?" I asked.

He laughed and then saw that I was serious. "I'm a tennis pro," he said. His fingers flew around the paper, making a tight cigarette. "I teach kids tennis."

He handed me the finished product and a lighter.

"Pot?" I asked.

"Right. . . ." He smiled.

I lit the paper and inhaled. I held it until his eyes widened and he said I'd better exhale. My whole body tingled, then fell away. I gripped the steering wheel, and immediately my jaw started clenching. A little too late, I remembered how poorly I mixed with drugs.

"I used to play the circuit," said the tennis pro.

I wanted to say, *Really?* but my jaw was clenched too tight. He handed me the joint again, and I shook my head. Moments later, my palms started sweating and I was grinding my teeth.

"What is this . . . really?" I stuttered. I couldn't turn my head.

He leaned back, relaxed. I wondered if we had been smoking the same thing.

"Okay, we've got to go," Track Suit said.

My eyes were abnormally wide. I couldn't blink. "We do?"

"Drive," he said.

"Drive?"

He patted my leg, then rubbed my thigh.

"What? What's going on?"

I felt lips on my face and turned away.

It's telling, the things that come to mind in bad situations. I thought of Jane first. She would have scared the life out of this man with one glance. Then I thought of my father. He would have forcibly removed him from my car. Then Mom. She would have pulled out a gun and fired.

I, of course, was paralyzed.

"This isn't pot," I blurted.

"Have you ever smoked pot?" he asked.

"No, but this isn't it."

"Relax," he said. "And drive."

I reached for my door, and he pulled me back.

He said, *"Drive,"* in a way that scared me. I put the car in gear and backed out of the gas station. I didn't know the streets in San Francisco sober, but in my current state we could have been in Hong Kong as far as I knew.

"Man, you *are* fucked up," he said as we crawled down a street. Which was painfully obvious to me. All of the street signs were moving, like animated cartoons. The road looked like water, and I actually felt my hair growing—it seemed to be sprouting at an alarming rate. The possibilities of what I had actually smoked ran through my mind like a poison label.

We arrived at a run-down high-rise, and I spent a long time trying to parallel-park. Finally Track Suit cursed and told me to turn the car off.

"You go on," I said.

"No way," he answered.

"I don't feel well," I said.

He gripped my arm. He told me to climb out.

"No, really. I'm not feeling well," I said.

"Get the fuck out of the car."

I got out.

We rode an elevator up. As the floors ticked by, I wondered what Jane was doing and if she was thinking of me. My father was probably just waking up, maybe getting his shoes on for a run. The faces of all my relatives passed by like ghosts. Scholars, doctors, housewives, and cousins. None of them, I thought, had ridden an elevator with a drug-dealing tennis pro clutching their arm. Once again, I was a pioneer.

We entered a dim apartment and walked toward what might have been a living room, had there been any furniture. Two women and three men sat on the floor, watching television. One of the women looked me over.

"Hey, Kevin," she said.

He let go of my arm. "Hey, Sheila," he said. "Got anything?"

"You're in the way," said one of the men, poking my leg. He was trying to watch television, so I stepped aside. My hair was bothering me. I kept one hand on the top of my head to stop it from flowing out the window.

Sheila pointed to me. "Who is she?"

"My wheels," Track Suit said. "We'll take a few lids to Emeryville and cop some bills."

He wasn't speaking English.

"Who *are* you?" she asked again, looking at me.

Kevin said, "What are you, a detective?"

Sheila pursed her lips. "It's coming," she said curtly. I looked longingly at the door.

"Sit down," Track Suit barked, so I did. Sheila, who was clearly fond of Track Suit and not at all of me, started rubbing his back. Before long his head was nodding.

I mouthed the word *bathroom* to anyone who might be looking and scooted backward. Sheila was happy to see me go. I made it to the door, turned the knob, and ran as fast as I could to the elevator. When I got outside it was daylight.

Back at home, I climbed into bed, shaking uncontrollably. I couldn't get warm under the blankets, so I submerged myself in a hot bath, shivering. I was in bed again when the phone rang. I heard my manager at Moby's on the answering machine, asking where I was. I kicked at my blankets and cursed.

"Come see me when you're in," she said. "I hope that's soon."

The phone rang again later and woke me out of sleep. The voice was unmistakable, Jane's mother, Linda Lowell.

"What's wrong?" she asked. "Your voice sounds funny."

Since I couldn't tell her I had inhaled something poisonous and been kidnapped by a junkie Harry Belafonte look-alike, I said I had a cold.

"Well, take some echinacea," Mrs. Lowell admonished. "Goodness."

I ducked under the covers and held the phone to my ear.

"Where's Jane?" she asked.

"I dunno," I said.

"Are you in a cave? I can't hear you."

I poked my head out. "She's not here, Linda."

"Did she tell you I might come for a visit?"

I kicked the covers again. "No."

"You don't sound very excited."

"I'm excited."

"You and I can see some movies. We'll go back to that place where they have the old movies. That was fun, wasn't it?"

"Um-hm."

"You do sound sick, Caroline."

"Yep."

"Well, tell Jane to call me."

I promised I would. Right after I found my hockey stick and bashed in my head.

TWENTY-SEVEN

Francine seemed distracted a few weeks later when I came inside and removed my sunglasses. She didn't even notice the new blue welt above my eye. I sat down, disappointed. Now I wanted her to ask about it. That was one ironic thing about me and therapy—I played hard to get, but I was paying to be gotten. It was almost kinky.

It bothered me that the first psychiatrist I'd seen—Mary-Lou, with her rhetorical questions and curling red nails—might have been right; that I had all the answers and 90 percent of this relied on my cooperation. The idea was to have someone else solve my problems—if I had to do all the work, then what was I paying for?

I paced Francine's living room and stooped to pet Sherry. "Did you bring anything today?" Francine asked. "The last few visits you gave up on props, I noticed."

"No props," I said. "Sorry."

"That's okay," Francine said, dismissing the idea with her hand. "I'd just hoped to see some pictures of your family. Or friends."

"I do have a friend at Moby's," I said, sitting down. "Piper."

"I like that name," Francine said. "Cheerful."

"She's part-time. She's a graduate student at Berkeley—literature."

I had gotten good at finding ways to hang out secretly with Piper, when Jane was either on a date or too distracted to notice my absence on lunch breaks at work. I told Francine that the lunches or coffees I had with Piper were precious to me. She had ambition and an innocent, serene way about her. Sometimes I wondered if she was what I might have been.

"You must be tired," Francine noted. She pointed to my pen. "Not a single click."

"Bothered," I admitted. "Every morning lately, I wake up thinking that I have cancer. Because I feel something weird in here." I patted my chest. "Itchy."

"Well, cancer is a pretty big leap from itchy. Have you seen a doctor?" Francine asked.

"No."

"Are you going to?"

"No."

"Well, either see a doctor or wonder, I guess."

"They don't spot tumors early on," I informed her. "Tumors take ten years to spot, and then it's too late anyway."

"I wonder if people *feel* tumors before they are visible, though," Francine mused.

My eyes widened.

"I'm not saying you *have* one," she said quickly, "I'm saying whatever you're feeling could arise from something else—"

"Hmn," I said.

"Hmn," she repeated. "Like . . . smoking?"

I stiffened.

"It hardly seems like something to hide here."

I put my head in my hands and kicked the ground.

"Hey," she said.

"But what will my father say?" I moaned. "My brother and sister? I mean, our mother dies of lung cancer and then I take up smoking? Not very creative. And what if I—"

"They might surprise you," Francine said.

I shook my head. "All this time I've been hiding it, and you knew?"

"Caroline, smoking anything is dangerous, and I do hope you stop with the cigarettes, but it isn't the worst problem I've seen in my career."

I pondered this.

She said, "Let's hold off on the smoking for a moment. I want to get back to you and friends. Anyone else besides Piper?"

"I really like one of Jane's friends," I said. "Her name is Stella, and she's smart. She's a doctor in an ER."

"What is Jane's reaction when you spend time with other friends?"

Francine was catching on. "Right," I said. "She hates Piper. And in the case of Stella, she doesn't want us seeing each other without her. She thinks it's weird."

"Why?"

"Because Stella is *her* friend."

"Ah."

"We have started sneaking dinners, though," I confessed. "On nights when Jane is working. We get a little drunk and talk about her. It's really refreshing. Without Stella I'd be over the edge by now. Or more over the edge."

"So you sneak with Piper, and you sneak with Stella?"

I nodded. "I sneak a lot."

"Well. At least it's good that you're reaching out," Francine conceded. "But is it stressful?"

"Very."

Stella had suggested our first rendezvous one day, after talking with me on the phone. I'd had a terrible fight with Jane and must have said something bleak enough to raise her concern. I remember wavering between guilt and relief when we first shared a booth at a restaurant in the city. But after a few drinks, I quickly succumbed to the relief. Stella had listened patiently to my litany of worries, and with her previous Jane experience, she could offer empathy and insights from life in the inner circle. I trusted her advice completely. Pretty soon we were talking on the phone in secret, too, forming a tight net of support between us. I understood her predicament, to be constantly placed on hold. And I think she understood mine—to never be put on hold for a second.

"Speaking of stress," Francine said. "Let's talk about the bruises."

I coughed and recoiled. A surprise attack.

"What is causing the bruises?" she asked.

The stirrings of an unwanted smile tugged at my cheeks.

"Right." I nodded.

Francine folded her arms.

As she waited, the awful thing started to stir inside me, the thing that took possession of my faculties, replacing common sense with the aching need to throw my head against something hard. Sitting there, I imagined the stinging relief, over and over again.

"Are you going to be sick?" she asked.

I vaguely heard her. I was busy searching for excuses—a bookshelf that fell on me at work—regularly. Muggers. Nosedives in the shower. Low-flying planes. Then I decided to stop playing hard to get. It was too exhausting.

"I do it," I mumbled. "I do it to myself."

"Oh," Francine said.

"I'm crazy. Go ahead and say it."

She frowned.

"Well, you'd have to be crazy to smash your own head," I said. "I'm going to the loony bin, I know it."

"Hold on," Francine said.

"The loony bin," I repeated. "I know what I'm talking about." I clicked my pen in the air and pointed to it. "Ridiculous!"

"We do need to talk about this," Francine said slowly. "But it does not help to beat yourself up over it."

I was struck by the sound of that. "Ha ha," I said.

"Ha ha ha," she replied.

"Who knew you could joke?"

"It's a hidden talent."

I took a deep breath. "What was I saying?"

"You've been injuring yourself."

"Oh. Yeah." I touched my head.

"When did this start, Caroline?"

I shrugged.

"You can answer that."

I clicked.

"You said Jane injures herself, isn't that right? Cutting?"

"That predates me."

"I was just wondering if that . . . inspired you. Or was something you did together?"

"God, no," I said. "God. That would be sick."

Francine let that lie. "Then tell me why you hurt yourself," she said.

"Panic, I guess. I'm trapped, and I feel panic. When I hit my head, the panic goes away, and I feel . . ."

"*Do* you feel?" she asked.

"No. I don't feel. And that feels good.

"Just like Jane described," I added.

"So that first time," Francine said, "when you felt panic, what caused it?"

"I had just been with Piper. I was supposed to be home, to bring dinner home, and I hung out with Piper instead. When I realized how late I was, I called Jane, but she was pissed. She almost ran me down."

Francine said, "Go on."

"So I came into our apartment and didn't know what to do. I saw my field hockey stick behind the door, and I picked it up. Then I started swinging."

I folded my arms. Her turn.

"Okay, let's rewind for a minute," Francine said. "Do you think Jane was rational? To punish you for visiting with a friend?"

"I was late—"

"*Caroline,*" Francine implored. For the first time she looked frustrated.

"Well, fine. I suppose it doesn't matter anymore if Jane is rational. I just want to keep us going. Get through the day and not be run down for making a mistake."

"What mistake?" Francine asked. "You had coffee with a friend—"

"But it's not *like* that for Jane," I explained. "It threatens her, and I know why. I know she can't help it."

Francine waited.

"Swa-*ha,*" I smiled.

"Well, are all your days like this?" Francine asked.

"Jane doesn't even take a bath without me sitting two feet away. If I'm quiet, she asks what I'm thinking. If I don't want to say, she says stop brooding. Sometimes she takes me on dates."

"You go on dates together?"

"I go on *her* dates."

"Oh. Do you have your own dates?"

"Are you kidding? There's no *time.*"

"Then why do you go on Jane's dates?"

"Because the alternative is worse."

"And what's the alternative?"

"Worse."

Francine considered this for a while, then said, "Do you keep a journal? Ever write how you feel?"

"Why?"

"I'm just wondering, because when you can't explain something, such as now, it might help if you wrote it, or tried to, anyway. It's just a thought."

"I don't have a journal, but I write stories all the time. They're crap."

"You don't have to be Eudora Welty to throw insight on a page," Francine noted.

That made me laugh—the Eudora Welty part. Then I remembered that Francine had written a book or two herself and might know what she was talking about.

"It's the process, not the product," she encouraged.

TWENTY-EIGHT

Ever since I'd first learned my letters, it had been my habit to write obsessively about whichever topic was foremost in my mind. My parents were an encouraging and patient audience for my earnest poems and dramatic, overreaching stories, which I sometimes performed in our living room. Along with running hurdles in the Olympics and winning Wimbledon, I had nursed hopes to make a life of inventing stories, first in prose and later on film. That dream had outlasted my athletic fantasies, but by the time I was living with Jane, my writing efforts, for screen or otherwise, had narrowed into one clumsy, transparent subject—resurrecting dead mothers.

The plots were repetitive, exhausted variations on that theme. I employed ghosts, reincarnations, vessels, and visitations to transform a naive young daughter from weak and indecisive to bold and reborn. The results were irritating and unconvincing. By the time Jane and I were working at Moby's, I'd shelved the idea of being an author and taken up photographing them instead, for the Moby's wall of fame.

. . .

After author events I hung around the signing table, asking each writer how they did it. One evening a novelist, possibly to make me stop, told me to join her at the café across the street when she was done signing. I almost dropped my camera in surprise.

"Are you a writer?" she asked me later, after we'd found a table at the café.

"Photographer," I said, patting my camera.

Right away I confessed. I explained that I could only write about one thing, and poorly. I had wanted to intersect the living and the dead and make it believable. Other people did it—I'd read the books and seen the movies—but I never believed my own stories.

"Maybe you're not approaching it right," she offered. "I don't know the details of your story, but for one thing it's usually dangerous to impose your expectations on characters. In my work, I try to put them in a compelling environment, give them problems, and see how they behave. And they do behave, in my experience. So for instance, maybe the world you've placed your characters in doesn't permit this life-and-death intersection."

"So I have to change my world?" I asked.

"Or listen closer to your characters," she said, smiling. "They are the ones stuck in the world you've made, after all."

Sometimes when I was supposed to photograph the authors, I spent more time scanning the audience with my long lens. I snuck photos of people who caught my eye, and often they looked like mothers. They weren't hard to spot. They were women who always entered the bookstore with purpose and schedules to keep. They had their to-do lists out as they scanned book titles and distracted expressions I recognized. And if they asked me for help in finding a book, I invariably discovered it was for somebody else.

One evening before a reading began, a middle-aged woman

entered the store pulling a blue oxygen tank behind her. She took a seat in the back row of folded chairs, just before a popular mystery writer started to talk. I hid myself behind a closed register and watched her through my telephoto.

Betty had been a prettier tank, but this lady's had better wheels. She didn't have children with her, but I knew they were there, on her mind, as she fished in her purse for something to write with. The to-do list, I thought.

After the reading, I found her browsing the biography section, with two signed mystery books under her arm.

"Can I help you find something?" I asked.

"Oh, thanks." She caught her breath and said, "My daughter is interested in anthropology. I was thinking of Margaret Mead."

I estimated that her daughter was in college, maybe a sophomore, taking her first anthro class. *"Coming of Age in Samoa?"* I suggested.

"No, no. She's read that already," the woman said. "Isn't there a biography? I think I read a biography once."

I reached up high and showed her *Blackberry Winter*, Mead's autobiography.

"Even better," she panted. "In her own words."

Standing there, I wanted to crawl into that woman's arms. Traces of gray touched her hairline, and I suspected there would not be time for much more to appear. I wanted to ask where she lived, what her daughter was like, if she liked to garden, knit sweaters, or play tennis.

But she was in a hurry, she said. On her way down her list.

I was daydreaming about that woman the next morning at home, when Jane came into my room with hot tea and another application. Since the priesthood and the law were out, I expected medical school might be next.

"You should check this out," she said, dropping the application on my desk. The "New School for Social Research" was printed on the front.

"Social research?" I asked.

"For you," Jane said. "They have a good film program—it's in Greenwich Village."

"Really?" I opened the application and peered inside.

"Stanford is all academic," Jane said, as if she'd studied their catalogs at length. "You need a practical place. The New School is cool. Much more open-minded."

"And New York," I said, relishing the idea. My first hopes after college had been to study there, at NYU. Apparently I'd told Jane that, and she hadn't forgotten.

"Would you move there?" I asked.

Jane shrugged, as if whether we lived together or not, it didn't matter. "The main thing is," she said, "you need to snap out of your funk. Stop worrying about me and *do* something."

Yes, I thought. But I'd never known that separation was an option, or moving to New York. I suddenly felt stupid and blind, as if I'd had the wrong impression of Jane all along.

"Think of it as an early Christmas present," she added. "Anything to cheer you up." Then she returned to a new wall mural she was building, out in the hall.

The mural had been growing for weeks and was now encompassing our entire front hall—almost twenty feet long and four feet wide. A base layer of white paper was covered by a collage of paints, photographs, and fragments of writing. Faded poems were carefully layered under cut paper shaped like limbs. There were disturbing photographs—erotic, aggressive, and sad images—manipulated by her paints and scissors into visions of survival.

When Jane went on an art jag, she couldn't be stopped. She threw herself into the pictures, words, and paint the way she did lovers, opening a vein, tasting the blood. With her arsenal of razors,

X-Acto knives, and scissors, she cut around heads, limbs, torsos, and eyes, pasting them as she wanted, coating them with washes of glue and color. Her MO was right there in front of me, but at the time I didn't see it—that Jane had shaped me the same way, trimming my edges, placing me in her frame. The parts that hadn't fit, like my family or my goals, she'd simply sliced off and thrown away.

But the application ran counter to this. It embraced my goals, and Jane's new suggestion of independence caught me off guard. I flipped curiously through the school's guidelines and saw the description of their master's in film. They taught editing, and production, and screenwriting. Some famous documentaries had come from New School alums. Several teachers looked accomplished, and a small hope grew in me, followed by a nagging suspicion that there had to be a catch.

Part of my confusion over Jane's apparent detachment was that she had been so adamant that I stay with her for Christmas. That conversation had been brief, as she got no resistance from me. I didn't want to be in St. Louis, because my home was with Jane, and the coming holidays only reinforced my sense that our family of two was where I belonged. We decorated the apartment together with lights and wreaths and snuck out on separate secret missions to buy each other presents. My humor was tested when Jane's outings for gifts had required my credit card, but she had sheepishly asked for it with a giggle and a wink, and it was easy to feel like a proud provider—indispensable to the end—when I handed it over.

Just before Christmas Eve, on a morning I had an appointment with Francine, Jane made her special scrambled eggs with onions, cream cheese, and milk whipped in. She read me the Anna Quindlen column while we ate and then trimmed her toenails over a trash can. That day, she was upset about Amanda, a middle-aged black woman in the last stages of AIDS whom Jane had signed up at her church to help. Apparently Amanda's son was on crack, and he had recently set their apartment on fire. She was about to be evicted. Jane announced that she was going to give her paychecks to Amanda, so that she could move to a better place and pay rent.

"But we can't pay our own rent," I objected.

"Do you want Amanda to die in a burned-out crack ghetto?" she asked indignantly.

It was pretty hard to say yes to that.

By then I'd learned that Jane had two speeds when it came to attaching to people—total hate or total love. When she loved, she fell hard, fast, and completely. She fell for odd things, like a person's limp, or a disease, or a crippled heart. I suspected that Jane loved Amanda in part because she was about to die.

Jane pushed the trash can away, and I noticed that she'd been crying.

"Do you think Amanda is going to die *soon?*" she asked.

"Yes," I replied.

She kicked the trash can and it spilled onto the floor. She went to the phone and dialed.

"It's pretty early—" I started.

"Amanda?" Jane blurted.

I started cleaning the floor. Jane paced as she held the phone and then kicked the wall. "Want to spend Christmas Eve here?" I heard her ask. She sat down and listened, and I left the room.

I sat on my bed and assembled some Francine props—a few more pictures of Jane, one of Sam, plus one of Jane's poems. Jane came in and sat on my lap. The phone was to her ear, and her thumb was in her mouth. Pinned to my bed, I waited.

"*Honey,*" she said into the phone, "you cannot heat your place with a hot plate, it's not safe." She glanced at my props. "I'll pick you up at noon. Pack a toothbrush." She hung up, threw the phone on the bed, and asked why I had pictures of her. I had been holding my breath and exhaled.

"For Francine," I said.

"Why? You're not showing her my poem, are you?" Jane snatched it back.

"She said to bring things that were significant to me—"

"Well, bring something else," she said. She took a picture of my mother off the wall and waved it in front of my face. "Bring this."

I batted the picture away and said, "So Amanda is coming for Christmas Eve?"

Jane leaned into me, worked on her thumb, and said, "She can have my bed." Then, struck with terror, she cried, *"Presents—*we have to get Amanda Christmas presents." Jane, who had witnessed my credit card declined on her last outing, said, "You'd better pinch some cash at work."

Sudden cash requests had come up more and more, and increasingly I imagined myself in prison, explaining to my father through thick glass that I'd had no choice, lives depended on me to rob the bookstore register. So far I had only taken money once, but even though that once still haunted me, the pressure was getting hard to resist.

"You pinch the register," I said.

"I'm not working today," she pointed out. "It's not like we're going to buy designer suits," she exclaimed. "Morally, it's the right thing. Amanda deserves a few nice things before she dies, and no one at Moby's will suffer. You've got to keep the *big* picture in mind. And the little people."

"But if I get caught, we won't have any money at all," I protested. "And I'll be writing you from prison. And then what will you say?"

"Swa-ha," Jane smiled. She kissed me and whispered, "Of course I'd break you out . . . and then we would hide in Switzerland, where Monny's relatives would have to take us in." She kissed me again and added, "Come on—see if you can break my record."

Just then I realized I was late for Francine, and the memory of her warnings to be on time sent Jane flying off my lap as I rushed for my coat.

"Get. The. Money!" she called after me. I shot onto the street, and she called from the window, "And presents! Presents for Amanda!"

"Well," Francine said when I arrived. "Only ten minutes late today. . . ."

I apologized and aimed for the couch.

"What news have you for me?" she asked.

I took my spot by the fire and thought that was an impossible question. It should have been easy to answer, people answer it all the time, but the weight of Jane's request—the weight of the past two years—crashed over me until I felt so small, I was invisible. I felt that if I spoke, nobody would hear.

"Not so good, I take it," Francine said.

I shook my head.

"Can you use some words?"

"Not so good," I said.

"Your *own* words?"

"Bad."

"Why?"

"Can I change the subject?"

"Okay."

"Well, it's just that lately, right before I fall asleep . . ." I bit my lip.

"Tell me."

"I imagine a baseball bat. Flying into my head. It's sick, but when I picture it connecting with my head, I relax. Then I can sleep. And I was thinking maybe, if I could just imagine that bat during the day, maybe I could stop the . . . bruises."

"Well," Francine said. "If imagining stops the doing, then that's progress."

"My thoughts exactly," I said. "So far it doesn't work, though."

"Do you realize," Francine asked, "that it sounds like you are trying to be unconscious?"

"I like the idea," I agreed.

"If conscious life is bad enough, I suppose that makes sense," she allowed.

"Really?"

"Well, I'm not saying it's a *good* thing . . ."

"I used to imagine my mother right before sleep."

"What was that like?"

"Better than not seeing her. I used to dream about her, too, all the time. I knew she was dead, even while we were talking. I don't miss the dreams so much, though. Waking up was awful."

Francine said, "You know, whether it's a hockey stick, a baseball bat, a brick wall, or Jane, it seems to me that you are getting increasingly creative at shutting down. That you are trying desperately to rest."

"But Jane is not restful," I said. I did like the creative part, though.

"Oh, I think she is," Francine countered. "I think surrendering your life to Jane is a lot like being unconscious."

"Well, I feel pretty much awake for it all."

"Describe your life right now," Francine requested.

"Oh, it's mostly basic survival now. I get money. Pay the rent. Stay employed. But Jane and I are always talking about something. We laugh. We laugh a lot, actually. And we go to movies. Sometimes it's great, and all seems worth it. I tell myself, Well, she is my family. And I love that feeling. She's rare. But then we'll have some argument or crisis, and, like I said, it's not restful."

Francine shifted in her chair. "I'm just curious," she said. "What if Jane won the lottery, and moved to . . . Finland, say, where she lived happily ever after."

"Finland?"

"Wherever. But let's say she doesn't need your help anymore. She's happy. No more crises. Let's say you're free."

"Well, that wouldn't happen," I said.

"We're imagining."

"Okay. I don't want her *gone*, Francine, I just want her well."

After some thought, Francine said, "You wanted your mother well. You've used that word exactly. Was that a similar feeling? Trying to make her well?"

"Well, I hope not," I said. "That didn't end happily."

I was thinking I'd made some kind of point when she said, "Let's ask Jane to come next week."

I stiffened. "What? Why?"

"Ask her," Francine said. "Ten o'clock."

"But what if she says no?"

Francine smiled and said, "She won't."

After leaving Francine, I stopped at the bank to see about honest money for Amanda. At the window, the teller explained that only $27 remained to be had.

"Are you sure?" I asked.

She looked behind me for the next customer.

"Not my savings account," I said. "Did you look in my checking account?"

She typed in my number again and said, "Twenty-seven dollars."

I backed away.

There was a time when I thought being poor was romantic. I envisioned artists and writers shivering in their garrets, producing great work, drunk and happy. With Jane I realized that being poor is only romantic when you have money. When the money is gone, every moment of every day is haunted by its absence. People start calling, saying the phone will be disconnected, or the check bounced, or the rent is overdue. A $3 latte is the stuff of dreams. Invitations to dinner or movies become complicated, declined. I was not prepared for this, even though I had seen it coming for months. My credit cards were useless, and reality had arrived. Family resources were too humiliating to request, given my reasons and the inheritance I'd kissed good-bye. So I turned my brain onto autopilot and aimed for the Moby's register.

In retrospect, I can see that Jane courted my money the same way she courted love. She had depended on people long before I appeared, with brief but serial success. Maybe I lasted longer because I had more money to give. Or maybe I thought I wanted what I paid for. Back then, I believed I was *offering* my funds, my time, and my love. And Jane would have stood up in court and agreed. She had a way of making it happen that way. She thought ahead.

At Moby's, one of the hippie old-timers, Jack, was wearing a Santa hat and ringing up books next to me. He started talking about the shoplifter I'd missed, who had run out the door with the two-volume *Oxford English Dictionary* under his arm. Now they were placed behind us in a glass case. Jack said it was ironic that someone who wanted the *OED* would also be a thief.

"He didn't want the dictionary," I said. "He wanted to sell it next door for cash." I had already sold most of my books to the second-hand dealer there, and they gave a fair price.

"Oh? How do you know?" Jack asked.

A customer approached me with a hardcover book. He handed me $25, and bypassing the register, I mentally calculated his change, placing the cash in a hidden spot along with the other twenty I'd secreted.

"I just know," I said.

At the end of our shift, Jack rescued me, and he didn't even know it. I had set aside $60 for Amanda, and had every intention of taking it, until he noticed the bills when he reached across my register for a pen.

"Oops," he said, fishing them out. "You lost a few."

I turned red as he popped open my register drawer. "Unless it's yours?" he asked, looking at me.

"No—no," I said. "Must have slipped off the counter." He dropped the money in the register, grabbed the pen, and started adding up his own register totals.

I wondered if he knew, as I pulled out my totals sheet. Now I would be $60 over, which would drive the Moby's bookkeeper crazy. Jack hummed and did his adding, and I did the same. If he knew how close I'd come to stealing, he never said a word.

On Christmas Eve, I came home from an afternoon of last minute Hail Mary shopping and found Amanda and Jane sitting on my bed.

"Hi, honey!" Jane called merrily down the hall. She'd strung more blinking white lights around the apartment and put the Tallis Scholars on my stereo. I smelled a feast already brewing in the kitchen. Jane had a good touch when it came to making a home feel special. The anxiety I walked in with was no match for her skills and faded quickly into relief.

I hid my bags of presents in the kitchen and greeted Amanda, who sat like an empress on my bed, surrounded by pillows. She sipped apple juice from a wineglass and raised it, toasting my arrival.

"You look tired," she said, waving me closer. "You work too hard."

Amanda was thinner than any living human I'd ever seen and very tall. She walked like a woman on stilts. Her skin was the color of chestnuts, she wore bold red lipstick, and she laughed at just about anything.

"I made fried everything," Jane announced. "And then we'll have protein milkshakes, and then wheat cakes with tofu—"

Amanda looked queasily at her toes. When Jane left to check on the food, Amanda drew her hands across my sheets and comforter and beckoned me to join her. "It's so warm here," she said. "It's a palace. Jane says you're the one who pays for it all."

"Oh, well . . ." I looked around the room.

"I'm so grateful to be here," she continued. "I just hope my son doesn't burn the house down while I'm gone. Or die."

"Oh," I said. "Oh, gosh."

She poked me. "Do you know what we saw today? This afty-noon?"

"No, what?"

"We saw a movie being filmed in Chinatown." She waited for me to be suitably impressed. "Jane was all worked up that you should have been there, since you're going to be a famous movie director. We went right up to the edge to see, and we saw that man—that black man, you know. You know his name?"

"Hmn—"

"Well, he was there, right there in front of me. I could have touched him."

"That's exciting," I said.

"I never thought I'd live to see that. A movie being made—and that black movie star. What's his name?"

"I don't know, what did he look like?"

Amanda winced and clutched a pillow.

"What's wrong?" I asked, shrinking back.

She closed her eyes and moaned. "It hurts sometimes," she said. "Boy." She opened one eye and focused it on my forehead. She looked closer, puzzled. "Is that bruises on your head?" she demanded. She zoomed in on my hairline. "It *is*. What happened?"

I smiled to reassure her and shrugged. She wasn't convinced for a second. "Just a bump," I said quickly. "It's nothing, Amanda."

"*Noth*-ing, Amanda," she mimicked. "Girl, you sound like my *son*. Crackhead boy don't ever have *nothing* happening. Not until the damn house burns down. *Then* he have somethin' going on." She eyed me and added, "And I know you smoke them cigarettes, too. Oh yeah, Jane says, Jane says. Don't even *try* to lie yourself out of that. Bruised and smoking. Good God. And you say, '*Nothing*, Amanda'?"

I waited to see if she was done and then started to speak. But I stopped midsentence, because really, she had a point. There she was, with weeks or months to live, and I was attacking my own body. It was an awkward moment.

"You're right," I said, touching my scalp. "But it's personal, okay?"

Amanda gasped and sat back, hand across her mouth. "Who hit you?" she hissed.

"No—I did this," I said, as if that explained everything.

Amanda recoiled even farther, leaning as far from me as she could, with two big white saucers for eyes. After a moment she said, "You must be pretty mad at yourself to do that." She nodded, gathering steam. "You know there ain't nothing you did that deserved no blow to the head. You better cut it out now, before the brains God gave you turn to mush."

When Jane came in with plates of dinner, Amanda reversed her expression, smiling brightly to show we were officially off the subject. The food was loaded onto my bed, since Amanda didn't like chairs, and Jane hoped to inspire her by eating enough for six people. I tried to do the same, and before long my stomach hurt so much that I had to lie down right there, among the fried eggplant and tofu pups. Amanda drank her milkshake and picked politely at the rest while Jane fell back like me, in a coma. On Christmas morning, I was sleeping under one of Amanda's arms and Jane was on the other side, nestled into Amanda's chest.

"Merry Christmas, baby," Amanda said, seeing me blink. "We made it."

She gently extricated herself and shuffled to the bathroom. While she was gone, Jane whispered about my Moby's take. She had saved $400 for Amanda, she said. That was her present.

"That much?" I whispered back. "*We* need that money, Jane—"

"*What?*" she hissed.

"It will be a miracle if I can pay our rent—"

"It will be a miracle if Amanda *lives*," she shot back.

"Whatever," I snapped. "I have a present for her. It's wrapped in the kitchen."

"What about the cash?" she asked. "I wanted to give her a big wad of cash."

"I don't have any cash," I said flatly. "I have the present. . . ."

"Forget it," Jane said. "Worry about your rent."

"*Our* rent," I corrected.

"Fuck you."

I stood up, frantic.

"Oh, simmer down," she said impatiently. "You'll be gone to New York soon anyway, thanks to me."

"What?"

"I saw you filling out the application."

"You *gave* it to me," I shrieked.

And so came the catch I'd suspected, like a noose slipping around my neck. I don't know if Jane had been sincere that day when she'd offered me my door to freedom. Maybe she knew she could afford to seem generous, because I'd never leave her. But looking back, I don't think she was always that calculated. I think often her motives, in the moment, were good. Only later, when she felt threatened, did her survival skills take over, and then all previous discussions were erased—sent to that recycling bin in Jane's mind called memory.

"And you sure took the bait," she snapped, glaring at me. She kicked at my bed, and I kicked my dresser hard, then clutched my foot and groaned.

Amanda stood in the doorway, perplexed.

"Good God almighty," she said. "You two is the strangest pair I ever saw. It's Christmas, for goodness' sake—the birth of our *Lord.*"

Jane and I stared at each other with thin lips, and then we looked at Amanda, skinny skyscraper Amanda, teetering at the end of her life. We both exhaled.

"I'll start breakfast, you get the presents," Jane said to me. She pointed a finger at my nose as we walked past Amanda, and we bickered our way down the hall.

I had found a red wagon for Jane that Christmas, a Radio Flyer, just like the one in the hardware store window, where she had stopped one day and looked longingly. What she would do with a wagon on the hilly streets of San Francisco was a mystery to me and Amanda, but Jane quickly shed whatever rage had just possessed her and hugged me with total affection. She especially loved that the wagon was piled with other gifts—a portable CD player, sweaters, paints, a wooden easel. She became fifteen, then twelve, then ten. A thumb-sucking, blinking child, begging Amanda and me to open ours next.

"Thank you," I said, holding a necklace from Jane. It was gold, with a cross, an anchor, and a heart. A J. Crew wool sweater followed, and a quilted jacket with pockets on the side. In a month they would all appear on one of my MasterCard statements, but for the moment I was charmed. I put everything on before my mirror and joined Jane in forgetting our argument.

"Oooh, sweet Jesus," Amanda cried. She pulled a thick red cable sweater around her, from Jane. I had no idea what Amanda could want other than a heated home and new body, so I'd settled on recycling a wooden picture frame for a picture I'd taken of the two of them—Jane in Amanda's lap, kissing her cheek. Amanda held it to her chest and squealed, "Me and my favorite girl. My best girl."

"I love you, Amanda," Jane said.

Amanda suddenly gasped, "But I don't have nothing for you girls. I didn't—"

"Stop it," Jane laughed. She turned to me and said, "Let's see what the Kraus family sent." I turned to a small collection of wrapped gifts. "Open them," Jane said excitedly.

First I unveiled a bottle of Chanel No. 5, which Dad got my sister and me every year. I took a sniff and smiled. It smelled like Mom before going out to a party. Then I opened our family's special Swiss cake and passed it around. Amanda tried to be polite, but the cake was an acquired taste, and along with Jane, she recoiled. There was a biography of Orson Welles from Dad and Gayle and the *Godfather* trilogy on video from Grant. My sister had made me jewelry, scarabs to match Mom's old watch.

"I miss them," I confessed, taking another sniff of the Chanel.

Jane said, "Sure, you miss them now, the one time a year that they remember you exist. But who is here the rest of the time? Who knows you the *best?*"

"They know me," I said cautiously.

"Whatever," Jane said.

Amanda looked between us and started humming.

"They *know* me," I said nervously.

"Uh-oh," Jane said, "Caroline needs to smoke."

"Oh no," Amanda said worriedly. "She doesn't."

Jane was right. I stood up and excused myself, muttering as I walked out the door.

When I came back from smoking on the roof, Jane and Amanda had started their own argument.

"But I've got to see my boy," Amanda was saying as I entered.

"I'm your family now," Jane urged. "I'll take care of you. Your son will kill you one of these days—"

"That's my problem," Amanda replied. "I love you, girl, but anyone can see we ain't family—you my *friend*, sweetie. And my boy is my boy, even if he is trouble all day long. It's *Christmas*. And he'll be wondering about me."

Amanda creaked and groaned herself upright, wobbling forward. "Time to go," she said, passing me with a pat. "Thank you for my presents, child . . . and for God sakes stop smoking and stay away from your head."

Jane ignored me as they went on down the hall, and she followed Amanda out the door to drive her home. She didn't come home all day, and I was half-asleep in bed when I heard her return with Gina, the disc jockey from Club 80. They giggled their way into Jane's room, and over the next hours the usual sounds serenaded me again into a state of severe anxiety.

Maybe it was the perfume, or the particular gifts my family had selected for me, but for some reason, when I had reached my limit, instead of sneaking a smoke or finding my hockey stick, that night I called home. Grant answered in a sleepy voice. It was late there, past midnight.

I whimpered my hello and he said, "Caroline? What's wrong?"

"I forgot to send Christmas presents," I moaned. "I forgot to call."

"That's okay—hey, hey, don't cry."

I stopped myself and wiped my eyes.

"Tell me what's wrong," Grant said patiently.

When I couldn't speak, he started talking. He said, "Well, we went to church last night. Bill Taylor asked after you. And I made the old broccoli soup. It turned out pretty good. And Madeleine baked the cookies this year. She painted them all Picasso-like, with limbs and faces all messed up. It was kind of grisly, actually."

I chuckled.

"And Dad's tree didn't fit *again*, so we cut the top off. It looks hilarious."

I pictured the house, with wreaths all around, the little Christmas bluebirds above our fireplace, with candles. Beverly Sills would have been singing carols, everyone dressed up.

Grant said, "We really missed you, C.K."

"Yeah?" I croaked.

"Oh yeah."

"You're not pissed?"

"Pissed? No."

"Because I've been such a creep."

"I wouldn't say that. You've been more like, absent. It would be a relief to have you be a creep if that meant you talked to us."

"Grant, I'm out of money," I confessed. "I'm so tired of worrying about money."

It should have shocked him to hear this, but he didn't miss a beat. "Money is not an impossible problem," he said. "We can help you with money."

"I lost it all," I said. "It's all gone."

After a deep breath he said, "Then we'll help you."

"I'm in debt."

"Hang on," he grunted. "I need to grab a blanket."

I held my breath.

When he returned I said, "I guess you want to know where the money went."

"Oh. I'm pretty confident that I know," he said.

"Well . . ."

"Yeah. I don't like her. But it was your money."

"I wish I'd come home," I said.

Grant was quick to jump on that. "*Come*," he said. "Come right now. I'll pay for the ticket. Dad would be overjoyed. We all want you here."

I thought it remarkable. My brother was just where he'd always been, beneath me, holding a net. And Dad was there, too. And my sister. And even Gayle. It was like seeing a mirage disappear, with my family standing real, behind it.

"I can't just leave," I said.

"Oh yes, you can," Grant said firmly. "Jane will survive. Jane is good at that."

Of course, Grant couldn't know everything. I had already imagined what she would do if I started packing. I envisioned razors and screaming. And worse.

"Well . . ." I sighed. "I just wanted to check in. . . ."

"Are you coming home, then?" Grant asked hopefully.

"Not now," I said. "I wish I could explain."

"Try," Grant said. "Please."

"Honestly," I told him, eyeing my field hockey stick, "I *can't*. I don't even know why myself."

And therein lay the root of my problem. I was not working from a perspective that made use of logic or introspection. I was too busy feeling to think, too buried under impulsive fear to spot my own unglued reasoning. Maybe I was like Jane in that way. Growing up, I'd always had trouble accepting reality, partly because I didn't see it. Now my perspective had warped into a funhouse of mirrors, with me running amok and bumping into glass. I was a prisoner on the bridge, believing the game; I was tripping on drugs, believing the hallucinations; I was escaping camp, because home was lost; and I was keeping Sam alive, thinking his death would be mine.

TWENTY-NINE

The sky was gorgeous as Jane and I drove across the Bay Bridge for our appointment with Francine. The sun hovered over the water and skyline like a monstrous burning balloon. I played with the radio while Jane reclined in her seat beside me.

"What do you think she wants to talk about?" she asked, batting my hand from the radio.

"I don't know."

"You must have some idea. What *have* you been talking about, anyway?"

"Stuff," I said.

"Well, I'm glad I'm coming," Jane said. "We need to accelerate your recovery. I mean, have you gotten *any* insight in the past months? Is she any good?"

"Yeah, she's good," I said.

Jane shifted in her seat so that she faced me. "Have you talked about me?" she asked sweetly.

"Sure. A little."

"Well?"

"Jane, I don't want to talk about it. Let's wait until we're there."

We drove in silence.

"Did you tell her about Easter last year?" she asked.

I cringed. "I'd rather forget about Easter."

Jane waited.

"No, I didn't tell her," I said.

"Then I'm telling that one," Jane said. "Someone has to speak the truth, or you'll never snap out of it."

"Fine," I said.

"Fine."

More silence.

I was sweating. For the first time in that godforsaken winter, I felt hot. I opened my window and breathed in the watery, January air. "Let's just be quiet," I said. "Please."

Jane was quiet for exactly ten seconds. Then she said, "Well, I'm going to talk in there, so you'd better get ready."

"Quiet," I barked. Jane shrank back, surprised.

Now I was fixated on that Easter. We had made the trip the past April, on Jane's insistence, just a week before moving into our Palo Alto studio. A few weeks later, we would make the dash out to New England to collect Jane's things, making for a dizzying month of familial unraveling.

Those last weeks at the Waverly house had felt like torture to me, and I had hoped that our three-day visit to St. Louis would provide a timely escape. I remember feeling united with Jane on the flight to my old home. We were about to embark on our first planned adventure as roommates, and I wanted my family to accept her.

Until Jane brought it up, I had blocked that Easter from my memory. Or, more accurately, I had revised the events so that they turned harmless and disappeared. Now, as we neared Francine's it all came back too vividly. That April, Dad had picked us up at the airport. Jane took the backseat and watched out the car window, seeing my town go by. When she brought up the idea of coming, she had said she wanted to see "my roots." I hadn't imagined that our visit would nearly sever them, too.

My brother and sister were also at home, and everyone was guarded, polite. Gayle came and joined us for dinner. Everything seemed bearable. At first.

We stood in the kitchen while Dad and Madeleine put the last touches on dinner. "How was your flight?" Gayle asked. She poured herself some wine.

"Bumpy," Jane said. "We slept, though."

"Hey, I meant to ask—did you photograph Studs Terkel?" Grant asked me. "I heard he came to Sorrell's last month. We're working with him on a case."

"We work at Moby's now," Jane informed him. She accepted some wine from Gayle and took a seat at the kitchen table. "Madeleine," she asked, "how are you liking Boston?"

My sister said, "Just fine."

"You look like you've lost weight," Gayle said to me.

"She's on my special diet," Jane smiled.

"Are you still running?" Dad asked me, chopping a tomato.

Jane guffawed. He had his answer.

Grant said, "It's been a while, Caroline. Do you still speak?"

Before I could open my mouth, Jane said, "She's tired."

With that, we all headed in to dinner.

That night, Jane and I lay in twin beds in my sister's old room. Madeleine was across the hall, snoozing in mine.

"Your family is so . . . in their *heads*," Jane said. "It's hard to believe you're related."

Most of the time, I thought the same thing. I loved them but had always felt vaguely other. I seemed to have a disproportionate amount of Mom's emotional genes, without enough of Dad's discipline to balance their effect. That's how I liked to reason it, anyway, blame the genes.

I started to hope there was an untapped gene I might have gotten from Dad, which would turn on and get me into grad school. This caused me to wonder about him and realize that when it came right down to it, he was something of a mystery—a fair-minded, thoughtful man who was emerging slowly, sadly, in his new role of sole parent. Who was this person who had come home every evening at six, had listened to and enjoyed us at dinner, then retreated to write his books? Dad had been only goodness in my eyes; he had rarely raised his voice or disciplined. He had been part of all the fun things, the bedtime reading, weekend trips to playgrounds, museums, and the symphony. I knew he loved classical music, wine, literature, and history. And science, of course. He was quiet but not shy, stoic but sensitive. A shadowy counterpart to Mom, with a separate identity I had yet to grasp.

Jane yawned and watched me, snuggling deep in her covers. "I really miss Monny here," she said. "Don't you? It's a sad house without her, isn't it?"

"It's sad," I agreed. "But they're moving on. They seem okay to me."

"It's easy to get along if your head is disconnected from your heart," Jane said. "Hey—you can put that in my quote book."

I did have a quote book for her, which was something she got a kick out of. She liked the idea of her thoughts living on in print.

I should have defended my family then, but I was too tired to argue. And because I was already feeling alien, Jane's words did have an effect. I figured if she saw it, then the space between me and my father, sister, and brother existed. And so I was grateful then, in the moments before sleep, to have Jane there. A person from whom there was no space at all.

"We'll visit Monny tomorrow," she whispered sleepily. "We'll be fine."

. . .

In the morning, after church, we went to Aunt Estie's house, where the whole extended family was gathered. Jane took a seat on the sofa and smiled nervously. I pointed out who everybody was, and relatives came by like a receiving line, greeting us and asking how I was.

"She's great," Jane would answer. Or, "She's a handful." Or, as I became more anxious, "She's hanging in there."

Aunt Estie pulled me aside before we left. "How *are* you?" she asked. "I haven't been able to get past your friend to ask."

"Oh, fine," I said.

She looked doubtful. "Can we have a visit while you're here? Just the two of us?"

"We're leaving tomorrow," I said. "Can we do it next time?"

"Is there going to be a next time?" she asked. It was my mother's voice that I heard. Her eyes that cornered me.

Jane walked over. "Thank you," she said to Aunt Estie. "It was a lovely party."

My aunt looked hard at Jane. "Thank you for coming," she said.

Jane and I left in a separate car, and as soon as we shut the doors, Jane let out a loud sigh. "Jesus, what a freak show," she said.

"What do you mean?"

"Everybody was so . . . *nice*," she said. "So *polite.*"

I put the car in gear and pulled away. "Stop it. They're my family, okay?"

"*I'm* your family," she corrected, as if for the first time. She jerked her thumb over her shoulder. "That's your gene pool." She produced a pale blue Easter egg, lifted from my aunt's centerpiece, and like an army general cried, "To the cemetery!" So I pointed the car west and hoped I remembered where it was.

The drive was long and scenic, a half hour through rolling hills and pretty homes in the outer suburbs of St. Louis. I got us there fine, but once we pulled inside the gates I paused, unsure. On instinct I headed for a big maple tree that looked familiar.

Acres of headstones surrounded us, lying flat against the ground. It was a massive, beautiful place, peaceful and groomed. It looked more like a park than a cemetery, except for one section of stone mausoleums that had cropped up since Mom was buried. I had heard that when people walked inside those monuments a recording of the dead person's voice said, "Welcome!" and actually started chatting.

I got out of the car and looked around.

"You don't know where it is," Jane said.

I took off, pretending at first to have a direction. I read headstone after headstone, brushing grass and dirt away to see the names. Bulah, Henry, Simone, Felix. Then I went back to the car. "I can't find her," I said. "I remember this tree, though."

Jane sighed and started browsing the headstones herself. We spread out to cover more ground. The more we looked, the worse I started to feel. It was such an awful, unnecessary metaphor, me in search of my mother. I started jogging, glancing at the stones and covering more ground. Jane and I intersected, and I said, "Fuck it, let's go."

"No way," Jane said, "I'm not going back without leaving this egg."

I pointed to a headstone. "Then give it to Mr. Kearny," I said.

Jane shielded her eyes and scanned the acres. "Are we even close?" she asked. "Jesus, Caroline, you might have said—"

"I remember that tree," I said firmly. "That's all." I went to the car and stood while Jane kept looking.

"What's her whole name again?" Jane shouted. She was crouched over a headstone, reading.

"Madeleine Martha Caroline Véron Kraus," I yelled back.

"Here's a Madeleine Véron *Moser*," Jane called.

My grandmother. This was progress. I jogged over, then knelt down and touched two headstones with our Swiss coat of arms carved into the stone. My mother's parents. "Okay, it's near here," I said. "She's close."

"See—your mother and I are connected," Jane said. "She led me here."

Jane was off, sniffing the air. Suddenly I wanted to find it first.

"What are you doing?" she asked as I scampered over the stones. Then she caught on and started sprinting, too, saying dead names as she went, her voice rising in pitch as we raced.

"*Ahhh!*" I screamed. "Here she is!" I dived onto the spot, a runner hitting home plate. Jane collapsed on top of me, laughing. I started laughing, too, and then crying-laughing, and then crying.

"Ha!" Jane said, crying with me. She pulled the egg from her pocket and placed it in the grass. We sat on Mom's grave and quieted. It was a bit of a letdown suddenly. After finding the grave, what do you do?

"Do you think she would have liked me?" Jane asked.

"Yes, I do," I said.

No one in my family would have agreed, nor would any of my friends or Jane's. But my mother had a way of penetrating people's layers and finding the parts that were good. She had embraced all of my friends, known them separately, and given some a sense of importance they'd never had. She would have embraced Jane at first, admired her determination, ironic humor, even her rage. Then she would have seen that parts of Jane had been manipulated, damaged, and destroyed, seen that these parts were now unleashed upon the world—manipulating, damaging, and destroying.

My mother might have loved Jane, but it would have been in the same way she loved my dog, Sam. Had she been alive that Easter, and found me standing beside Jane in our different kind of cage, she would have said that Jane had to go—had to be removed from my world. But as with Sam's life, only I could make the decision.

When Jane and I returned from the cemetery, Easter dinner preparations were already under way. At our house, especially around holidays, we moved from meal to meal. Even as we ate one, we were discussing the next, always in a state of anticipation.

Dad had prepared a sweet ham, with brown sugar and honey. We would have had salad, too, and maybe new potatoes with a lemon butter dill sauce. I had no idea that after Dad said grace, my family would pounce. And it seemed that this was just what Jane had wanted.

It started right away, with Dad asking Jane where she went to college.

"Why?" she asked.

He was taken aback. "Oh. Just curious," he said.

"I studied art and photography." Jane sighed and glanced at me, as if to say *See? Aren't they as I said?*

"Where?" Gayle asked, genuinely interested.

"She's a poet, too," I said. "Really good."

"I'm a feminist," Jane announced, surprising me along with everyone else. "Gloria Steinem came to Sorrell's not long ago, and she really inspired me. My plan is, I'm going to be the president of the National Organization for Women."

"Oh," Gayle said, trying again to make a connection. "That's quite a goal! Gloria and Betty Friedan are Smith alums with me—have you joined any grassroots groups? Or participated in any of their events?"

Jane's enthusiasm waned, and she said, "No."

Gayle absorbed this with a puzzled but polite smile.

Jane switched gears and turned to Grant. She asked how he could be a labor lawyer for the side of management. She wondered if that weighed on his conscience. She made sure I was paying attention.

"No," he said, frowning.

"When labor has no voice?" she asked. "No money, no power?"

All eyes bore down on her except mine, which were scanning my family, who seemed to be locking arms. I knew how intelligent the brains behind those eyes were, how versed they were in politics, law, medicine, art, finance, and anything else Jane might bring up, and then I looked at Jane, who had missed chunks of high school and paid little attention to facts in college. I felt a surge of anxiety.

"That's just wrong," Grant said. "Sorry."

"Think of Margaret Thatcher's policy," Jane went on. "Now that is a model."

Gayle, who had met the prime minister, raised an eyebrow. "Hold on," she said. "Margaret Thatcher is a member of the Conservative Party. She supports policies for a strong market economy, which differs quite a bit from the Labour Party—Labour relies heavily on governmental programs to address social and economic needs. Margaret Thatcher is not a great defense for your argument here. . . ."

Jane didn't think through what to say next. She just bellowed, "I know that," and ate a bite of ham. I felt like clawing the walls. My family was on to her. They collectively moved in for the kill.

"Do you know what a union is?" Grant asked.

"Ever heard of labor laws?" Dad added.

"I'm not talking about that," Jane said. "The economics of working-class life means there is no equality."

That puzzled everybody. "You mean capitalism?" Dad inquired.

"Have you read Adam Smith?" Madeleine wanted to know.

Grant was chewing ham like a steam engine.

"Think of the coal miners in Latin America right now," Jane started. "Or the Soviet Union."

That tipped Gayle over the edge. She could have schooled the president on Latin American fuel resources. In her trips to the *former* Soviet Union, Gayle had worked with coal-mining labor movement leaders. I could see her working hard to stay composed.

"Maybe we should stick to the U.S.," she suggested. "Here, labor has actually improved its bargaining leverage—our economy has a high job growth rate and an improved standard of living for blue-collar workers. And if you check the statistics, you'll see that membership in labor unions has actually declined, which is a pretty good indication that labor doesn't feel unions are as essential as they once were. Meanwhile, I might add, organizing efforts in the white-collar service sector are increasing."

I raised a hand. My fingers trembled. "Stop it," I said. "*Stop* it."

Jane said, "Oh, but this is just getting good."

"We're on to something interesting," Dad agreed. "I'd like to hear more."

Then, to everyone assembled, Jane said, "So, you are obviously a pack of Republicans."

I stood. "We wouldn't be having this discussion if Mom were here," I said angrily. And then I stormed out of the room into the kitchen. But they were unstoppable. Behind me the voices of my family became louder and Jane's more hostile. I grabbed my purse, walked outside, and hid by the fountain near my parents' bedroom to smoke. After that, I circled the house, muttering. I peeked into the dining room and saw animated faces, exasperated gestures, and lips moving fast.

Jane was outnumbered and outclassed, and I hated my family for it, for hating her. I left the window and headed for the garage. I found a tennis ball and hurled it against the wall. It came back and I hurled it again, harder. I let loose a howl and kicked a gardening basket. I kicked it until it broke apart, then pulled tools off my father's workbench and hurled them out onto the blacktop. I howled again, kicked the wheels on Gayle's Jaguar, then bashed in our five big aluminum trash cans with my best soccer kicks. In a daze, I turned around, screaming and growling, and saw my father, Gayle, Madeleine, Grant, and Jane, watching with astonishment in the doorway.

"What's wrong?" Dad asked, afraid to move.

Madeleine stepped toward me, but Jane raised a hand.

"I know what to do," she said. She walked calmly over to me, suppressing a giggle. "Honey?" she said. "Everything okay?"

I glanced over her shoulder at my family. They stared back with worried eyes. In that moment I believed Jane was right. They didn't know me anymore, if they ever had. Only Jane knew me. And by attacking her, they had attacked us both.

THIRTY

Jane and I parked near Francine's, and the memory of that Easter had me unraveled all over again. Since then my family had grown more and more concerned. Grant's trip to see me, and his appalled reports to Dad and Madeleine, had only reinforced their fear that I was moving further from their grasp. My father had even asked if I was on drugs, which was an ironic suggestion, since drugs were about the only self-destructive habit I'd failed to acquire. In truth, I later realized, he wasn't far off.

Jane had to coax me to Francine's door, and when I rang the bell a sinking feeling told me we were in for another ambush. Francine put us side by side on the sofa facing her. Sherry was banished to the outdoors.

"First of all, thanks for coming," she said to Jane.

My pen was out, poised. Francine gave me a reassuring smile.

"Sure," Jane said. "You know, I read your book. I really liked it."

"Yes, you told me," Francine replied, "on that first phone call."

"Oh yeah." Jane nodded. "Well."

Maybe to fill the silence, Jane added, "I'm a writer, too. I have some poems coming out in a collection at my church. Do you know the church? St. Marks?"

"I do," said Francine. "So you are both writers." She looked at me, then Jane did, too.

"Caroline?" Jane asked. "She's kind of stuck in that department. Wouldn't you say, honey?"

"I'm stuck," I agreed.

Jane said, "You should take notes, Francine. They all have the same plot." She gave me a sympathetic pat.

I looked up at the ceiling and muttered.

Francine said, "Is it too personal, Jane, or would you share what it is that you write about?"

Jane's face turned light pink. "Well," she said.

I said, "Sex and death." Two plots.

Shadows encroached upon Jane's cheeks like a gathering storm. "We're not here to discuss my writing," she said.

"I think you brought it up," I said.

Jane shot me an ugly look. Francine intercepted it, saying, "Well, moving on, then. Caroline, I thought you might want to share, with Jane present, some of the things that we have been talking about these past months."

At that moment, I could think of nothing I wanted to do less.

Jane said, "She has lung problems for a start. Chronic asthmatic bronchitis. Which is obviously grief—grief is held in the lungs—" She nodded to emphasize the point.

"Interesting," Francine said thoughtfully. "Although she also smokes." Looking at me, she added, "And she is in the room, so let's include her."

"But don't you think it's curious that she would be attacking her *lungs*?" Jane asked.

I listened, fascinated.

"Caroline?" Francine redirected. "Are you feeling verbal today?"

Jane giggled.

"I don't know what to say," I admitted. That was my big piece.

"The thing about Caroline—" Jane started.

"Hold on," Francine said, raising a finger. "Let's have Caroline talk for herself, and you talk for yourself."

Jane closed her mouth.

Francine looked at me.

Jane cocked her head slowly and looked at me, too.

"Okay," I said, looking at Jane. "We're in trouble. I know you say we're a team, but—"

"We always get back to this," Jane interrupted. "We are *friends*," she said firmly. "Period."

"But not friends in the usual sense," Francine said. "You are friends who, for instance, share a bank account."

Jane said, "The way I see it, Francine, we are married. Caroline and I have an agreement just like any other marriage."

"I did promise to stay no matter what," I said. "And I promised I'd take care of the money."

Jane was rocking a little, intent on the carpet.

"I'm wondering, Jane," Francine said, "have you married other friends? Is Caroline the first?"

"That is a hostile question," Jane snapped. "Have I been arrested or something? Do I need a lawyer?"

"Let me rephrase," Francine continued. "Do you think this is a fair arrangement for Caroline? What is your part in this agreement?"

I groaned inwardly. Francine was escalating us into nuclear territory.

"I look after Caroline," Jane said bitterly. "She's sick a lot, and depressed, and stuck in this . . . in *grief*, which is what we should be talking about, by the way. I'm the one who boils the herbs she drinks, who throws the cigarettes away, who cooks, and shops, and keeps the damn bathroom clean after she steams it all up and leaves

Q-tips everywhere. I'm the goddamn maid, if you want to know——"
Jane was breathless, excited. "I earn every penny."

I listened, amazed.

"Well, that sounds like hard work," Francine admitted. "And
you signed up for this because . . . ?"

"Because I love Caroline," Jane said. "Aren't you listening?"

"And she can't take care of herself?" Francine looked at me.

I hemmed and hawed.

Jane released a vindicated sigh.

Francine said, "Okay . . ." It looked as though her head hurt,
what with all the contradictions to keep straight. "So, if I've got
this right, Jane takes care of Caroline, and Caroline takes care of
Jane, but nobody is taking care of themselves. Is that about right?"

"This is ridiculous," Jane snorted. To me she said, "No wonder
you're getting worse."

I glanced at Francine, offended on her behalf. She seemed
unfazed.

"But Jane," I said, "she has a point. And I am worried about
us—about money."

Looking at Jane, Francine added, "Did you know that?"

"Hold on," Jane said. "Why are we back to me?"

"I'm in debt," I said.

"And that's my problem?" Jane looked at Francine. "What *is* this,
man? I've never been to therapy like this."

"Where does your money go?" Francine asked me.

"Our rent," I said, "Jane's car payments; our groceries; her
phone calls to Europe; odds and ends, like the wet suit she needed,
and the surfboard. Her therapy, lots of clothes, special face soap——"

"Hey," Jane interrupted, "I paid for my face soap."

"Did you know that Caroline can't afford this arrangement?"
Francine asked.

Jane was entering a full-scale sulk. She checked her watch.

"Does it seem reasonable that a friend should be paying for you this way?"

Jane shook her head in disbelief. "Jesus," she said, "I can't believe it. Is that all you two talk about? Money? Is money more important than loyalty? Or love?"

"What do you think?" Francine countered.

"Money is irrelevant," Jane said. "I tell Caroline this all the time. She's constantly moaning about it, and missing life while she's counting pennies. It's becoming a problem for me, really."

I stiffened.

"So you don't worry about money," Francine said.

"Not a bit," Jane said. "I worry about my friend who's dying of AIDS, and the millions who go without food in the world. I'm worried about the old woman on Mission Street, who talks to the air and sits in a dirty wheelchair, and all the children who are fucked and abused every day—every sixty seconds a new one joins the fold—left to hide in corners, with razors and empty promises." Jane sat back. "That's what I worry about, Francine. Not whether I have lunch money."

Francine came right back with, "Have you ever been without lunch money?"

Jane slapped the couch. "The point is, I don't *worry* about it. If Caroline wants to back out of our life—"

"Then you *would* have to worry about it," Francine said. "I mean, you do have to live somewhere, right? And eat, at least? Or would you choose the dirty wheelchair on Mission Street."

"Over obsession about money, I'd choose the chair," Jane said. "But it's a moot point because I can take care of myself. Believe me, I survived before Caroline came along."

"Ah! But Caroline obviously thinks she *needs* to take care of you," Francine said. "Maybe you should let her know you can take care of yourself—let her know how unimportant the thousands of dollars she has given you were, make sure she hears that you will be fine when she doesn't cover your part of the rent, or your car payments, or the nice boots you are wearing."

Jane looked at me and said, "Would you say something, for Christ's sake?"

I blinked like a mole hitting the light.

Jane was coiled like a spring. She threw up a dismissive hand and said, "Caroline can do whatever she wants with her money. I don't need her money—that's her decision. If she wants to give in to her family's values, then what the fuck am I doing here anyway?"

"You said you'd be out on the street if I didn't help," I said. "Do you need help or not?"

Jane folded her arms and said, "If you are going to reduce our relationship to money, then it's time I left."

I looked to Francine for help.

"Okay, let's put aside the money for a moment," Francine said. "Jane, how would you describe your attachment to Caroline?"

I groaned, out loud this time.

"My *attachment?* So I take it we're not even going to touch a relevant subject," Jane said. "We're going to keep going down dead-end paths."

"Maybe it's not a dead end," Francine said. "Give it a try."

Jane said, "Caroline's problem isn't me, in case you're under that impression."

"I'm not," Francine said. "My impression is that she is her own problem, and you may be cultivating that problem, for reasons of your own survival."

That was a conversation stopper. Even Jane looked blank. She started to say something and then looked at me.

"Hmn," I said.

Jane brought her thumb up to her lip and ran it back and forth. She wanted to suck it as much as I wanted to smoke. After some thought, she smiled and said, "You're really something, Francine. Very good."

"Oh?"

"I take it back. I like you. I think we are a lot alike."

"Really. How?"

Jane's eyes were suddenly warm and sweet. "I can see it now," she said. "We recognize each other. I know. I know what it's like."

"What is it like?" Francine asked, very curious.

I might as well have been wallpaper.

"You've been hurt, too," Jane said. "Something happened to you. Something that opened a hole."

Francine's expression was solid, impenetrable. "Why do you think that?" she asked.

"It opened a hole, and you've been searching for ways to close it ever since. You think you'll find the answer by mending people like us. And when we don't fit your remedy, it hurts. I understand."

Francine leaned forward and in a low voice said, "If you want to know the truth, Jane, I think everybody has 'holes.' Everybody has holes, or rips, or severed limbs. We all cross lines, leap borders, get lost in the woods. The metaphors are endless. It's an inevitable fact of living, that loss or trauma will occur, to varying degrees, to all of us. So if you are looking to single me out as special, as some kind of kindred spirit, you are not looking far enough. Look beside you. Look out on the street, in bus stations, at work, in your parents' home. We are not so special, you and I."

Francine crossed her arms and said, "Now, who survives? That's a different story. Some of us really thrive. Others manage. And a percentage is destroyed, little by little, from within. They may survive, but they don't exactly live."

Jane opened her mouth, and Francine raised a finger. "So, it would be just fine with you if Caroline took care of herself now?" she asked. "We never did hear that answer."

I looked at Jane, on the edge of my seat.

To me, Jane said, "Sure. Have a party, honey. I believed you were different, but maybe Francine is right. Maybe I was wrong. You can smoke and cry and write about dead mothers forever. I have better horizons planned."

That was it. I had been twisted, rung out, and thrown back in deep water. I was done. I looked at Francine and said, "Isn't it time to go?"

Jane was out the door without so much as a wave, and I lingered behind. Francine caught my arm and said, "It's going to get bumpy, but hang on, Caroline."

Jane waited by my car, her mind already racing, already calculating what had to be done. She didn't speak to me for the whole ride home, and when we walked into our apartment she disappeared into the bathroom. I knew what she was doing. Under her pressed slacks new red ridges were growing, along with prescient fear.

"Well?" she said, standing in my doorway. She was wrapped in a bathrobe, scrubbed and pink from the bath. "What are you going to do? I need to know now."

"Can't we just stop this and be normal?" I asked. "Friends? Like other people. We could be neighbors, have our own friends, date people and not care, be *happy* . . ."

"Don't be naive," Jane said.

"Why can't we?"

"Because that is not reality," she said. "That is not who we are."

"We could try."

"Wrong," she replied. "All or nothing."

She was so calm. So assured and confident. I envisioned the Void in me opening again, the horrible vastness of being disconnected, alone.

"All," I conceded.

"I don't want to go through this again," she warned. "Not ever."

"No," I assured her. "Okay."

That night, we ate popcorn in front of the television. Jane wore heart boxer shorts that revealed her shiny new cuts. I cut a switch in my brain and drifted back into numb compliance. We watched the *Late Show with David Letterman*, and *I Love Lucy*, and *McCloud*. And the hours passed.

THIRTY-ONE

When I called my father later that January, it was strictly to ask for money. I knew that my voice was anxious and desperate, but eviction had turned into a real possibility, and I wasn't cut out for robbing registers, that was clear. Dad picked up on my frantic tone, and he said yes right away.

"I don't want you dipping into your nest egg," he said. "So if you need something to tide you over, I'm glad to help."

I thanked him sincerely and then silently thanked my brother for not spilling the beans on my lost inheritance.

"As long as it's for *you*," he added. "Only you?"

"Right," I lied.

"Okay. How much do you need? What's it for?"

"I was thinking of taking some classes," I said, "to get ready for graduate school. A GRE class, and some film courses, and maybe creative writing." It was a tired refrain, but it still sounded so good.

"Will you have time for all that?" Dad asked. "Maybe you should cut down on hours at the bookstore—I can help make up the difference. I think it's a great idea to get rolling on graduate school."

It should have made me sick that I had predicted this. "That's great, Dad," I said. "I'm so grateful."

"How much do you think would get you going?" he asked again. I summoned my courage and said, "Two thousand dollars."

"Okay," he said. "I'll mail it today."

The visit with Francine seemed to linger in the air between Jane and me, though we never acknowledged its impact or brought up that day again. Instead, Jane settled back into her old routine and started dating a new woman from her church—a woman who looked eerily like any one of the tennis ladies back home in St. Louis. She was an attractive soccer mom type, who wore plain belted dresses and matching pumps. Her name was Ruth Evans, and though she was without the husband she'd had for a dozen years, her two children and breezy maternal style added a new category of lovers to Jane's repertoire.

As with all of Jane's other conquests, at first I resented her. As the $2,000 gradually ebbed away, I found myself alone more and more at night, contemplating where all my friends had gone, while Jane immersed herself in the early stages of wooing, which was the one period when she did not want me along.

During most of these nights I parked myself in front of my television and swirled through channels until the monotony put me to sleep. Sometimes I found a movie to transport me, in the way only movies could do, and for a while I'd forget about my debt or Jane's last round of cutting. I'd see Henry Fonda in *The Grapes of Wrath*, or Jack Nicholson in *Five Easy Pieces*, or Meryl Streep in *Sophie's Choice*, and disappear in their magnificence and their fictional ordeals. Generally, I flipped past depictions of reality on my way to these clouds, but one night my hand froze on the remote as fragments of sound from a PBS documentary caught my attention.

In a modulated voice, a narrator said, ". . . such individuals may exhibit frantic efforts to avoid real or imagined abandonment, sudden shifts in mood, inappropriate anger, and self-destructive acts such as cutting."

I leaned forward then and nudged up the volume. The voice said something about "impulsive behavior," such as promiscuity, compulsive spending, shoplifting, and reckless driving, along with "uncertainty in things like sexual orientation, career choice, friendships, moral values . . ."

Bullet points appeared on the screen, under the words *Borderline Personality Disorder.* I grabbed a notepad from beside my bed and began writing down what I heard. The narrator went on to describe individuals who were "bright, witty, charming, and creative." Also charismatic and "highly manipulative." Numbly, I wrote down what appeared to me a narrative of my alter ego, my supposed partner for life. Phrases like "broken trust" and "sexual abuse" were followed by descriptions of people who had been "stripped of their boundaries." I wrote down words like "damaged" and "stolen" and "violent rage."

My astonishment grew as people who lived with the objects of these descriptions said their pieces, too. They talked of continuous guilt, financial ruin, intense love, and fear of punishment. Unconsciously, I added my own word: *"trapped."*

As the program unfolded, I felt as if cameras had been planted in my life with Jane and the footage was rolling now for all to see. I felt a heavy sinking in my chest, combined with the small hope that maybe I was not alone in my experience, that maybe there was a name for Jane and me after all. There was dread, and there was hope, because it looked as if a minefield of disasters awaited me and yet these people who came forward had survived.

When the program was over, I instinctively reached for the phone and dialed Stella. Since moving into the Hancock apartment, Jane had tired of her again and had taken to replaying Stella's phone messages just to make fun of her awkward attempts to reconnect. From what I could tell, Stella's worst crime had been that she was both reliable and well-meaning, which to Jane had amounted to dull. For my part, I had grown to count on Stella more and more as the only friend who could possibly understand what I was going through.

It was late at night when I called her, and on her answering machine I asked if we could meet for dinner the next night, while Jane was on a camping trip with Ruth. I mentioned the topic of the documentary I'd just seen and left it at that.

Stella picked a small Italian place with cozy booths. When I saw her walk through the door, I stood up at our table and eagerly waved my arm. I was always hungry for these periodic visits, when we shared our Jane troubles and joys and then gradually got tipsy enough to help them recede. That night Stella poured us each a glass of white wine, and I started asking questions right away.

"Did you know that self-injury is one of the *main behaviors* of people with a borderline personality?" I asked. Stella watched me refer to my notepad, mildly amused. "In the program last night they also said that—and I quote—'individuals diagnosed with borderline personality disorder usually have a pattern of undermining themselves at the moment a goal is about to be realized'—like dropping out of school, or destroying a good relationship just when it's clear that the relationship could last. They described people who had sudden shifts in mood, unstable, intense relationships, and inappropriate anger. And they mentioned *cutting*. And impulsive behavior—they mentioned sleeping around, compulsive spending, shoplifting, and reckless driving—" I looked up at Stella. She had polished off her wine and was pouring herself another glass. Eventually she returned my stare.

"Well?" I asked.

"Yes," Stella said. "I know what you're asking. I've thought about this on and off, Caroline, but I've never really let myself dwell on it."

"So you know about this borderline thing?" I asked. "Is it real?"

"I learned a little about it during my psych rotation, but not very much. I was just there for three weeks, but there was one patient who was supposedly borderline."

"And?"

Stella laughed and winced at the same time. "And she was attractive, obviously smart, with long blond hair. She was totally captivating, and the only person that my chief resident warned me about."

"What did he say?"

"He said that I should be careful with the borderlines, because I would want to save them," Stella replied. "I remember that comment vividly. He said that I should be very careful not to get drawn in by them."

Jokingly, I said, "Uh-oh."

"I took it personally," Stella recalled. "I thought my chief was saying that *I* was vulnerable for some reason, specifically *me*. And to be honest, I still don't know if that's what he meant or not." She picked up her menu and, after a long sigh, studied it.

"On the other hand," I said, thinking aloud, "lots of people have shifts in mood, or inappropriate anger. And people drop out of school all the time. And I'm not a great driver myself—"

"Right," Stella said. "Although cutting is not exactly like running a red light." She paused, then said, "But then again, look who you're talking to. I've been in love with Jane for years, so I'm not very objective. Even now I still can't stop hoping that the best in her will win out. I suppose I should know better, but there it is."

"How long have you been thinking about this?" I asked. "Why didn't you tell me?"

"Well, Jane cut herself the first week we were together," Stella said. "I actually found her while she was doing it, in the bathroom of my old apartment. She was taking a razor up and down her arms. And that's when I remember thinking, Oh *God.*"

Stella took a deep breath as I shredded my napkin and waited.

"I mean, just imagine," Stella went on. "There she was, possibly the one type of person against whom I'd been specifically warned, sitting in my bathroom and bleeding." After a pause she added, "And why didn't I tell you I was worried? I guess because I've been busy not telling myself." Ruefully, she added, "Well. At least I didn't go into psychiatry."

After some thought I asked, "Did the woman on your rotation get better?"

"I don't know," Stella admitted. "I wasn't around long enough to see."

A waiter approached, and both of us delivered our orders. After he left I leaned forward and said, "You know, all last night I was wondering, is someone necessarily borderline just because they develop defenses after suffering a really serious trauma, like Jane did?"

"Are you sure she did?" Stella asked quietly.

"Oh no," I groaned. "You too? Why is that so hard to believe?"

"I'm not saying it didn't happen," Stella said. "I used to believe everything Jane said. But if you're going to become a student of borderline traits, don't overlook a big one—manipulation."

"Which might be a product of trauma," I pointed out.

"You could be absolutely right," Stella nodded. "Or absolutely wrong."

"But it all makes sense, given the way she is—I mean, *something* has made her deathly afraid that people will leave. *Something* drives her to cut herself, and wreak havoc with money."

"Other people's money," Stella clarified.

The food arrived, and I watched Stella disappear in thought as she ate her salmon. She seemed different to me that night, more secure than before, more confident. I wondered if it was only a coincidence that she had also been separated from Jane for weeks.

"You seem good," I ventured. "Happy."

"Almost," Stella agreed.

"Not being around Jane has done wonders?" I suggested.

"Heaven and hell at the same time." Stella smiled.

Lucky girl, I thought. I envied her that smile.

Stella said, "But getting back to your point about whether or not Jane could be borderline, first define it, and then maybe we'll get somewhere. Speaking generically, yeah, it makes sense to me that a person would develop ideations—or defenses—as a result of some kinds of trauma. But then again, some people can become unhinged for no reason at all. And what about others, who by all rights have suffered enough so that they *should* become unhinged, but come out completely grounded and fine?"

I looked at Stella, exasperated. She smiled back sympathetically and said, "Okay. How long do you think we've both been trying to save Jane?"

"A long time," I admitted.

"A long time," Stella agreed. "And do you know the old joke about the definition of insanity?"

I thought for a second and then frowned. "Doing the same thing over and over again . . . , " I said slowly.

"And expecting different results," Stella finished.

"Ha ha," I said glumly.

"*Swa*-ha," Stella corrected.

"Believe me," I said, "I've thought of that before." Mentally speaking, in fact, I'd been keeping score for some time. As far as I was concerned, my hockey stick habit, combined with smoking, spending myself into oblivion, and then departing from my sexual preference, had put me right up there with Jane. Maybe I was even ahead of her, since I couldn't claim a reasonable cause for my slide into the abyss.

"Hey," Stella said gently. "I was just kidding."

"I'm not," I said weakly.

"Caroline, you're struggling now, and I am, too. But don't put yourself in Jane's league, if that's what you're thinking."

"Why not?" I asked. After a pause I confessed, "I've been injuring myself, too."

Stella frowned. "Cutting?"

I shook my head and then, thinking better of providing details, said, "Never mind."

"Caroline—" Stella started.

"I've also lost all of my money," I continued. "And trust me, I could go on."

Stella said, "Hmn."

My voice wavered as I gathered my nerve and said aloud the fear that had been deep in my heart for years, going all the way back to my mother's depression. "What if there is no way to get better?" I asked. "Jane and I could be stuck like this forever."

Stella put a tractor beam on my eyes and said, "You want to know the remedy?" I nodded, holding back tears.

"We have to separate ourselves from the thing that is hurting us. From Jane. We both have to stop with the guilt. You're right—being away from her has done wonders. So I speak from recent experience."

"Easy for you to say," I replied. "I can't just disappear—she'd be homeless."

"Did you injure yourself before you met Jane?" Stella asked.

"God, no," I said instinctively, then I realized what she meant.

"Were you in debt?"

"Not like this," I admitted.

"Or whatever else is in your bag of secrets?"

"I didn't smoke, either," I mused.

"So just think about it logically," Stella said. "Look at Caroline before Jane, and look at her after."

We were quiet for a while, and in our silence I gradually imagined Jane and myself in a new light—as two people who might have the kinds of problems that could be fixed, but, as Stella suggested, not if we stayed together. The seed was planted, and I felt simultaneously freed and crushed. One by one, I began flipping the switches in my brain to on, so that even drunk I felt alert. Primed. My image of Jane was changing steadily in my mind, from the wronged child I needed to save to an irreparable adult that I might have to flee. But leaving her homeless still seemed insurmountable.

"It's scary," I said as Stella and I left the restaurant. "This idea of borders and lines. I mean, I'm on that spectrum, too, somewhere. It makes me wonder how thin these lines are. They always seem so hard to see, until after you've passed them."

Stella said, "Tell me about it." We stood between our cars, reluctant to part.

"Do you ever wonder what Jane would have been like if nothing bad had happened to her?" I asked. "Assuming that something bad did," I added.

"What would any of us be like?" Stella replied. "Jane hasn't cornered the market on being traumatized."

I let that linger, then shrugged and gave Stella a hug before stepping into my car.

A week later, Jane was watching for Ruth out of our second-floor window. When her wood-paneled station wagon pulled up, Jane shouted, "Honey!" and ran down to the street to greet her. This was to be my "meet the parents" visit with Ruth, and I was trying hard to get in character as they came up the stairs, full of happy chatter.

Jane had a typical dinner going, a carrot soup of her devising, then pasta with peas, and my contribution for the occasion, store-bought bread and wine. I stood by the stove when they came in and tried to look busy in one of Jane's aprons. "Okay," Jane called, "now it's a party!" She brought Ruth into the kitchen, twitching with delight. "My two favorite people in the same room," she smiled. "Perfection."

Ruth greeted me with a lightweight handshake, and I returned in kind. She said she'd heard wonderful things about me, and I returned the compliment, mirroring her smile.

"Wine," Jane said, looking nervously between us. "We will have wine." And with that, she disappeared around the corner.

While Jane was gone Ruth inspected our kitchen, and then she whispered, "May I use your loo?"

"Of course," Jane said from the doorway. "And bundle up, honey," she said to me. "It's up to the roof garden for hors d'oeuvres."

"No," I groaned. "It's *January*, Jane."

"Quit your whining," she chirped. "The Cabernet will keep us warm."

"But first may I use the loo?" Ruth asked hopefully. Jane winked at me and took her by the elbow, offering a tour of our place as she went.

"This is Caroline's room," I heard her say from down the hall. Her voice got slightly louder when she added, "And that's the Monny wall. The dead mother shrine."

Up on the roof we sipped our Cabernet and watched the sun cast long shadows before sinking over the roofs of the city. Jane put her feet up in Ruth's lap for a rub. "Tell us a story," she said, looking at me. "Tell Ruth the one you wrote about *running away*."

"Which one?"

"That one you showed me—about *running away* from home when you were little. It's classic Caroline, Ruth—all about leaving because things get tough. Very insightful, I thought. And of course it ends with the grand exit of all time—a goddamn dead mother."

Ruth gaped at that comment, but I didn't flinch. I knew that underneath our apparent truce, Jane was still fuming about Francine. In the past, her sarcastic appropriation of my mother had been welcome—somehow it had diffused the reality of my longing and comforted me, as if Jane were my one ally in the fight with grief. But after our visit with Francine, and then my discovery of the word "borderline," things had started feeling different for me, which Jane sensed.

Looking back, I realize that neither Stella nor I could with certainty name the source of Jane's troubles. Diagnoses like that require years of training that neither of us had. Nevertheless, after talking with Stella, I'd started to see both Jane and me through a new prism of possibility. Diagnosable or not, I saw us differently that night, and her words about my mother were infuriating.

"What's wrong?" Jane asked. "Cripes. Don't be offended. You've nailed your niche, honey. Death, dying, and all things dead. And running from problems instead of facing them. Come on, treat us. Ruth has never heard you tell a story, and that's your specialty."

"No thanks," I said. "And lay off my mother."

Jane looked startled for a split second before she grinned. "Then fuck it," she said cheerfully. "Let's eat!" And before Ruth could get a word in, Jane shot down the ladder and disappeared. Ruth and I watched her go, and then we stared at each other.

"It's fine with me if you don't tell the story," Ruth whispered.

"Thank you," I whispered back.

"Don't be mad at her," she added. "Jane loves you so much. She never stops talking about you, like you hung the moon. I guess she must be having one of her moods tonight. Sometimes she can really switch gears, don't you think? I just tell her what I tell my kids: Don't take life so *seriously*. Because if I can survive being battered, and then divorced, she can survive anything."

I suppressed the urge to choke and then to smile. I looked at Ruth with sympathy. We'd only just met, and already I had discovered the broken part that had drawn Jane to her. As I saw it, the only problem for Jane was that Ruth seemed to have overcome it, or at least she seemed on her way. If she really was as spunky and grounded as she seemed, then her future would not contain the woman who was currently fuming downstairs.

After a prolonged dinner—in which Jane flattered Ruth, stroked her arm, and wooed her with profoundly loving eyes—I left them with the dishes and went back to the roof for a smoke. No mints this time, no lotion. I was lost in my head when Jane came up behind me.

"Hey," she said.

I spun around.

"Honey? What the hell am I supposed to do if you die?" she asked, reaching for my cigarette. I let her take it, and she took one long puff before dropping it under her shoe.

"I have no idea," I said, watching my moment's relief being ground into the terrace.

"Right," Jane said. "Thanks for thinking ahead."

I shrugged.

"So are you going to snap out of it or what?" she asked. "Ruth thinks you're mad at us."

"I'm tired," I said, hoping that would suffice. But Jane's eyes narrowed, and her body tensed.

"You are embarrassing me," she said angrily. "I told Ruth you were so smart and funny—the point is for us all to have fun *together*. You haven't even tried to get to know her tonight."

"She's your friend," I said.

"And *you* are my wife," she replied. "I need both of you."

Later, it occurred to me just how true those words must have been for Jane. Ever since our beginning I had been joined to all of Jane's lovers, as if to complete some ideal in her mind.

"Sorry," I said sincerely, aiming for the ladder. "What do you guys want to do?"

"Forget it," Jane muttered, coming down behind me. "I'm tired now too, thanks to you."

That night I lay in bed staring into the darkness as Jane and Ruth rocked the wall between our rooms. They murmured and shrieked, and I knew the show was for me. I saw my future clearly: spouse and guardian to a bottomless pit of need, to a broken person, a woman whom I could not stop from sinking and who would take me down beside her.

It was a grave I'd been digging all along. And I was halfway into it.

Chapter
THIRTY-TWO

I heard Ruth leave before dawn, and in the morning I found Jane in the kitchen with coffee, reading the paper. I sat at the table and drummed my fingers until she looked at me and said, "Spill it."

I tried to smile.

"You look like you're about to give birth. Spill it, honey."

"Jane?" I said.

"Yes, dear?" she replied.

"I'm going to move back to St. Louis."

I let that hang for a moment, then added, "I'm broke, and tired, and I can't take it anymore. I'm not sure when, but pretty soon I'll be gone, so we should figure out somewhere where you can stay."

Jane said, "I should get a medal for all the times I suffer through this conversation."

"I'm giving notice at the store," I said. "Today."

Jane simmered behind her paper. I felt her seethe and saw the profile of her jaw jutting forward. Feeling the heat rise, I went to my room and started dressing for work. Moments later Jane was behind me, holding a long butcher's knife.

"Out of the *blue*," she hissed. "You fucking liar."

I stared at the knife.

"I won't survive it," she said. "You promised you wouldn't give up. You said *you* would be different." She came closer. "Everything you said, man, a fucking lie."

Her tough-girl street-talk mode usually preceded violence, so I raised myself to my full height and backed up. Jane grabbed the telephone and threw it at my head.

I yelled, "Shit!" as it bounced off my cheek and hit the wall behind me.

"You're a fucking idiot," Jane said, spitting. She came toward me.

"Jane," I said, "look at us. We are *killing* each other." I backed up, inches from the wall, and tripped over the phone cord. "I'm black and blue, and your skin is ripped to shreds. We are a goddamn freak show."

Jane rushed forward and pushed my shoulders, sending me hard into the wall. "You," she seethed. "You are *worse* than the rest. I trusted you, man. I believed you. Now what am I supposed to do? I have *nothing*. You have *everything*. The only difference between you and a molester is that you have fucked me in the head."

She threw me on my bed and straddled me, squeezing one hand around my neck. "Here's what it feels like to be *me*," she said, tightening her grip on my throat. My ears started ringing, and then she let go. I heard the knife drop to the floor, and she fled the apartment.

I lay there, shaking and turning cold. The phone was off its hook, and a recorded voice repeated, "Please hang up," over and over again. I slid off my bed, crawled over to it, and dialed home. Dad picked up, still chewing his Sunday lunch.

"Hi!" he said cheerfully.

"Dad," I croaked. I rubbed my throat and tried again. "Dad . . ."

"Yes?"

"Dad . . . I'm completely . . ."

I heard a chair scrape against the floor, and he waited.

"I—I'm in trouble here," I stammered.

"Are you hurt?" he asked. "What is it?"

"Jane threw a phone at me, and—we've had a bad fight."

"I'm coming," Dad said. "I'll come tonight."

"Oh *no*," I exclaimed. "No, God. Please don't come here."

"Well, I'm either coming there or you are coming here," he said.

"Yes, I'll come home," I said. "Please don't come here."

"Can you really pull yourself together and leave?"

"I can. Except I don't have any money left. I don't know how to—"

"*All* of the money is gone?" Dad asked, incredulous. "The money from your mom? And the two thousand dollars I sent you?"

"I know. I know. I'm sorry, Dad."

"Can you at least use a credit card?" he asked.

"No."

After a silence he couldn't resist saying, with venom, "*Jane.*"

I said, "Dad, she's really upset. She's carrying a knife around and—"

"Okay," he said. "You need to stay away from Jane. I'll hold off coming if you get organized *now*. Call movers, and book a flight. I'll buy the ticket for you. I'll pay the movers."

"But my car," I started.

"Ship it," he interrupted. "I don't think you'd better drive through that desert again. We'll ship it. I'll pay."

"Okay," I said.

"Okay."

I squeezed the phone, hopeful and terrified at the same time.

"I love you, Caroline," he said. "I don't fully understand what's happened, but I love you. When you've got the details, call me.

Actually, call me regardless, tonight—every night until you're here. I expect you to stay in touch now, all the way. Or I'll be on your doorstep."

That put the fear of God in me. Dad and Jane squaring off on Hancock Street would be the worst kind of surreal nightmare. After we hung up, I frantically flipped through a phone book and called the first moving company listed—A-1 Movers. For a price, they said they could act quickly, have my things en route to St. Louis within the week.

A few hours later I was at work. When Piper said the phone was for me, I expected Jane. Instead I heard Stella's voice, frantic on the other end.

"Jane just called me," she panted. "I'm on my way over to your place now."

This shouldn't have surprised me, but it did. On another day, I might have worried for Stella or even felt a twinge of jealousy that she'd been called in for the rescue. But something had snapped, finally, in me, and with complete detachment, I said, "Good luck."

"She's really devastated, Caroline," Stella said.

"That makes two of us," I replied.

"Are you mad at *me?*" she asked worriedly. "You sound funny."

My voice was giving me away. I wasn't mad, exactly, but she was right, something had severed. I was beginning to think that Stella could be my way out.

"No, but I'm leaving," I said.

"How soon?" Stella fretted. "Jane said immediately."

Well, I thought. So Jane was ahead of me. I held the phone and realized that Jane had already put Stella on deck as her next place to land if I actually left. And if I made that happen—if I made it too hard for Stella to say no—then maybe I could be rounding the bases for home before the week was out. As Stella started pleading, it occurred to me that immediately was good.

. . .

Later that afternoon I went to the manager's office at Moby's and knocked on her door. Lisa was a no-nonsense type, with short dark hair, Woody Allen glasses, and burgundy lipstick. She invited me in and wasn't at all surprised when I said I was quitting on the spot.

"Caroline," she said, "I know something has been wrong with you. The bruises, for one thing." She tapped her forehead. "I hope this means you're getting help."

"I'm going home," I admitted. "I've been a mess here, I know. I'm sorry."

"You and Jane Lowell have been a strange pair," Lisa allowed. "We've been wondering what was in the water at Sorrell's."

I laughed and said, "Yeah, good question." Then a wave of guilt that had been at my back for months caught up with me. And before I could stop myself, I stammered, "Before I go, I should mention that there are some . . . loopholes in the register system. A way people might be . . ." I cleared my throat. "Setting money aside . . . when they ring up books."

I felt my face turn pink as Lisa leaned forward over her desk and said, "Oh? *Who?*"

"I can't say."

"Have you seen this happen?"

I nodded.

"How is it done?"

"A book comes to the register. It's not rung up. The sales clerk takes the money from the customer, calculates the change in their head with tax, opens the register to give the change, then pockets the original cash."

"I see. And you've seen this happen?"

"It happens."

"And you won't tell me who has done this?"

"Really, I can't."

Lisa removed her glasses and eyed me. "It's not very hard to guess," she said.

I waited.

"But I won't," she sighed. "Thanks for letting me know."

It wasn't much of a redemption, but it was enough to get me out the door.

Stella's car was parked in front of our place when I pulled onto the median after work. A meter maid paused as I stepped out. "Hey!" she called. "Finally I get to meet the person who thinks this median is a parking space." I paused as she started on my ticket and then flew past her with an overdue glare.

Inside, our apartment was quiet. Moving down the hall, I heard low voices in the bathroom and peeked in. Stella was on the toilet lid, holding Jane's towel. Jane sat in the tub, her head between her knees. The room was steamy and smelled of jasmine soap.

"Hi," I said.

After a moment Jane rose out of the water and stood, dripping in all her nakedness. When I saw three raw razor cuts etched into her face, I screamed.

Stella could not look at me and I couldn't face her, either. She was all nerves as she wrapped a towel around Jane and helped her out of the tub.

Jane smiled at my horror. Stella looked completely drained and wore a defeated expression as she put antibiotic ointment across the cuts. Jane said, "Get packing already," and pointed me out the door.

Later, Stella came to my doorway, holding packs of razors. "I'm throwing these out," she said flatly. "I'm going to take them to the dumpster."

"Okay," I said.

"And Jane's expecting to stay with me," she added. "Did you know that?"

I squirmed and looked away. I had always seen myself in Stella, but never as painfully as I did right then. She was trapped, just as I had been a million times before, but even after all of our dinners, and all of the times she advised and rescued me, I was determined to save myself, regardless of what my exit did to her.

I said, "Just until she gets her feet under her."

Which both of us knew would be never.

Stella said, "Shit. I don't want her to move in, Caroline. You of all people should know why."

"You'll be all right," I assured her. And in Stella's face I saw something break then, because she knew I had left her behind.

When Stella went outside to toss the razors, I tiptoed to Jane's doorway. She was on her side in bed, knees tucked under her chin, thumb resting near her mouth. Her eyes were closed, her face a nightmare of raised red lines.

"I can hear you breathe," she croaked. "Your lungs are a mess."

"I have to go," I said.

"Then go."

"I want us both to be happy."

"Too late," she murmured.

"But it's not the end of the world, right?"

"Whose world?"

When I stepped closer, she cracked an eye.

"You shouldn't smoke," she said.

"You shouldn't cut yourself."

"You shouldn't bash your head in."

The front door opened, and Stella's steps came down the hall.

"You shouldn't go," Jane whispered. "Please don't go."

She closed her eye.

That night, I was watching television in bed when Jane walked in looking catatonic, holding the knife again. I sat up, wide-eyed.

"What are you watching?" she asked.

"The *Tonight* show," I said, slowly.

"Who's on?"

My eyes were glued to the knife. "Geena Davis."

"How appropriate," Jane said, stepping forward. "Thelma."

"Uh-huh."

She came to the edge of my bed and said, "Scoot over."

"First put the knife down," I suggested.

She dropped it on the floor and climbed in with her back to me, facing the television.

"They were lovers, you know," she murmured. "Thelma and Louise."

"I know."

"You have to look between the lines to see it."

"Yes."

"Do you think they made the right choice?"

I didn't answer.

"Honey?" Jane cocked her head. "Off the cliff?"

"What I remember most about that scene," I said, "is that we never see them hit the ground."

Jane's forehead wrinkled. In went the thumb.

"In movies, you can stay airborne forever," I said. "Which is why I like movies."

"But you do agree they were in love," she mumbled.

"Yes. I see that now."

"Good."

She was quiet in the morning, still lying in my bed as I brought in empty boxes from my car. "Going to work?" I asked, seeing she was awake.

"Nope. I quit. Yesterday."

I started strapping tape around the boxes, filling them with books.

"Phoned it in," she added.

"Then what are you going to do now?" I asked, trying to keep my temper. Her timing for becoming unemployed was unbelievable.

"Well, my razors seem to have disappeared," she said flatly.

"Maybe you could get a better job—"

Jane cut me off with a look.

"Or not," I said.

"You know I won't make it without you," she said. "I don't want to anymore. I'm tired, Caroline. I give up."

"Don't say that."

"Okay."

"You've got Stella," I reminded her. "And other friends. You've got Ruth—"

"Blah blah blah blah," Jane blurted. When I opened my mouth to interject, she shouted, "Blah!"

I put my head down and returned to packing. But I kept worrying about the knife, our drawers full of knives, and finally I said, "Really, Jane, what are you thinking of? If you stay with Stella—"

"Killing myself," she said calmly.

I stopped packing and said, "Whoa. *No*, Jane."

"Okay."

I came over to the bed, packing tape dangling, and said, "Are you serious?"

"Are you leaving?"

"You would kill yourself because I'm leaving?"

"Maybe it's a coincidence. We'll never know."

I sat on the bed and put my head in my hands.

Jane found my remote and clicked on the television.

I clicked it off and said, "Let's go," pulling at her arm.

"Where, honey?" she asked sweetly.

"The hospital."

"The *loony bin?*" she cried. "Are *you* insane? I've been there. That's worse than suicide."

I let go of her arm, then went to the kitchen and called Stella.

I whispered into the phone, "Please help me. Jane is going off the edge and I don't know what to do. Can you come? She's carrying a knife around—"

"Oh, shit," Stella said.

"I know you're at work, but I'm supposed to see my therapist in an hour, and I'm afraid to leave the house."

"I'll come over," she said grudgingly.

When Stella arrived, I pointed her toward Jane and took off fast to see Francine.

"She says she wants to die," I cried even before I'd removed my coat. "She's carrying a knife around. She cut her face. Her *face*, Francine." I was out of breath.

Francine said, "Okay, okay. Come in and settle. . . ."

"It sounds like all hell is breaking loose," she said, sitting across from me. "I expected that. It had to happen eventually, Caroline."

"You're not kidding," I said. "Do you think she could do it?"

Francine pressed her fingertips together and considered the question.

In no mood to wait, I demanded, "Well? Do you think she could actually kill herself because I'm leaving?"

"Leaving?"

"I told her I was leaving. I called my dad and set up movers."

"Well . . ." Francine smiled. "Progress."

"I feel sick," I said.

"You can do it."

"No, no. I don't know. If Jane died, I'd be destroyed. She'll take me with her."

"That's not true," Francine said.

"Off the cliff with her lover," I muttered. "Brilliant."

Francine looked puzzled.

"Never mind," I said.

"Caroline. I can't promise that Jane won't kill herself," Francine said. "But I *can* tell you that people who commit suicide—who sincerely want to kill themselves—generally do not announce it. They do not advertise. The suicidal mind is secretive, bent on a goal. It does not want to be observed or stopped."

I remembered a girl then, when I was in college, who had walked with me to class every Tuesday and Thursday. We didn't know each other beyond those walks, but I had always looked forward to meeting her on the path to the English building. Her name was Diane, and she was the most careful, studious girl I'd met at college. She was an academic wonder.

One evening I was studying in the English building, scribbling a rushed essay on Shakespeare's use of metaphor, when Diane walked past and headed up the stairs. I was intent on my essay and barely waved.

At some point, I heard a loud blast several floors above me. I didn't think anything of it. A short time later, paramedics rushed past with a stretcher, and when they came back down, they were carrying Diane. She was bloody at the head and covered by a sheet.

I had waited outside the English building with other students as the ambulance drove away, and we stared at one another in collective shock. "But we were planning a party together," her roommate said. "She just made Phi Beta Kappa."

"I had a tennis date with her in an hour," said a sorority sister. "What could have happened since we made that plan?"

For the rest of that year, I had walked alone down the path where Diane and I had built our brief friendship, past the initials she had scratched on the trunk of a tree just days before she killed herself. "For posterity," she had said. And I had only laughed.

· · ·

Francine watched me. "It's the cruelest trick," she said, "to manipulate with suicide, if that's what is going on. And it's effective, too."

"*Is* that what's going on?" I asked. "I mean, this isn't a time to roll the dice."

"Will she go to a hospital?" Francine asked. "That would be the best—"

"Right," I said. "No."

"Then you have to roll the dice. If you don't, *you* might be the one in a hospital."

"I can't do it," I said. "I can't risk her life."

Francine leaned close and said, "Do you really think you have the power to cause or prevent death? Are you *that* powerful?"

"According to Jane—"

"Can you prevent death, Caroline?"

"Well, if I stayed—"

"Can. You. Prevent. Death."

"No," I said, "but I—"

"Caroline," Francine said loudly.

My fists were hitting the sofa like pistons. "No. I can't."

"Anyone's death?"

"What?"

Francine waited for me to catch up.

"You mean my mother?"

"Okay."

"But I couldn't have stopped that," I said. "I can't cure cancer—"

"That's right."

"Except—" I felt my heart contract.

"Except what?" said Francine.

"If I'd *done* something. Done something different. She needed help and—"

"Who?"

"My *mother*."

Francine exhaled and sat back.

"She kept looking at me, and I couldn't find the thing—"

"What thing?"

"Whatever she needed. The . . . lotion . . . or water . . . or, something so she'd breathe. I couldn't make her *breathe*. And she kept waving her arms—"

"Were you alone?"

"Oh God. I don't know, I don't know. Yes. And Dad, he was jogging, and I fell with the lotion, and—"

"And what?"

"And I shouted, 'Fuck!'—I shouted, 'Fuck!' and told her to stop. It was *happening*, you see? She was dying there in front of me. And I couldn't stop it. All my life I couldn't stop it. And now—"

A dam was breaking inside my chest, releasing every organ onto the floor.

"It's too much," I said. "I can't stand it anymore."

"Nobody can stop it," Francine said.

"But . . . I was *there*," I moaned. "I was the one there."

"Thank God you were there," Francine said. "You are *lucky* you were there."

"No, you're wrong," I said bitterly. "Because when it counted, I let her down. I ran like an idiot around the house—while she was trying to die—and I cursed at her. And then, when Dad came, I just walked out on her, without a word."

Francine waited. "Is *that* it? That you didn't see her die? Or say something?"

"But I should have *stayed*. I should have been calm and told her it was okay . . ."

"Was it okay?" Francine asked.

"*Fuck*, no!" I shouted.

"No," Francine agreed.

"But I shouldn't have screamed at her. The last she saw of me, I was *cursing* her. I meant to say good-bye. Or I love you. Or whatever people are supposed to say. But I didn't. So now it's all wrong. And she's gone. And I don't get a second chance."

We stared at each other.

"Maybe you do," Francine said.

"What?"

"Maybe you can say good-bye."

"Oh—do you have the pipeline to the other side? Because it never works out in my stories. Not once."

"You can say good-bye, Caroline. Walk away."

"What do you mean?"

"Get on an airplane. Start your life. *Your* life. Jump, Caroline. Say good-bye."

"To Jane?"

Francine waited.

Finally I said, "To both of them."

She answered with a nod.

When Francine and I stepped outside onto her porch, I hugged myself and tried to look hopeful. "I don't expect to see you again," she said.

"Yeah, but if—"

"You'll go," she said.

"But . . . in case, could you hold my spot?"

"Nope."

I turned back toward her open door, and Francine shut it behind her. "Go on," she said. "Write to me. From somewhere good."

I took two steps down the porch stairs and hesitated.

Francine wrapped her sweater tight and fluttered her hand. "Go on now . . . shoo, shoo. You walk away first. See how it feels."

I ran.

THIRTY-THREE

I found a note in the kitchen when I got home, in Stella's hand. *Jane is with me,* she wrote. And that was all.

I discarded my coat, and everywhere I looked I saw remnants of Jane. The shiny metal soup pots we'd bought together, the photographs I'd taken of her, her art. I looked around our place, and even as I savored my freedom, I missed her.

I took the day to pack and tried not to linger over Mom's things or the reminders of Jane. I faltered a few times. First I came across Mom's rolled-up journal from the psych ward. I couldn't resist opening it, and when I did, I landed on a page I could have written myself.

I have lost the path, she wrote. *I have lost the path. I cannot find the old familiar signs to guide me. Why can't I find them? Maybe they are the wrong signs. Maybe they are there, but I can't see them. I am falling backward. I cannot see where I am going.*

I took that page, put it in my pocket, and kept packing.

· · ·

After a few hours, I ran out of tape. I took my last paycheck with me out the door, walked along Dolores Park, and stopped at my bank. After cashing my check and closing my account, I was back on Castro Street. I made a left for the hardware store, and on my way I passed a fancy shop with tall leather boots in the window. I stopped and admired them. Leaning closer, I saw they had a nice heel and zipped up the back. They were black. At the top, a thin braid finished at the knee.

I went inside.

"You want to try them on?" a young man asked, already sniffing a sale.

"Actually," I said, "I've tried them already. I'll take an eight."

Moments later I met my boots at the register and let a piece of my paycheck go.

Back at home, I called Stella's and left a message saying that my plane was to leave the next afternoon, a few hours after the movers came. I'd left boxes for Jane, and the apartment was hers until the end of the month.

In the evening, I stayed up on the roof garden until it got too cold and then went to Jane's room and sat on her bed. Everything was there and waiting, as if normal life would continue. Racks of clothes waited on hangers in Jane's long, open closet. I lay back, taking in her perspective. Boxes of art supplies sat among unfinished pieces, along with the photographs that we'd transported from the East, with ideas of permanence. On the wall she'd taped up pictures of poets and artists, and there was the one I'd taken of Jane, sitting like a queen on Amanda's lap.

I read the quotes Jane had tacked up and flipped through the books on her bedside table. One was a novel about a man who had set his family on fire, another was an anthology of poems, and tucked between them I found clues to Jane's next spiritual quest—a copy of the Bhagavad Gita, with laminated pictures of a smiling

Indian guru inside. I could see that this latest passion was gathering momentum—packages of incense waited to be burned, and the scent of sandalwood still lingered in the air. Jane had been waking early the past weeks, chanting prayers and meditating. And now there were altars of flowers and stones, and more pictures of the guru, all around.

The floor was scattered with other pictures too, cut from magazines, waiting to become part of Jane's next collage. And there were her sketches of landscapes, paper lamps, and random jars of shells and sand. All around me I felt her spirit, distilled and eerie in her absence. In the rawness of Jane's art I had always seen her potential, and that night I mourned it, even as I reached for my own.

I thought of the things I had just packed—my quotes and pictures, my poetry books, my own jars of shells and sand—all that I had acquired in our time together. I thought of Ed and Marlene, and our first meetings on the bench, and, consumed by a sudden sadness, I realized that the prelude to leaving Jane had begun.

The next morning, after the movers left, I shut my travel bag and wondered if I had actually seen Jane for the last time. I raised the window overlooking Dolores Park and lit a cigarette, wondering how I could find her to say good-bye.

"Perfect," a familiar voice said behind me.

I coughed and twirled, dropping the cigarette.

Jane folded her arms and sighed.

Outside, my cab pulled up, and Jane said, "Tell him to go," as she jangled her car keys.

After I waved the cabbie on, I said, "I was worried you wouldn't come."

Jane peered around my stripped room and stuck her head into my empty closet. "Well," she said, "you are a worrier."

In the car, Jane had Bob Dylan on the stereo. He was singing "Shelter from the Storm." A picture of Jane's new guru was on the dashboard, along with a tiny altar of beads and flowers beneath it. The guru was a radiant dark skinned woman, with red lipstick and enormous eyes. Jane's next impossible romance, it seemed, was in high gear.

"Remember the first time you played this song for me?" she asked, pointing to her tape player. "That night when we went driving?"

"I do," I said. "I knew I liked you when you said you liked Dylan."

"It was an easy test," Jane conceded.

"So are you okay now?" I asked, turning the music down.

"Okay?" she asked, as if nothing had ever been wrong.

"You seem happy," I remarked.

"I have the guru," she replied. She gave me a peaceful smile. It was creepy. Jane seemed submerged, distant, and overly calm. She blinked and smiled, blinked and smiled, as if she were gone already—subsumed in the same way so many had lost themselves in her.

"The guru has an ashram in New York," Jane said. "A few hours from your film school, in fact, in upstate New York."

"I haven't been accepted yet," I said.

"You will be." Jane turned the music back up. Her jaw shifted left and right. She rubbed her forehead and said, "Stella's house is so moldy. I've been cleaning the bathroom for hours."

"Our place smelled like turpentine," I offered.

"Yeah," she said. "Well, I like turpentine."

We rode on.

"So when will you know about film school?" she asked. Her voice was detached again, too polite.

"This summer. I have to take the GREs."

"You'll get in. And you'll love New York. I used to go there all the time with my mother."

"Art shows."

"Exactly."

Jane was smiling now. She seemed to be getting more and more serene as we neared the airport, which made me downright gloomy. "You'd better visit my parents if you move to New York," she said. "Mom would be hurt if you didn't. She really loves you."

"So what are your plans, Jane?" I asked, hoping that would shock the guru out of her or at least dent her unnatural grin.

"The guru will guide me," Jane said confidently. "Who knows, maybe to New York." She winked. "Don't be sad. We both have our paths."

I was fully disconcerted then. Had I just failed Jane and been forgiven for my weakness? Was she newly enlightened or full of shit? I felt like I was back in the funhouse, bumping into mirrors that each looked like an exit.

"I won't take you to the gate, if that's okay," she said. She pulled to a stop outside the terminal and turned to me with a genuine smile. I loved that smile. Then she removed a gold bracelet from her wrist, snapped it around mine, and said, "I love you."

An avalanche of good memories struck me mute—all of Jane's moments of brightness, her companionship and wit—and none of the bad memories came to my rescue. I stepped from the car with dread.

Jane threw my bag on the curb and kissed me. "Don't smoke," she commanded, punching me in the arm.

I was without words, ready to climb back in Jane's car, when Francine's directive came to mind. This was my moment to say good-bye, and I had to force myself to do it.

"You're not making this easy," I said.

Jane's eyes narrowed, and I sensed anger infecting her now.

"Would you rather I take a swing at you?" she asked. "Because I could do that, too."

I retreated and shook my head.

"It's not supposed to be easy," Jane said. "This is heartbreaking,

Caroline." Her voice cracked as she leaned into my ear and whispered, "You broke my heart."

I could see the shift in her as she stepped back. Now the old Jane was talking.

I was dizzy. And it was heartbreaking. And for the record, she broke my heart, too. And there were no good words to make our separation otherwise. And I had to go.

"Good luck," I said, hugging her.

Jane cocked her head, and as she smiled, tears overtook her.

"We'll both need it," she blurted.

The guru's spell had washed from her like a painted disguise, and just as swiftly, my funhouse mirrors fell. What was left between us, as we stared at each other, was just as frightening. But at least, for a moment, it was real.

Jane backed away. When she climbed into her car, I held my breath, and I did not exhale until her taillights were gone.

In the airport, it was my turn for tears. I stood amid rushing bodies, already lost. A perfect ending would have me smiling and confident, newly sure of myself, and rid of my need for Jane. But those endings are always lies.

I found a chair at my gate and removed a cardboard box from my bag. A sleepy, silver-haired man cracked an eye when I took off my shoes and raised the pair of tall black boots to the light. I looked at the man. He nodded, impressed.

My flight was called on the PA, and I slipped them on. Stood. The heel was tricky, and I teetered a bit, aiming for the lady taking tickets. On my way I stumbled headlong and caught myself before hitting the ground. A passenger gasped.

"New shoes," I explained, collecting my bags.

I steadied myself and walked forward.

New life.

Epilogue

Seven years have passed since I last saw Jane, and in those years, increasingly, I have recognized the indelible mark she has left on me—on how I see myself, interpret people, and move in the world.

The summer after we parted at the airport, I was accepted into the New School film program in New York City. I found a roommate named Paulette—a busy young woman who wore Brooks Brothers' suits and dramatic glasses and worked on Wall Street. Before I moved in with her, I made sure she lacked the sort of personality that might seek anything resembling friendship. She had a steady boyfriend, which was good, and when she showed no interest in my background, family, or feelings, I felt confident that all she would take from me was rent. These were my new boundaries, formed by my post-Jane philosophy: Trust no one.

I couldn't be too careful. I'd already spotted a number of Jane-like women lurking in my classes. They stood out as especially clever, funny, and dynamic, variously tortured by childhood traumas, and drawn to me by what seemed like a gravitational pull, as if my emotional résumé were printed on my forehead: "Experienced crisis addict. Three years of inappropriate caregiving, and bottomless well of misguided empathy. Now available."

When I countered their early advances with polite detachment, I witnessed with amazement what might have happened had I been a different person when I met Jane—these damaged souls hovered briefly but then moved right along, without looking back.

Maybe it was hubris that ultimately knocked me down again, just as I began my second year of film school. Or maybe it was my punishment for abandoning Stella, who, it turned out, had had the last laugh on me. Only weeks after I'd left her in the lurch with Jane, she withheld money, and then her body, and soon enough Jane went away.

But whether hubris or penance, or both combined, I was still poised for another fall. With my fine-tuned radar and proud new confidence, I had thought I could spot every threat and never lose track of myself again. I didn't realize that keeping dangerous people out was far different from managing the one who had gotten in— that Jane had become part of me, like a scar or fractured bone. She was an itch that had quieted but never fully left. And in spite of my careful vigilance and veteran experience, as summer came to a close and my fall term approached, I opened my door and allowed Jane back into my life, for one more round of pain.

Her timing was beautiful. She showed up on my West Village doorstep just days after Paulette had moved out to live with her boyfriend, catching me with an open spare room, where she happily dropped her bags. It should have been telling that the moment I saw Jane beaming at my door I felt joy instead of fear. But it took time for me to recognize that the old ghosts were still inside me, rematerializing as if from sleep, to harbor and welcome trouble again. I was about to learn that changes in geography did not result in changes in attachment—that just as I had held on to my mother, I still in some measure held on to Jane. I was about to learn that buying new black boots was one thing and walking in them was quite another. To stay upright, I had to not only separate myself from Jane's chaos, but stop wanting it, wherever I was. Short of that, I had to at least want my freedom and independence more.

Luckily, while on my own in New York, I had tasted freedom and independence long enough to become hooked. I had had a future building when Jane showed up, was learning the craft I loved, and was at last finding my own artistic voice. When the time came to choose between Jane's needs and mine—in an inevitable conflict so familiar that we both actually seemed bored—that foothold in my emerging identity became my salvation, and again I chose to leave, this time without reservation.

Jane and I parted for the second time in a dusty parking lot, near her new lodgings in an ashram in upstate New York. There was no fanfare to herald the moment, no angels singing that I was free. Just Jane and me again, at another crossroads, saying good-bye. And even as I drove away, I didn't know if it would be the end. And even now, I cannot swear to it. Good-byes, I've learned, are necessary but frail. Lost friends and mothers keep returning, in our dreams, in passing faces, in the wind. They keep returning, and we keep going. One good-bye at a time.

For years after I last saw Jane, I used to lie awake at night, eyes wide and worried, and wonder why an advantaged young woman like myself, being fairly smart, strong in spirit, and raised with unconditional love to succeed in anything I tried, willingly surrendered my inheritance, followed by my ambitions and goals, my self-respect, and all sense of right and wrong. I could not fathom what had caused me, at twenty-three, to embrace and support an adult as if she were my child—someone who could turn vicious and violent and who was slipping across her own dark borders faster than I could run. Before meeting Jane, I had never imagined I could be drawn so fully into another person's troubled depths that I too became unhinged. Only by going back have I found that the seeds were planted long before I met Jane, just as her troubles took root long before she knew my name. Our collision was the worst possible train wreck, yet the experience has delivered me.

Because of Jane, I have discovered that people are not as they seem—they are much better, and much worse. I have seen stable minds break and broken minds soar, felt personalities merge and emotional boundaries vanish. I know now that loneliness resides in every heart, that even souls of integrity can lie, cheat, injure, and steal, and that ultimately it is sheer survival that drives our best and worst desires.

I have been amazed, along the way, to find other "Jane people" in the world, all with their own stories of strange personal surrender. Like me, they are tainted by wariness, by extreme caution whenever new people approach. Occasionally the dam breaks between us, letting loose bizarre secrets and stories that only Jane people can understand. In these circles specific words are used: manipulative, damaged, beautiful, seductive, childish, sweet, and cruel. This is our Jane language, and we speak it to be rid of it. But the words are carved tattoos; they sting and swell and never leave.

We envy those who are somehow immune to the "Jane" experience. We wonder, was there an inoculation that we missed? Did we fall out of line when special pills were handed out? But eventually we all break down and use the word that fits—addiction. What else do you call craving the very thing that destroys you? And when I go back to see how it started, like all good addicts I have to admit that the problem began in me, in my own skidding perspective, in the lines I had already crossed—the profound attachments, separations, and deaths—which made the borders with Jane difficult to see.

Ultimately, surviving Jane gave way to my first real independence from anyone who would remove me from myself—real or imagined, living or dead. Jane provided me with a dangerous education, but in the crucible of her vivid extremes I came into my own.

Somewhere, a mother is cheering.

A few months after graduating from film school, I returned to St. Louis to attend to some unfinished business. On a cool November afternoon I invited my aunt Estie to a private viewing of my first film. I had edited the 16 mm footage shot by my grandfather and added music, narration, and stills. The movie opened with my mother's face, her cheek pressed against mine at a track meet, and then it dissolved into motion, going back in time to my grandparents' youth and a scratchy record of so many ancestors gone, mixed with those of us left behind.

At the end, Mom's moody eyes filled the screen, and then they faded, blinking her silent exit before the picture went white.

I looked at Aunt Estie. She was quiet, still staring at the screen.

"I'm not sure how to end it," I confessed. "It's not supposed to just go white like that and end."

After some thought she said, "I know how."

I leaned forward hopefully.

"To be continued," she suggested, as if this were the most obvious thing.

I laughed and then quieted, realizing she was right.

What else can we offer those who are gone, except the promise of our own separate lives? Legacies are made like films—by cutting, connecting, and splicing. Attach the end of one life to the beginning of the next and roll onward. Millions of souls have stood where we are, and millions more will come after.

Keep moving.

Because the human mind is tricky.

And we ought not to linger in its dark places.

Author's Note

When I began writing *Borderlines*, back in the short, cold days of January 2001, only two people knew that I was embarking on this story. As active, successful writers, each offered me the same caution—pursuing this genre usually comes with a price.

Not pursuing it, they added, can cost more.

Over the past two years, I've learned firsthand that both caveats were wise, well timed, and true. Eventually I did tell more people that I was writing this book, and right away, the most startling questions followed.

"So is it fiction, then?" friends invariably asked. "Will you use real names?"

The term *memoir*, I could see, was confusing.

"The genre is *non*fiction," I learned to say.

"But you are so young," a friend once complained. "What have you done yet that merits autobiography?"

That's when I usually said, "Let's start over."

"It's *memoir*," I still find myself repeating, as if the word itself should suffice. Not autobiography, which suggests a notable life, lived on grand scales of world importance. And not history, which promises objective clarity and airtight sources to support each event, spoken word, or exchange.

Then how can you know that what you're writing is true?

This has been the collective refrain. It's a valid and important question, and one that points directly to issues of nonfiction narrative and perspective. Memoir is, fundamentally, a literary investigation—a mystery that is cracked by re-creating dialogue and translating setting and action into words. But these are the vehicles to truth and not in themselves the end. There are the facts of this story, and then there is what I make of them. The curved lens of memory adds its angles to the process, shaping every setting, stretch of dialogue, and scene. But the aim of memoir—to transcend personal experience—is a corrective voice to that lens. In the end, the most distilled, captured "truth" is what the author has gleaned, with earnest motivations.

Over time, my family has gamely adapted to the challenges of being written about, and I am grateful for their unconditional support. They have endorsed my mission, permitted me my voice, and allowed me my lens. And while I have hopes for similar equanimity from the other names herein (yes, all changed, along with—in many instances—other identifying characteristics), I realize that the perils of perspective are significant.

Nevertheless, my goal here is not to expose other people, but rather, in my depictions, introspections, and experiences, to make sense of what happened to me; to yield larger meaning to my experience; and, in so doing, to transform devastating and difficult events into the most hopeful of outcomes, which is wisdom.

—Caroline M. H. Kraus
June 2003

Acknowledgments

My quest to tell this story found its first guide in Hope Edelman, whose workshop at the Iowa Summer Writing Festival provided me the confidence, momentum, and narrative tools to overcome high hurdles along the way. Hope's faith in my work, and her bridge to my first literary audition, made this book possible. I cannot adequately thank her for cracking the window to my dream.

When my agent, Elizabeth Kaplan, raised that window, my good fortune took off like a kite. Her tenacity, sharp instincts, and honest guidance propelled *Borderlines* from dream to reality, and her steady, grounded support gave me the courage to keep charging ahead.

My editor at Broadway, Ann Campbell, was a brilliant partner in the development of every page, and her commitment, fortitude, smarts, and enthusiasm won my heart. Ann's gift for understanding my intent with this story, and her confidence that it was all there to be told, brought us all across the finish line.

Also at Random House, Linda Steinman's wise counsel kept me

on course to the end. Her belief in this project, her objective eye, and her sensitive, diligent insights cannot be heralded enough.

Family and friends who played starring roles include my father, Frederick Kraus, who issued me one piece of advice: *Don't let anyone stop you.* His mantra carried me through the most difficult writing, as his strong character has carried me through life.

Not to be outdone, my mother, Madeleine Véron Kraus, equipped me with a lifetime of archives, which turned me into the sleuth she had always envisioned. Her trail of papers, and her absence, were profound companions for this ride.

My sister, Madeleine Kraus, and brother, Grant Kraus, both embraced my efforts to write about our family, and their trust has made all the difference. My stepmother, Gayle Jackson, was an irreplaceable ally as I tackled this work, and perceptive, as always, to the end. And my mother's sister, Estie Pruett, was a touchstone throughout—for all she has done to support this endeavor, her big sister would be grateful and proud.

Finally, four friends undertook to help me as readers and cheerleaders: Camilla Lindan, whose patient ear and words of wisdom delivered me time and again; Nina Barrett, whose early confidence gave birth to my own; Lisa Chipongian, whose intuitive, insightful comments kept the bar high; and Anna Forrester, who saw the first fragile pages and demanded more.